# The Stan

Dan Talley

*Jason,*

*God*

*Bless*

*America*

I have tried to recreate events, locales and conversations from my family's memories, journals, letters, and pictures and share our true story. I have changed all names of individuals and places and combined some conversations and events. The essence of our story is as accurate as a disabled veteran can creatively tell them.

To:
Those who serve
Those who changed
Those who never return
Those they love.

# CONTENTS

# INTRODUCTION

Josh, my son, and our experiences together in combat and my internal struggle in such context is one discussion you will read in our story. My son's perspectives, my wife's and daughter's emotions, worries, and problems through a third deployment are included as well.

I am Dale Sanderford. I am nothing special, just one of millions of men who understand his country is worth defending. One man who, like my son, believe our family, our freedom, our rights, privileges, and those of this country are more important than we are. Such difficult decisions were not my plan in 1986 when starting my military career. Who plans to see his son in a disabled gun truck on a road in Afghanistan? After all, I went to Iraq in 2005 in an effort to prevent his deploying. Every man's hope as he goes to war is to "finish this so our children won't have to." Yet here we are.

How does a man describe going into combat with his son? We could list facts as an intelligence report would. Karen, my wife, says we should share emotions, fears, and celebrations. How does any soldier, or spouse, communicate what he or she did, saw, and felt in combat? Not all civilians can understand or even care to try.

Perhaps to review who we are and how we came to this point we can communicate much of this. It is a difficult task. As with many returning soldiers, we do not know who we are now, and neither does our family. Perhaps our journey within these pages can lead us all, you, my family, and me, to who we are and where we go from here. Perhaps this telling will help us to find a purpose for life beyond places we have been and actions we have taken. Our families discoveries aside, we pray soldiers, families, and friends understand each other more as we express things many never say.

It is easier to remember where things happened than it is when. Like Smith picking his nose and wiping it on our interpreter Mahmud's shirt as he slept. Which mission it was and when we were there is unclear. We remember winter versus summer based who was in our truck and cold, wet, hot, or dry. However, specific dates escape our memory, due to monotonous boredom, and indifference to such information. Only when R&R leave draws near, or it is time to come home, are dates or even days of the week relevant.

Clearing over one thousand klicks at three to five klicks per hour is tedious. Many people will not understand the lack of clarity such repetitious experiences create. I recommend you load your family or at least four people in your car and sit on an abandoned dirt road for eighteen hours a day, two days in a row. Thirty-six hours should allow you to taste the wonderful monotony broken by uncontrolled violence and humor we in route clearance call "another day at work."

Within military families, numerous emotions, experiences, hurts, pains, and fears remain unspoken. Often, the only way for a relationship or an individual to remain healthy is to discuss most if not all good or bad experiences. Once we admit our issues, we can discuss them, attempt to understand and grow both as individuals and in relationship with others. This book is not a lesson in political correctness, openness to others, or acceptance of others' beliefs. It is not an attempt to offend anyone. Instead, we share thoughts, ideas, and emotions from different times, experiences, and seasons of our lives, both the positive and the negative.

While some people will take offence by our family members' honest thoughts, we do not imply this represents all service members, nor attempt to convince, satisfy, or push any agenda on a reader. This is our story, and we are sticking to it.

My wife and I have been married for twenty-eight years. To her, I have to say thank you for being my support, my home, my love, my counselor, and my nurse all those years. In no way could I have done what I have without you by my side. Thank you also for including your perspectives in this text. Hundreds of thousands of military spouses sacrifice to support our nation's conflicts. Such dedication is often unappreciated, unrecognized, misunderstood, and glossed over by political noise. This is difficult as you stand next to your service member who has been through so much to come home. Who must learn a new way to live. What we have gone through as troops is only half a story. Karen for your unwavering support and love, your willingness to share your journey, I thank you.

Josh is twenty-three years old and the pride of my life. Knowing he watches pushes me when I want to quit. I pray his son brings him similar motivation. Josh's intelligence, questions, honesty, and perspectives included here expand this text from an *old Joe's* book to contrasting perspectives on war.

My daughter finally stopped saying, "I like pie" any time emotions come up. Even commercials on a cartoon channel would cause her to blurt out,

"I like pie." Our nine-year-old daughter's additions to this text surface buried emotions. Reading her thoughts as she experiences this war is enlightening, heart breaking, and hilarious. I love my little girl and am so proud of who she is after all her struggles.

## Karen's Introduction

I am glad we are writing this book. We feel it is what God wants. Published or not, does not matter. It is good to put down our feelings, gratitude to God, and other details of our journey. We pray God uses this book for His glory. We want to reach out to people on a similar path and say there is hope, and you will make it. Soldiers, first responders such as Firemen, Policemen, Emergency Medical Technicians, and others in harm's way live out their lives in constant anxiety. Such a life takes a hard toll. We hope our experiences offer some spiritual truths and practical tips to help them cope.

I would not want to live these last few years over, but I would not want to lose things gained from it either. I have seen strength in our marriage, and it is solid, rock solid—thanks be to God. You wonder sometimes through the busyness of life if your relationship with your spouse has the moxie to see it through any situation. As Post Traumatic Stress Disorder (PTSD) hits home and everything familiar is lost. If you find your marriage has that moxie, you are thankful.

One night while going to sleep, Dale thanked me for being such a good wife. My immediate response was, "I've waited all my life to be a good wife."

I believe, in that moment, I spoke an important truth. In any marriage, at times, one is building faithfulness and loyalty, and we do not even know it. We are in day-to-day routines of cooking, cleaning, loving, and listening, and sometimes we think, "Where is this going? Does it matter?"

When a test comes to put our relationship under fire, it withstands the heat and we realize what seemed mundane was consistent training for an intense time yet to come.

Dale supports me so often, in therapy for "my issues," three children's births, loss of one, college, work, and life's insecurities. I have waited all my life for this moment, for a time to stand by my husband when he is totally lost in a world unfamiliar to him. I will guard him with my life. When he believes he should leave us through suicide. When his mind does not work, he feels people stare or talk about him. When he watches both military and civilian careers slip away in a few short weeks, everything he built through a lifetime of education and service disappears. I will stand by my husband. I will believe in him. God will do it through me.

We were tested by fire. I thank God He considered us worthy for such a trial but often have felt fear and insecurity. I have made decisions for us—tough ones—and the devil whispers in my ear, "When Dale is better, he'll blame you for this."

Each day and sometimes each moment God gives His word to assure, He is helping me. I now clearly see his assurance in our journey.

I am at my best, my strongest, when I lean most on God. He works through our faith. When we agree we need Him and accept He loves us and our battles REALLY are His, the journey with Him is amazing. I have learned not to care about Dale's career or having a nice home. I care about Dale and about our family. A test by fire burns all chaff away and gives a renewed sense of living, a clean slate allowing for choices as to where to go from here.

Dale and I want to stay close to God and continue praying for His direction. Please pray we will keep our newfound intensity and desire to seek Him in every area and not to fall back into a routine or mundane life. We would be most grateful. We pray the same for you.

*Dale's last words of introduction*

Many of our friends lost marriages during or after our deployments. Others lost jobs, other relationships, and some even lost their entire social structure.

Our family has dealt with three conflicts over as many decades. Each was different. Just as we approach each one with a varied perspective and purpose, each has a different effect on us. Our third deployment completed a set of experiences to create within me depression and Post-Traumatic Stress. Mental and physical limitations prevent my being who I was, doing what I did, or understanding what to do next.

We hope our story will lead readers to understand themselves better, to support, and love each other. I Am not who I was. God, counselors, and family help me learn how to live again, to become someone new.

# Number and Spoken As for Phonetic Numerals

| Numeral | Spoken As | Numeral | Spoken As |
|---------|-----------|---------|-----------|
| 0 | ZERO | 5 | FIFE |
| 1 | WUN | 6 | SIX |
| 2 | TOO | 7 | SEV EN |
| 3 | TREE | 8 | AIT |
| 4 | FOW ER | 9 | NIN ER |

To avoid confusion and errors during voice transmission, special techniques have been developed for pronouncing letters and numerals. These special techniques resulted in the phonetic alphabet and phonetic numerals.

Numbers are spoken digit by digit, except that exact multiples of thousands may be spoken as such. For example, 84 is "AIT FOW ER," 2,500 is "TOO FIFE ZE RO ZE RO," and 16,000 is "WUN SIX TOUSAND."

The date-time group is always spoken digit by digit, followed by the time zone indication. For example, 291205Z is "TOO NIN-ER WUN TOO ZE-RO FIFE ZOO-LOO." Map coordinates and call sign suffixes also are spoken digit by digit

# Glossary of Military Terms

| Acronym / | Pronunciation | Definition |
|-----------|---------------|------------|
| AAR | Ay-Ay-Ar | After Action Review |
| AFCOP | Af-Cop * | AFCOP - Afghan Combat Outpost |
| AO | Ay-Oh * | Area of operation |
| BC | Bee-See * | Battalion Commander |
| BIP | Bip (ryhmes with dip) | Blow In Place |
| CAB | Cab | Combat Action Badge |
| Commo | Cahm-oh | Communication be it radio, computer, |
| COP | Cop (police officer) | COP - Combat Outpost, coalition |
| CQ | See-Que * | Charge of Quarters, NCO responsible |
| Deuce and | Standard English | Two and a half ton truck |
| DFAC | Dee-Fack | Dining Facility |
| EOD | Ee-Oh-Dee * | Explosive Ordinance Disposal |
| ETS | Ee-Tea-Es * | End Tour of Service |
| FM | Ef-Em * | Radio Communications |

* <--Letters are spoken as in American English alphabet

| Acronym / | Pronunciation | Definition |
|---|---|---|
| FOB | Fob (ryhmes with corn Cob) | FOB - Forward Operating Base, small secure location for coalition forces |
| Guidon | Guide-On | The guidon is a company, battery, or |
| HME | Ayh-Em-Ee * | homemade explosive |
| ID | Eye-Dee * | Identify |
| IDF | Eye-Dee-Ef * | Indirect Fire, mortars, artillery etc. |
| IED | Eye-Ee-Dee * | Improvised explosive device |
| IG | Eye-Gee * | Inspector General |
| Lt. | El-Tea * | Lieutenant |
| Kill Sack | Standard English | The location an ambush attempts to |
| klik | Click | Kilometer |
| MOB | Moab (ryhmes with Robe) | Mobilize |
| MOS | Em-Oh-Es * | Military Occupation Specialty |
| NCOIC | In-See-Oh-Eye-See | NonCommisioned Officer in Charge |
| OP | Oh-Pee * | Observation Post |
| Papa | Standard English | Pee break |
| PMCS | Pee-Em-See-Es * | Preventive Maintenance Checks and |
| POO | Poo (ryhmes with Sue) | Point Of Origin (location from which IDF originates) |
| PTSD | Pee-Tea-Es-Dee * | Post Traumatic Stress Disorder |
| RPG | Are-Pee-Gee * | Rocket Propelled Grenade |
| RTB | Are-Tea-Bee * | Return To Base |
| RTO | Are-Tea-Oh | Radio Transmitter Operator |
| S3 | Es-Three * | Operations Officer |
| SAF | Es-Ai-Ef * | Small Arms Fire, AK-47 etc. |
| SOP | Es-Oh-Pee * | Standard Operatiing procedures |
| TOC | Tock (ryhmes with Stock) | Tactical Operations Center |
| TC | Tea-See * | Truck Commander |
| TTP | Tea-Tea-Pee * | Techniques Tactics and Procedures |
| VICs | Vick | Vehicles |

* <--Letters are spoken as in American English alphabet

# Glossary of Foreign words

| Word | Pronunciation | Definition |
|------|---------------|------------|
| Kandak | Can-Deck | Afghan army brigade size force |
| Hadji | Hah-Gee | Nickname used for locals in the |
| La | Lah | Arabic for no |
| Awgaf | Ah-Guh-If | Arabic for Halt or stop |

# Military Time

In English-speaking Canada and the United States, the term "military time" is a synonym for the 24-hour clock. In these regions, the time of day is customarily given almost exclusively using the 12-hour clock notation, which counts the hours of the day as 12, 1, ..., 11 with suffixes "a.m." and "p.m." distinguishing the two diurnal repetitions of this sequence. The 24-hour clock is commonly used there only in some specialist areas (military, aviation, navigation, tourism, meteorology, astronomy, computing, logistics, emergency services, hospitals), where the ambiguities of the 12-hour notation are deemed too inconvenient, cumbersome, or dangerous.

Military usage, as agreed between the United States and allied English speaking military forces, differs in some respects from other twenty-four-hour time systems:

No hours/minutes separator is used when writing the time, and a letter designating the time zone is appended (for example "0340Z").

Leading zeros are always written out and are required to be spoken, so 5:43 a.m. is spoken "zero five forty-three" (casually) or "zero five four three" (military radio), as opposed to "five forty-three" or "five four three".

Military time zones are lettered and thus given word designations via the NATO phonetic alphabet. For example, 6:00 a.m. US Eastern Standard time (GMT-5) would be written "0600R" and spoken "zero six hundred Romeo".

Hours are always "hundred", never "thousand"; 1000 is "ten hundred" not "one thousand"; 2000 is "twenty hundred".

# Phonetic Alphabet

To avoid confusion and errors during voice transmission, special techniques have been developed for pronouncing letters and numerals. These special techniques resulted in the phonetic alphabet and phonetic numerals.

The phonetic alphabet is used by the operator to spell difficult words and thereby prevent misunderstanding on the part of the receiving operator. The words of the phonetic alphabet, which is a word alphabet and not a code, are pronounced as shown in the table below. The underscored portion indicates the syllable or syllables to be emphasized.

The phonetic alphabet is also used for the transmission of encrypted messages. For example, the cipher group CMVVX is spoken "Charlie Mike VICTOR VICTOR XRAY.

| Letter | Word | Pronunciation |
|---|---|---|
| A | ALFA | AL FAH |
| B | BRAVO | BRAH VOH |
| C | CHARLIE | CHAR LEE |
| D | DELTA | DELL TAH |
| E | ECHO | ECK OH |
| F | FOXTROT | FOKS TROT |
| G | GOLF | GOLF |
| H | HOTEL | HOH TELL |
| I | INDIA | IN DEE AH |
| J | JULIETT | JEW LEE ETT |
| K | KILO | KEY LOW |
| L | LIMA | LEE MAH |
| M | MIKE | MIKE |
| N | NOVEMBER | NO VEM BER |
| O | OSCAR | OSS CAH |
| P | PAPA | PAH PAH |
| Q | QUEBEC | KEH BECK |
| R | ROMEO | ROW ME OH |
| S | SIERRA | SEE AIR RAH |
| T | TANGO | TANG GO |
| U | UNIFORM | YOU NEE FORM |
| V | VICTOR | VIK TAH |
| W | WHISKEY | WISS KEY |
| X | XRAY | ECKS RAY |
| Y | YANKEE | YANG KEY |
| Z | ZULU | ZOO LOO |

*Therapy Session Number 81*

Children's books on shelf by size, toys in box, last step to set these damn bead puzzles straight, one hundred colorful wooden hoops to align right, uniform, systematic, done yet they remain a chaotic rainbow of colors in improper order. No kids are here so all should be stored properly.

*I wonder if I can take its deformed wires loose and order the colors properly, better not, ain't mine.*

Center couches in Doc's lobby cradle two women and a teenage female who chit chat and click their phones. Both moms panic to verify subordinate family members' assignments for tonight are clear. Big mama says the same crap a third time. Who will take whom, where, and when?

*Really woman, so complicated, so much panic, even cussing, over a damn soccer practice you high-strung yuppie. Like to see you deal with the sh' we did. I love my wife.*

I sit alone in kiddie corner, away from the dramatic duo female officers. Any time people are in central waiting area I sit alone, away from everyone, and watch cartoons, with my toys. I organize this sh', restack magazines, and play phone solitaire, anything to keep my mind busy here, not where I was.

*Ole Sarge best ignore late practice discussions or whatever horrific tragedy has driven Mom to freak out.*

Miss Teen in her Gucci outfit clicks, taps, and stares at her phone. Only an occasional eye roll at Mom interrupts her frantic multi-person texts.

Doc opens the lobby door and calls me back. I pass him, clear the doorway and lead him toward his office.

*Carpet's been cleaned, door one left secure, opposite door right open to work room, no one there, door past copier open to other hall, clear. Second door left open, female at desk, lights dim, no one on couch, shade covers her window. Slow down, peek around corner, r to right, right turn, door far end open, man on computer, beard, bald, insecure, I make eye contact.*

*Doc's door left, enter, scan left to right, room empty, lights dim, French doors secure with see through white curtain drawn, chair right empty, room clear, turn left, b-line to couch seat, opposite corner from French doors.*

Doc secures his office door, sits to my twelve o'clock, and asks, "How've you been since our last meeting?"

I get out a journal and stare out his French doors. "I'm ok, same ole sh'."

"What's on your mind, Dale?"

"I found myself in a freedom from defining myself."

Doc stares over his tablet and says, "Help me understand what you mean, Dale."

I wave my left hand, glance at Doc's beard, his leather footstool, baggy pants, and his damn tablet. "Everything I've used to define myself is gone, civilian career, military career, leading men, and soon my house. None of that sh' is who I am. Doc, I am more than any of it. Started thinkin' like this when my son and I were in Afghanistan findin' bombs."

"What about your shared experience took you in this direction?"

*Something moved outside, what the, oh, wind on a rose.*

*"We're often used as bait, to draw out bad guys. We get shot at or blown up so infantry behind us see where the mean people are. After a while, you realize how little you matter. None of this does. If I die, no title matters."*

"Is there a particular event you see as a turning point for you in these thoughts?"

I glare outside, not at a red rose, or a crooked retaining wall beyond. I see a chokepoint on our route to my son.

***

Thursday, mid-August 2010, zero four thirty, Mathews prays before our Route Clearance mission back to our Forward Operating Base. We have been away from "home" seven days. In a week, we got three IEDs, an ambush, and three days in Sharana's transient tents for vehicle (VIC) repairs. Today we head north back to Paktya province. My son Josh's platoon clears south as we meticulously do so moving north. I am a Platoon Sergeant while Josh is a driver today.

Our zero-five-hundred Start of Patrol (SP) insures we miss morning civilian city traffic. It has been a long uneventful day as we close on Josh's platoon at sixteen-thirty. Our VICs bounce and rock through old IED holes. Sunset begins to our west and mountains are visible fifty klicks east. Wind carries dust clouds we stir up westward, interrupting the sunbeams' journey to our path home.

I see Josh's platoon icon on my computer screen, but we cannot yet reach them on their radio frequency. Another quiet afternoon clearing roads and easing through crater after crater, some we remember, and some we do not.

*Back home Karen, my wife, is getting Charlotte out of bed about now. Maybe I will talk to them tomorrow.*

"THERE IT GO," my gunner RC yells.

His matter-of-fact clarification is simply, "Blast north."

A surreal second later, Rollins, my lead vehicle operator, says, "One Nine, smoke cloud north."

I radio, "Husky One this is One Nine, roger, we see it."

A husky operator's search, mark, and tell our Buffalo operator where to interrogate for possible IEDs.

"One Nine, this is One Two Alpha, want us to lead us out and get up there, over?"

"Negative One Two Alpha, break, Husky One, Husky Two get us up there, clear as you go, don't get us blown the hell up, over."

"Husky One, roger"

"Husky Two, roger"

We still have no radio communication with our brothers. I get a text report of Small Arms Fire (SAF), Rocket Propelled Grenades (RPGs) and Indirect Fire (IDF). U-shape ambushes from behind are common. We had one here last week moving south. We Charlie Mike (CM, continue Mission) north as our sister platoon responds to today's aggression.

*Who got hit?*

A poke of a One Thirty Seven vehicle icon on my computer screen will display the corresponding vehicle's status. I poke Smith's icon, a popup opens, and his speed data reads 5 KMPH. I close his popup data; click the next in line, popup reads 7 KMPH.

*That's Donner, he's moving. Wait. Rear ambush; check the trail Vic dumb ass.*

A spark in my peripheral vision, I glance at Miller, he looks at me, he lights a smoke, neither he nor I speak. I go back to my screen.

Miller says, "Your son out today?"

"Roger, he's drivin' Top."

"Tops out, what the hell?"

"He's fillin' in for Lt. Martin, Martin's on leave."

I click another icon, Smith's rear vehicle.

*Duke is rolling. Sh', who the hell got hit?*

Smoke ejects with Miller's every word, passes his steering wheel to cover our windshield in a gloomy fog. "We need to get up there, Sarge."

I poke another icon.

One more data popup opens.

This icon's velocity caption reads "0.0 KMPH"

*First one at a halt.*

*Gotta be the one that got hit.*

"Sar'nt Sanderford, we gotta roll," Miller says.

RC's feet shift on his gunner platform. "Get my ass up 'ere, lemme get some."

Text on my screen blends with and gives way to images of what "0.0 KMPH" means, on the ground, an immobile vehicle taking small arms fire.

*Smith's hands are full, bet he's screamin' and cussin'.*

*In that open field with qal'ats north and south, drainage ditches east and west.*

*How is Josh handlin' this one? How many and what weapons fire on him?*

The human mind is unbelievable. Our brains process data, recall memories, assume answers, and reconsider it all several times before blast smoke disperses.

Concern and anxiety birth hunger for facts. Letters on screen break through Miller's smoke. Force down memories of other fights. Facts in text form chop away estimates of this one. I choke down paranoid assumptions. Must search for and deliberate on current facts.

*Focus dumbass, read the vehicle designation.*

*Josh*

I toke my smoke.

*Josh's hit*

I look around, front, right, at Miller, and focus on the soft gray and brown smoke cloud to our north.

*Josh is under that sh'.*

I see tracers rise, and arch to an unseen distant impact.

*Under fire.*

*Bullets hurt.*

Smoke plumes emit above the tree line, friendly tracers, and theirs.

*Karen's gonna be pissed.*

I retrieve a cigarette pack from my right sleeve pocket, pull one out, grip it between chapped lips, light it from the butt of my last, stow a burning butt in the Gatorade bottle latrine/ashtray beside my computer screen.

*No confirmation from Sar'nt French, he is pissed. We all wanna fight; help our brothers, and my son. Self-control Sarge, mission first, you last.*

"One Two Alpha, this is One Nine, you copy?"

French's standard sarcastic response, "Aaaand a roger," confirms his frustration.

Silent minutes pass as we creep north.

\*\*\*

Doc says, "I'm sorry to interrupt, Dale, but please clarify for me. You chose not to rush to your son's aid?"

"Yessir. Not right to risk my men to save my son. The NCO creed says, 'I will not use my grade or position to attain pleasure, profit, or personal safety.' To risk my men and forgo my mission, just to save my son." My head shakes; I squeeze my red journal, leg taps like a Thompson machine gun. "Ain't right."

"How do you view your decision now?"

"It was right. His platoon and mine needed an IED-free route after the fight. I chose to leave my son in that ambush, in the kill sack, to Charlie Mike clearing for bombs. It was right, irrespective of risk, fear, or emotion. It was right."

My head leans left and I lock eyes with Doc.

"Like I said Doc, I don't matter."

"Honestly."

My arms cross my chest, journal tucked under my left armpit. I stare at him but see my son.

"At that time, in that place, neither did my son. No more than any man on the ground."

Doc makes notes; I stare at my son's truck beyond the rose. Blast marks and bullet dings around his window, an AK-47 bullet hole through his storage box door.

*Leave my son in it.*

*Should I have rescued him?*

*When he fell as a toddler, I was there, but not now.*

*Why did I bring him?*

*Just to leave him here.*

*As if he meant nothing.*

A headshake, glance at Doc, and hard stare at his footstool brings me back.

"Doc, I'm done for today. That's enough of this sh'."

"Ok, Dale. They will reschedule you out front. Thank you for sharing. Any time you're done, take a break, leave, have a smoke, whatever you need to do."

"Roger. I'm out."

*Josh's Journal*

June, 8, 2010, Gardez

I finally got to go out on mission. I found out on the 5th about a mission we were going to do on the 7th with special forces. ODA was camped out at COP Tashnab, an ANA camp on Mierda. It was with RCP 137. The mission was regular route clearance.

Once we got to a point, as always the Taliban would fall into their ambush positions. The idea was that before that ODA would have already occupied these positions and they'd take them all out. 137 would basically be bait.

Once drawn out by a convoy rolling, anything with a weapon in the area around the RCP would be destroyed. I really wanted to be on this one. I waited for Captain Wayne to come in the morning of the 6th so I could ask him if I could go.

If 2nd platoon was going to be bait I was going to be bait with them. To my surprise he let me. I rode over with One Fifty Four to Gardez later that day. I had all my stuff ready.

Magazines, clean weapons, and body armor. I spent the evening hanging out with Mike and the guys.

At 1900 LT. Martin gave us a rundown on the next day. We were to clear to CP Jug. Only one RCP has ever made it that far without having to fall back. It was the elements of a hell of a first mission for me. I wanted to be on Mierda and I wanted to dive right into the action. This mission provided the perfect opportunity.

Sergeant Smith read off the trip ticket. Douglas wasn't on it but I was. I was riding in the Buffalo.

We rolled out at 0100 so I didn't sleep. I was running off the 4 hours of sleep from the previous three days.

It started pouring down as we were rolling out.

Our Husky wasn't picking sh' up. We let battalion know but they told us to roll anyway. That's what I thought would happen. There'd be nothing keeping us from rolling out. We were then relayed that ODA was not yet in place. We turned around to go park when they told us to go ahead and roll out.

We rolled through Gardez and reached the start point of Mierda and halted to wait for daylight. During that time we were told that Zombie element, the ODA, had been compromised.

They were falling back to COP Tashnab.

Our mission was now to clear all the way up to Tashnab.

We rolled out and didn't have any occurrences for a while. We stopped and interrogated a few suspicious spots for bombs.. Our Husky driver, Sergeant Dupre was being cautious, as he needed to be on this route.

We finally reached an intersection of a few qal'ats. Dupre came over and said he was picking up heavy readings over a fresh dirt spot on the road. We went up to interrogate with the Buffalo. We knew this would be something. We fell into place and started digging. We dug for a while and as we relayed we were about to Charlie Mike Sergeant Harwell, who was operating the arm, found some wires.

He tore the wires from whatever they were connected to. Then he put the fork into the ground next to the wires.

"Oh sh' ," he said.

I gripped the handle above me. He pulled up and showed the yellow container which his fork was completely stuck in. He started bashing it on the ground and finally got it off. We backed away to let EOD do their thing.

EOD then dismounted and took a sample from the yellow container. He then started pulling up on the wire, breaking it from the ground to see where it led.

During this people started appearing from their qal'ats. One elderly man was outside the whole time watching.

We sent some guys up to talk to EOD. He was putting stuff into the computer.

"Holy sh' we barely missed that look," Specialist Norton said.

I looked up and saw the EOD guy picking up a pressure plate. Then he continued tracing the wire. We were sent up again to interrogate further.

We found nothing. We pulled forward and waited for EOD to get the word to BIP (blow in place).

At this time, our air support told us about the guy in the white that I had spotted. He was in the distance at our nine o'clock while we were interrogating.

They said he was playing with something then he put it back in his pocket. CAS then told us 10-12 armed individuals were approaching with RPG's and AK's.

We all started to laugh in the Buffalo, our interrogation vehicle. I guess after you are in a position like that for a while you really don't care what happens next.

Our dismounts ran back to their VICs. Using our Gyro cams we saw these guys were just ANA. EOD blew the HME behind us. 30 lbs of HME. That was cool.

We Charlie Miked and not 25 meters down the road we were taken by surprise. To our 12 on the route we saw a big explosion.

"*IDF, IDF,*" multiple guys yelled over the radio.

We kept going right towards it. We couldn't fall back on this route it was too dangerous. Plus, it was our mission to draw out the enemy.

"That wasn't mortar fire," said Sergeant Harwell. "That's usually gray/black smoke."

I didn't think it was IDF. If it was then it was centered perfectly directly on the road. Our husky reached the blast sight.

We passed too and EOD got out to look at it.

There was a burned truck 15 meters behind that point.

The EOD guy said it was an IED that was set off too early. It was a big one. One that would have done some pretty big damage.

We would have also been stuck out in the open in front of this qal'ats intersection place. EOD's gunner relayed that EOD Actual was looking for body parts. Possibly a fu'up PPIED." EOD Actual continued, "This is EOD over, I found a hat and sunglasses but no body parts…break…I have no idea what happened here."

Maybe an animal set off the charge. We didn't see any blood though. A few parts of a camel but they didn't look fresh. Decomposed a bit.

We Charlie Mike'd and reached COP Tashnab. I just knew we were going to get shot at soon. People rolling around with AK's and sh'.

We started coming back. We made it back to FOB Gardez without incident.

It was a pretty uneventful mission for Mierda. We reached our objective. That hardly ever happens. We found our first IED as a company.

When I got back to Gardez, I hung with Mike then Lt. Martin told me that a clip from Alpha was on the way. I got on it and got back to Alpha.

I was passed out for the ride back in the TC (Truck Commander, front passenger) seat. I was tired as hell. We got in and I saw Dad at the gate with some guys trying to leave.

"Have fun?" he asked.

"Well, hell yeah," I said.

We both laughed. We parked our VICs, and I went to the TOC. Captain Wayne was on the porch talking to a lieutenant and reached out to shake my hand before I went in.

He told me we did a hell of a job and made the company proud today. I checked in with Sergeant Hatfield, and he told me to go get some rest and come in tomorrow night.

I went back to my room and just sat down for a minute and thought about the day.

I had fun. I loved being out there. I got naked and crashed hard as hell in my bunk.

# 2

To my twelve o'clock Karen sits on Anita's red couch. We visit Anita, our Christian counselor, once a week since I came home. I am, as always, in my corner chair. Anita is in the twin chair to mine at my three o'clock. She has a nice office, even though her "modern art" above Karen's cushy couch hangs at a slant.

*Why does a female Christian counselor have blood red velvet furniture? A Baby doll in her messy corner basket needs a hairdo. Dolly's butt faces me.*

Anita says, "Dale, last time did you learn more of how Karen feels? How she felt?"

Date time group written on my journal's next blank page, after my last week's session with Doc, I close it and place it to my left, pen secure inside it. "I knew before. She tells me all the time. I grasp how deep it is, why it's so strong, still strong."

Karen raises a knife hand toward me like a Drill Sergeant, leans forward, glares at Anita and says, "That's even worse." She chops air with her knife hand. "He says he knew how I felt and he did not care." Knife hand falls on a pink mini notebook in her lap; she stares through me. "You just proved you care more about the army than you care about me, what I want, what I need."

"I love you, Karen. I do care."

"But you went in spite of how I felt."

Anita says, "Let's talk about your choice to go."

*Deep breath Sarge, here we go.*

I give a fleeting look to each woman and a glance out the window to my ten o'clock.

*Wow, that is one fat squirrel. LOL*

Another glimpse at Karen, I focus on Anita's damn multi-color checkerboard rug between us.

*Hold it in, Dale. Two non-military women and one discussion's gonna help 'em understand me. Make me understand them, BS. Stay in the game, this is about Karen, not you, ya selfish a-hole.*

I say, "Spring 2009 deployment rumors increase."

Anita squints at me, tilts her head right, and taps her fingers. "Did you tell Karen these rumors?"

Karen inhales half the air in the room and bellows, "No, he didn't"

Anita waves a hand at Karen.

*Bad mistake lady, do not cut her off, best let her finish, your 'bout to get an earful. Woman, do not touch her knee, you'll be in arm's reach.*

Anita eyes me; hand on Karen's left knee. "Dale, did you talk to Karen about these rumors?"

"No, we always have rumors. I don't bring 'em home till I know for sure."

Anita's hand retreats, she settles back in her chair. "At what point did you know for sure?"

"Not till April. Orders were due in at summer camp that May. I told her then, in April."

"So, Karen, he told you as soon as he knew for sure."

"Yes, but acted like he might not go. Said he wanted to stay home. What a bunch-o-bull. He knew he was goin' the whole time."

Anita turns to me. "Dale, did you act as if you might stay home?"

*Face Anita, talk to her Sarge. Karen don't wanna hear it.*

"I wasn't sure. I'd just got a promotion at the college, several big projects, our kids, church, Karen, work, I didn't wanna go. War ain't fun; people get hurt. I had a Sergeant Major tell me, 'You can't keep goin' and nothin' happen to you, sooner or later it's your turn.' I didn't want a turn."

Karen straightens up and slams her notebook on the center couch cushion. "You knew you were goin'. Twenty-four years in, coulda' retired at twenty, and none of this would'a happened. But no, you kept goin' till everything got worse, till you went again."

"Karen, how did Dale decide to go?"

"He didn't for like months. We were in limbo, wondering what Dale wanted to do."

*There it is. That sh' again, 'what I wanted,' not what I had to do, not what God said to do. Not what the army or my men need me to do. What that selfish jerk Dale wants to do. Honor, integrity, and dedication mean nothing anymore.*

*Y'all think we flip a damn coin, no thought of spouse, kids, no one but ourselves.*

I zone out to Karen's perspective re-run.

*I am not the only one to make this decision...*

***

*Williamson sits motionless on the lawn mower between our platoon gear cage and the bay door, hundred-yard stare on his face. I plop down next to him and further bend the chair's metal leg.*

*Williamson needs to talk.*

Williamson glances at me as he takes a drag off his cigarette. "What's goin' on Sar'nt Sanderford?"

"Same ole, same ole, you?"

"Hell, I dunno," says Williamson. "Thinking 'bout oh five, you were there Sar'nt, you know the sh' we did." I began to get confused as to who was talking. The industry calls this talking heads.

"Yeah."

A deep drag burns his smoke to the filter, he thumps ash and fire through the bay door to field strip it, and lets white smoke trickle from his mouth in rhythm with his words. "I don't know, Sergeant Sanderford. Do I re-enlist knowin' we goin' again? These young guys think."

His head shakes side to side as he fidgets in the mower seat. "Sh', they don't know what it's like to zip a buddy in a bag. I should be there. They think it's a big freagin' adventure. It ain't. Sh' sucks, man. My times up in three weeks, we ain't on a stop loss, I could just walk away, ya know?"

*Our struggle to go or not, when we don't want nor have to is worse than bein' over there.*

Williamson stows his cigarette butt in his pocket and retrieves a red box and lighter from his left front pocket. He does not blink. With empty eyes, he stares outside, lights another cigarette, shoves his lighter in the box, closes it, and shifts on his green mower-recliner to pocket his smokes.

Silence deafens me as my eyes shift from him to the half-open bay door, past aligned trucks, to Iraq. Owesat's river road, our Observation Post (OP) above it, and the Euphrates Bridge replaces my motor pool view.

My eyes return to Williamson's, his sole motion is to place his brown filter cigarette in tight, chapped lips to draw deep drags of relaxing nicotine.

*He don't see a motor pool any more than I do. What to say?*

"I know, Williamson; I could retire today, right now. Walk away from you, my men, all of it. On the other hand, do I walk away from family and friends, civilian career? What's right?"

Like a rock band drummer Williamson's right hand pounds his leg. "Zactly, Ser'nt Sanderford, egg-freagin'-zactly." Right knife hand points to troops outside on trucks. "I love these guys. We been through some sh', ya know. I just don't know if I wanna do it again." Williamson's back slams back to his yellow chair, right hand drops to his lap, cigarette hand waves at shoulder height in route to his mouth. "I just don't know."

My rusty metal chair screeches in relief as I stand, pat his back twice, and rest a hand on my young friend's shoulder. "Every man has to decide for himself. I can't steer you in one direction or another. We'd love to have you with us. You gotta pray and make your own decision. No one can do it for you."

My hand slides across his back as I ease past him to the bay door. His steel eyes focus on a memory outside, he nods once and tokes his smoke.

*What a load-o-crap. I spewed the same crap at Rollins and French this morning.*

Wright was begged to stay in for Iraq in 2005. Newlywed, good wife, great civilian career, he did not want to go. We wanted him with us, strong Christian, awesome NCO technically and tactically. He died, our first loss that trip, day one.

*I miss him.*

*I will not push people to stay in. NCO's should. I'll let everyone make his own decision. I don't need more regret, stress, and self-blame. Or more dead friends.*

Done with Williamson, I take my motor pool stroll. Old Sarge needs to check today's Preventive Maintenance Checks and Services (PMCS).

Left brain punches right brain, right kicks left in the balls, both ignore little heart's opinion. I creep between vehicles, ask squad leaders what is complete, and what needs attention.

*"Let" everyone make his own decision. I can't even make my own.*

Emotions, options, responsibilities, and commitments fire from opposing brain sections to thwart any intelligent thought, progress on this decision. All thought slows to a crawl.

\*\*\*

Something outside catches my eye, it streaks by, my head snaps left, and eyes focus in time to see a car hit a parking space curb.

*Damn, is your cryin' session that important? Slow down.*

I look back to Karen. Her script on my 'wanting to go' is almost complete.

"Anita, why would he go? Why would he choose to leave the kids and me again? Don't we matter?"

*Don't cuss, swallow your thoughts, let her get it out, maybe then she'll stop her endless anger cycle.*

I say, "Karen it did take a long time to decide, it was a tough decision."

Anita is back in her gentle momma voice. "How did you make your choice Dale? Tell Karen and I what finalized it for you?"

*Might as well tell her, Karen still won't believe me, maybe Anita will.*

*"Prayed it through, took months, but I prayed it through."*

\*\*\*

Bird songs calm my thoughts as I smell their pine forest home beyond our yard. Our back patio is a peaceful place to read Scripture and pray. God gave us an awesome place to live. We moved here six months before my last trip over, February 2004. Our home nestles amid pine-covered hills on three sides and a lake on the fourth.

All days start in a similar way. I ask God to take away my desire for alcohol. It dulls the debate rattle in my skull. Only way to sleep is rinse my head with a beer or two after everyone goes to bed. Without it, I lay awake to review past deployments or contemplate one to come.

My largest project at work is to purchase and redesign a 70,000-square-foot facility and create a hub for workforce education and training. Stress rises as coworkers grip comfortable familiar methods and see no reason to change.

My promise to our college president, and my boss, to stay and see this through unless my unit goes to combat further confuses my loyalties.

Back to Iraq's sand box a third time. Our mobilization (MOB) orders will be here any day now.

Karen says retire, Josh does too. Charlotte cries. My boss asks how long I will do this. My men assume they can depend on me. Captain Wayne talks to me about this and that to prepare our troops, unit, gear, techniques.

*I wanna have a beer and forget it all.*

*Gotta go to work soon.*

*What was that, a tiny dog?*

Agent F, the neighbor's asthmatic pug dog, tries to bark, probably at my boxer outside his fence, teasing him again.

*Back to now, to today's decision.*

I will fast and pray through lunch today. Karen and I pray for God to make His will clear, to give us a unified direction.

We both have trouble hearing God, or listening to Him. Our minds garble with thoughts, memories, and emotions. She says my love for troops is greater than for her. Feelings of rejection and deep concern for our children block what communication she and I attempt to share. Those same garbled thoughts, no doubt, block our hearing God's still, small, voice.

*Should I leave Karen and go again?*

*I should go. My wife needs me here. My projects at work are incomplete. Is "third time's a charm" true? I won't return, at least not in one piece. Karen will die while I'm gone.*

*Do I allow these fears to stop me? Stop me when others are dead. Some died this week in Iraq and Afghanistan.*

*Most Americans will not or cannot do their part.*

*To go is to leave my civilian missions, my roles as Father, Husband, Brother, and employee for Soldier, Leader, and possibly Casualty.*

*Staying home is disrespect to lost friends, quitting, giving up on protecting my country, for a comfy-cozy life with family and friends.*

*Comes down to one question, 'Whom shall I walk away from? Who will Dale choose, and who will he disappoint?'*

Everything suffers in my confused zombie-like existence. Alcohol brings escape from aggressive memories and estimates of battles to come.

*I am an indecisive alcoholic. Why in the hell would anyone want me around anyway, back here or over there?*

I stare through pine trees and pray aloud, "Lord, please give me direction, a clear answer. This limbo state of confusion wrecks everything. My life is sh'. I'm back in the bottle."

Karen, I am sure, prays a similar prayer inside. Its zero-six-thirty-five, we will wake Josh and Charlotte soon and trudge through another day.

"God, I really want to begin today with your answer," I beg.

A relaxed warmth engulfs me, as if hot chocolate flows from head to foot. A comfort and peace I have never known consumes my being; forehead, ears, neck, shoulders, gut, legs, bare feet, and warms my chilled toes.

Like a baby in Mom's arms, I am comfortable, relaxed, and secure.

*My reason to enlist remains. Dale's initial purpose in 86 is unchanged, even in today's pile of emotional sh'. There it is, time to leave Karen again. Regardless what we will face, or my growing certainty I will not return.*

*Those of us willing must do for the country we love. The United States asks us to go, again, go we will.*

*At some point we all say, "I've done my part." but it's not my time yet.*

*Protestors in our liberal society won't go.*

*If someone has to die to in our country's wars, it won't be those who try to tear down our country, our morals, religion or heritage. Those willing to serve must go. I must go.*

\*\*\*

Karen says, "'Yeah, right."

Anita looks at her. "Karen, you don't believe he prayed it through?"

"Why would God separate us again? A third year without him, Charlotte with no Dad, then he took Josh with him. I don't see why God would put us through this."

Both my palms turn up, my arms rise from red armrests. "I don't either, Karen, I don't either. But that is what I understood, so that is what I did."

My hands drop to my lap. Karen looks away, shakes her head, looks back at me and raises her right index finger toward me.

Anita raises both hands, one palm to each of us like a referee to separate heavyweights in a title bout.

"Dale, you believe you acted in God's will. Karen, you disagree. We won't settle definitively today which of you is correct. I encourage you to pray about this, together, and let's discuss it again at some point."

*Well that's the end of that sh'.*

Karen pinches her lips, closes her notebook, and stows it in her purse. I stand and adjust my pants, perform a window check and step off for the door.

Anita stands, hands Karen a paper from her desk, and says, "Reschedule out front. Y'all take care."

Karen schedules us for next week, exits the building, walks to her car, gets in, and leaves. I walk past my car, to the woods and light a smoke.

*Karen's Journal June 2009*

A third time? Really? Don't ask that of me. It's too much. Do you not like to be around me? Do I not matter enough to stay home this time? Asking you the last four years when you would retire and knowing you had no intention really hurt. I've never liked the one-weekend-a-month–two-weeks-a-year deal. We could have had that time together. Family time, too. By the way, he told me a few days before my 40th birthday. Our first Valentine's Day married he told he wanted to go active duty Army. Dale's timing is rotten.

How do you find the enthusiasm, the goal as a third-deployment spouse when he could have chosen to stay home? He's served—you have served. Let's move on. The hurt is so personal—such abandonment. He says it is *God's will* but if so how could it be so hard even when, at times, I'm really, really trying?

\*\*\*

Anita says, "We have a few more minutes. Shall we shift gears? May I hear your conversation with Josh? How did he take it?"

*Sh', Let's keep talkin about Dale's choice to trash his family.*

*Bottle your emotions and answer the question.*

*Tell the story Dale.*

\*\*\*

Josh knocks on my tiny pinkish college office door at lunchtime; a few days after "we" chose to deploy again a Monday early April 09.

Josh's first semester here, he consistently finds his way to my office just before lunch. I wave him in and finish my phone call. He sits left of the door.

The receiver hits its base and, in the first three sentences of our, "what's up, whatcha doin' today" conversation, Josh asks, "So, uh, Whatcha doin' for lunch?"

With half-a-smile I say, "Mexican."

"Great."

I lift the phone handset. "Let me call and see if Karen can meet us."

Second ring she answers with her long office script which ends in, "May I help you."

"Wanna meet for lunch, Baby? Josh's wants to eat with us."

"Wow, Dale, really? He wants to spend time with his parents?"

"I'm not sure it's a time with us thing, but he wants to eat."

"Oh, of course, we get more time with him now than his last two years of high school."

"I know. How's Mexican sound?"

"Over here or out there by y'all?"

"Over here, twelve-fifteen good for you?"

"Okay, see y'all there."

"Love you, Baby."

A hesitation to remind me I should stay home precedes Karen's matter-of-fact "Love you too."

*I hope she didn't hear my "well sh'," as I hung up.*

"Well sh' what?" Josh asks.

"Nothin', your Mom and I have a little disagreement, not a problem."

"You ready, Dad?"

"It's not twelve-O-clock, can't go till twelve."

We leave and drive a mile north to a quiet Mexican restaurant. We arrive and find Karen in a corner booth. Her two-hour lunch allows her to get to restaurants early, reserve a corner booth so I can position my back to a wall, and order my usual.

*It's great to have a wife who knows me well enough to get a good booth and the right lunch.*

Josh and I walk to her table. I kiss Karen. Josh teases me for doing so.

Karen is still trying to come to terms with my decision. She feels she had no input; I did not listen to her concerns or opinions or even ignored her emotions. Beyond all her struggling, she strives to be supportive.

We have not told Josh or Charlotte yet. Our decision is only two days old. I sit across from my wife and son as we chitchat about Josh's classes, Karen's work, and our afternoon plans. We devour our chips and signal our waiter for another basket. Prayer is complete before more chips arrive.

Karen opens our conversation. "Josh, Dad has something to tell you."

I glance at her, surprised and using my expression to ask if we want to deal with this during lunch, in public. Her blank look tells it is time to put it out there.

"Our unit is being mobilized for deployment to Iraq for a route-clearance mission."

Josh's eyes water, he must deal with his own 05 memories, fears of losing Dad, separation difficulties, and what this all means to him. I remember how emotions and problems in 2005 caused his freshman of high school year to be such a struggle.

His first comment is, "What about Charlotte?"

*Wow! Our self-centered nineteen-year-old's first thought is for his nine-year-old sister.*

"I understand this is what God would have me do, Son."

"What about the college? Charlotte? Why don't you just retire?"

Karen and I have known, argued, and struggled with this for months. Only now does Josh hear about it. Maybe describing how hard this decision has been will help him understand why I have to go.

"We've prayed about this for a long time, Son. This is what God would have us do."

Josh says, "Why would he want to split our family up again? Why?

He motions for Karen to let him out, she does, and he goes outside.

Karen says, "Did you hear him? His first concern was for his sister."

"I saw that, he's a fine young man. He'll be okay. He'll get through it."

We have our food when Josh returns. He sits down without making eye contact, obviously still upset, he asks, "So, when's this gonna happen?"

"We'll get official orders this summer and start our mob. We'll go on active duty early 2010. It's not like last time. We'll only be on active duty twelve months. That includes our pre-deployment training and demob. In country should only be about ten months. They're trying to make it easier on us. Only a twelve-month separation rather than seventeen like last time."

Josh takes sarcasm to an art form when he says, "Oh, only a year this time? Well that's *much* better, Dad. Only a year...shah. Just a year of your life? No big deal. What does the college say? You gonna have a job when you get back?"

"I will. They don't want me to go, but I'll have a job when I get back."

Josh shakes his head and says, "Seems stupid to me. I mean you already been twice. Why are they makin' you go again? Why don't they get people who haven't gone yet?"

*I must negate arguments of our mission completion, perspectives that our company and especially our family have done enough.*

"It's our turn, Son. Our unit is called, it's our turn. Besides, some people have been four and five times. Why should I get off with just two?"

Josh continues jabs at my decision's logic. He says, "Cause you have over twenty years, you can retire and be done. Twenty years means you have done your part. Let someone else do it."

Thousands of men have this conversation with their families. The point is always the same.

*All right Sarge, TRY again to explain a soldier's perspective.*

"I joined to serve, and I'm still in. I won't turn my back on my men."

Josh's right hand waves his fork, almost hits our chip basket in route to the table. "Oh, but you'll turn your back on us."

Karen adds, "You can turn your back on your family, but not your men."

*Two on one, awesome. I wonder if Captain Wayne and Sergeant Duke are having these same conversations. They are in the same boat; we all have twenty years and don't "have" to go. Let's cut this off before emotions run away and our conversation gets louder.*

"God says I should go, I'm going. I do not look forward to it. Route clearance is a bit dangerous, but here we go."

Josh wrinkles his brow and stares at me. *He looks like me tryin' to make a point, that's cool.*

Josh says, "What is route clearance? What are you talking about?"

"We'll go out and look for IEDs, to keep roads safe for other troops."

His head tilts left and right, both hands wave above. "Oh, we're just looking for bombs, bombs that are killin' people, no big deal, and God wants me to. God wants me to try and get killed so you won't have a father... Great lunch, Dad! You tell Charlotte yet?"

Karen says, "Not yet, Son, not yet. We decided to tell you first."

"Well, there it is, great. I gotta go. Y'all have a great afternoon. I gotta go to class." He stands up to leave and adds, "I still say you've done your part, Dad."

"God said I ain't done yet, Son.... Have a good afternoon."

Anger and disgust deform his face. He turns to go. "Yeah, bye."

Josh, like most his age, struggles with "religion," and, "people at church." He questions who God is, and a myriad of other concepts and beliefs. I wonder what effect my "God wants me to" answer will have on his beliefs.

As important as his confusion is, it must take a back burner. We get to tell a nine-year-old Daddy's-girl that Daddy is leaving again.

Karen says, "Love you, Josh."

"Love you, too, Mom. I'll be praying for y'all."

After he leaves, I look at Karen and say, "Well, that went well."

"You have to expect him to be a little hurt. You're choosing to leave us again."

"I know. He needs time. We all do...we all do, Baby."

***

Anita looks at Karen. "Is that how it went?"

"Yeah, Dale just told him. It was nice to see Josh's first concern was for Charlotte. Not a good lunch."

"I don't know. It sounds like it went fairly well. I can't imagine having that conversation with my girls. That must have been tough for you, Dale."

"Yes, Ma'am. Two on one is always tough."

"I refer to the emotions you must have had. What you both must have felt as your son put forth Karen's argument for not going."

"Yeah, that sucked too."

Karen says, "But he still went. In spite of how we felt, how it was sure to affect us, he still went."

Anita says, "Y'all pray about that. Dale still feels God wanted him to go. I understand you disagree Karen, but are those Karen's emotions or what you understood from God?"

"I don't know. I just don't see why God would do that to us a third time."

"I don't either, Baby, but He did. That is enough for today Anita. It's time to go."

Anita says, "Your right. Our time is up for today. Y'all promise to pray and talk about this right?"

"If Dale will, I will," Karen says.

"Yeah, we'll do that. I gotta go see the back doc now."

"Ok. Karen, Dale, y'all have a good day."

I stand, retrieve my green journal, and motion for Karen to exit first.

Karen exits Anita's office. "Are you coming by the office?"

We shuffle down the hall, her ahead of me.

I say, "Yeah, I gotta get my back cracked."

"Wanna get lunch first?"

I open the lobby door for Karen and caress her back as she exits.

I say, "Nah, I'll just get done so I can pick Charlotte up from school."

"Ok, I'll see you tonight."

*Dale's Journal*

182345APR2011 - At home

Back to work at the college, shaky day. I still see Afghan roads when I drive but time to get back into life. I have had over a month, time to suck it up and drive on.

I get to work early, first day back and all. Everyone is "happy" to see me. I am quiet and reserved. We had some issues before I left. Alcohol consumption, lack of sleep, depression, and confusion was dragging down my work drastically. Now here we are ready to "pick up where we left off."

Only I am not trusted with as much as before. Fair enough, I was messing up spending so much time remembering previous deployments, being indecisive and making stupid mistakes.

I am blessed they held my job for me. Thank goodness, I came home. If I had gone to Fort Benning, I would be in the bottle right now. Despite the rules against drinking at a Warrior Transition Unit (WTU), I woulda done just like Josh is. Try to wash the memories out of my head. I have done that before and it took me down a bad road.

I've had no alcohol since I got home this time. That should help. They gave me some simple projects to work on to "ease" my way back into things. I actually have a window in my new office. Nice to be able to look outside when I can't stand being in here.

I go out for smoke breaks in the morning and afternoon to get away from the work, people, and being inside.

I say "ease" back into things. I was given three projects no one has been able to complete in 5 years. Yeah, that's easing back into it. Toughest one is working with someone even the president of the college fears.

Great, let me deal with him and see if I maneuver without any waves. He is very protective of his little world. Yet, they tell me just start doing what I need to for this to move forward.

They have made no progress. Then when he sends out an e-mail slamming me for not "being a team player" I am told I need to learn how to work with other departments more. By the same people that said, "If he won't do anything to start the project you need to move forward with or without him."

Now I'm a sorry excuse for a government employee because in doing what I was told I stepped on toes. Let me go back to the Stan, or Iraq. The politics here suck.

Make everyone feel good about doing the same thing they have always done, but make them do something different so we can have progress. Whatever, I still don't understand these damn policies. I wanna get away from everyone.

# 3

I leave my boss' office, exit our building, cross a parking lot, take four deck stairs in two strides, turn right on well-worn deck boards, halt in a smoking area, light up, and call Karen.

Unable to stand still I pace, smoke, thump ashes, pace, lean on a splintered hand rail, pace again, and observe any movement or sound around me.

"Thank you for calling…"

As I exhale a white cloud, I interrupt her office sales pitch. "It's me."

"What's wrong? Dale, what's going on?"

"You know my improvement plan?"

"Yeah, what happened?"

"I have three days to complete stuff. Sh' no one here has ever done. Gotta do it without permission or authority to do it. I'm not allowed to…"

"Calm down, Dale. Slow down. You have a good boss…"

"I don't have time to calm down. This improvement plan has deadlines. I've already missed some. I can't do this sh'. Hell they want crap done that ain't never been done. I throw up on my way to work every day. I can't take this sh'. I don't understand. Numbers don't make sense. I can't even count change. Ain't worth a sh' at anything. I'm done with this. I'd be better off goin' back over."

"Let's see if we can see Dr. Taylor. Maybe he can help."

"I…I don't know. Ain't sh' he can do—damn brain don't work. I misunderstand everything, can't communicate, can't focus. The more I stress, worse it gets. Sh' gets worse every damn day."

"Dale, you wanna call Doc or you want me to?"

"Go ahead. I'm gonna smoke."

"Ok, I'll call you back in a minute."

"Thanks, Baby."

"It's gonna be ok, Dale. God's got this. I love you and we're gonna be fine."

"Roger."

"I'll call you back as soon as I get in touch with him."

"Roger."

"Go outside, take a break, get away from everyone, and clear your head."

"I try, it don't clear like it used to."

"We will get through this. I'll call you right back."

"Roger."

"I love you, Dale."

"Love you, too."

This smoke area is my refuge from anxiety and stress inside.

*If I can't handle stress in education. I can't be worth a sh'.*

First smoke gone, I light another, finish it and light a third from a half-inch cherry flame on my second before Karen call's back.

"What's up?"

"Dale, are you doin' better?"

"Not really."

"I'm on my way to pick you up. Doc can see us as soon as we get there. Ok."

"Roger. I gotta get outta here."

"Will it be ok for you to leave for a while?"

"Roger. Don't know. Ain't been to lunch, I can sign out for lunch I guess. Maybe I won't get fired for that."

"Sounds good. We'll get you some lunch on our way to Doc's."

"Not hungry, just wanna get outta here."

"Ok. I'll be there in five minutes. Go ahead and lock your office, sign out for lunch, and wait for me outside."

"Roger. See you in a few."

"It's gonna be ok, Dale. I'm coming to get you and we'll figure this out."

"Roger. Out."

Karen picks me up. I smoke two more in route to Doc's office. Karen checks us in while I burn another outside.

*I ain't sitting in there. People stare at me.*

*Worthless piece of sh'.*

*I freak out, throw up, and get edgy, at a low stress job.*

*What the hell happened to me? Why can't I understand how to do this sh'? Two years ago, I wrote state policy. Now what I wrote don't make sense!*

We get in Doc's office. I have been here twice. He did not seem to care either time, asked generic get to know you BS same as all those other shrinks.

Doc Taylor sits to our front, gets out a notebook, and pulls out a calm voice.

*Shrinks all use soft voice crap to make you think they care.*

"Well Dale, Karen, how are we today? I understand we've run into an issue this morning?"

Arms tight across my chest, with a slight rock forward and back I stare at him. "I can't do this sh' Doc."

"What's that, Dale? What can you not do?"

Karen pats my right knee as it bounces. "He's full of anxiety, stress, and confusion. His work suffers. After being back to work for like a month and a half, they have him on an improvement plan. That put even more pressure on him."

"Is this new, or were there problems before you went to Afghanistan?"

"I had problems before I went."

"What kind of problems did you have before, Dale?"

"Same sh'. Last six months at work all I could think about was past deployments. What we'd face on the next one. Lost friends, injured buddies, bodies, all that sh'. Only way to get it outta my head was to have a few drinks."

"And did alcohol affect your work before the deployment?"

"I never drank at work. Nor did I go to work after I did. My confusion, lack of focus, inability to make simple damn decisions, all started before my last trip. It's freakin' unbearable now, though."

"Tell me what you are going through, Dale. What is horrible now?"

"I throw up in route to work. I burn two or three smokes at a vacant lot on my way in. One with good 360 fields of view. Try to calm the hell down. Drivin' gets me edgy. I know I can't perform when I get there. That really pisses me off.

Simple phone calls, even to long time customers or old friends, suck. Every day I gotta call people back to clarify or re-ask questions. I forget what they said, don't understand my notes, and even forget to ask sh'. Questions off a checklist I made eight years ago, damn list is right in front of me.

None of this *crap* makes sense. It don't work, scared to talk to people, can't stand makin' cold calls and can't stand people I have to work with. Great idea, take a guy who wants to punch a kid at Walmart, yeah, have him be your change agent.

I wanna get away from these stupid people and all their petty protectionism, neglect, self-importance and two-faced comments. Everyone's out to prove I screwed up.

My boss's assistant has to explain policies to me. She says one thing Monday, and the opposite on Tuesday. Everybody changes what their story, even my boss.

I have a great wife. But she wants to eat lunch like every day, like she missed me or some sh'. Why would anyone miss a man who can't do his damn job? I still ain't had a drink but I think about it. I need time away from all these f'in people, from all this sh'. Ten-minute breaks morning and afternoon ain't getting it. A stop before and after work to clear my head don't even work anymore.

Sunday at church, I almost brought up my M-four to yell, "get the fu' back." I was back on that checkpoint lookin' for MIA navy guys. Wednesday I saw mortar rounds fifteen meters north, and five meters west, in church. What the hell is that sh'?

Why can't I do sh'? Why's everything so damn confusing? I work till eight or nine at night to finish projects. I still miss freakin' deadlines. I did turn in a second business plan for approval last week.

Boss ain't asked a single question about it. I can't do sh' without her, the college and our damn lawyer's approval. But hell, it's all Dale's fault we don't sell. Kiss my ass people. Approve a plan, allow me to act on it, or leave me the hell alone.

Doc says, "Is this different from your work before the deployment?"

"No, it's similar, same project work, same sales issues, but I don't lead people, I'm just a worker bee."

"I assume very different from your days on deployment."

"Hell yeah, over there I had 35 troops, VICs, equipment, ammo. I got commander's intent and made sh' happen. I'd motivate troops to get it done, no matter what. I was good at it. Friday I had to get a lady at work to help me decide if I was authorized to move a f'in bookshelf in my own office. I can't decide sh' without stressin' about bein' second-guessed."

"That must frustrate you."

"Damn right it is. Let me do my damn job. Give me guidelines, tools, people, and let me make it happen."

"You don't have freedom to make decisions?"

"I can't decide if I can go to the damn latrine, don't produce like before, and I told you I can't understand this shit. I'm on an improvement plan. My work here has been so bad I get evaluated every week. Is this supposed to help my stress level? We meet on Wednesdays to discuss my transition progress. Ain't done well in one damn meeting.

"Kiss my ass. I have led men where others would not go. Give me freedom to execute what needs to be done and I will make it happen. With these stick in the mud people, policy, and political constraints nobody can make sh' happen like that. I don't have the patience all this.

"I throw up every day drivin' in. Half my workday is spent puttin' things in place. I'm f'in OCD. Even pencils in my drawer gotta face the same way, words up, and be sharp before I leave.

"To fight my poor memory I keep staff journals. Write down every word anyone says, my response, what I need to do next and whatever else I gotta remember. Every project has its own log. I do a log for conversations with my boss.

"I'm a damn cry baby. I had mission changes multiple times outside the wire, 'specially on multi-day missions. Now I'm scared to go take a piss cause I might get in trouble."

Both my legs pound carpet. I stare out French doors, bind my arms across my chest to stop waves in tirade, and lean back.

Doc looks to Karen. "Karen, what changes have you seen in Dale?"

I look at Karen, she looks at me eyes watery, grasps a mini notebook in her lap, and hesitates as our eyes meet. "He's distant. He is here, but his mind is somewhere else."

I gaze outside, she looks at Doc. "He tells me the same things a lot. The other day he told me the same thing, like three times, in fifteen minutes. Each time he acts like he hasn't said it before. He doesn't remember anything, forgets what I tell him, and stresses out quick. He snapped at our daughter last Thursday. Dale never does that, he's always been a great father."

"Have there been any physical confrontations?"

*What the hell Doc? What kinda piece-o-sh' you think I am.*

"No, Sir. He leaves the room or goes outside to smoke."

Karen eyes me, and forces her words. "One time... but that was before."

"What was before?"

"After his 05 deployment to Iraq, he had a couple issues with our son. Josh was sixteen, and pushed us on everything. They got physical with each other a couple times. As soon as Dale realized what he was doing, he stopped and basically let Josh win. No one was hurt."

"There hasn't been any of that recently?"

"No, Sir. He yells and cusses, but never gets physical."

"Is it normal behavior for Dale to yell and cuss?"

"No, Sir. He's never been like this. He's completely different."

"Dale, what goes through your mind as you listen to Karen?"

"Doc, I can't do this sh' anymore. Nothing makes sense. Nothing works. Everyone's against me. No one will help. They just wanna find a reason to fire me, be disappointed with me or to watch me screw up. You heard Karen. I'm worthless at home. Yelling, mad, don't want to spend time with anyone."

How will I take care of my family? How can I find another job when I see bodies at work? How can I learn a new job when I can't do one I've done for eleven years? Who would hire someone who can't produce enough at a government job to stay on? Everyone knows these are low stress jobs. Who would want a dude with an MBA who can't understand his own damn spreadsheets? I sit at my desk and can't think, I can't focus.

I'm a pain in the ass to my family. They'd be better off without me. I ain't doin' nobody any good, none. I've become a stupid, worthless, piece of sh' and everybody knows it.

I'd rather be over there in a fire fight than dealin' with all this emotional out of control BS. Everyone would be better off if I just was not here.

Doc says, "Have you had any thoughts of hurting yourself?"

"Roger. Thought about suicide, friends have done it. Karen, my kids, the college, the church, everyone'd be better off not havin' to deal with me. All I do is screw sh' up.

Doc looks at Karen, rests his pen hand in his lap, and crosses his legs. "Karen does he have access to weapons at home?"

Karen wipes her tears, nods her head, and blows her nose.

Doc says, "We need to take care of that today. Can you do that for us Karen?"

Karen puts her tissue down, picks up her pen, and shifts the notebook in her lap. "Yes, I will." She writes in her little notebook and looks up at Doc. I look at her, but she won't look at me.

*Karen has always been a list maker.*

Doc says, "Dale, would you be able to take some time off? Give us time to focus on you, on these issues."

"Yessir. I have sick leave."

Doc changes notebooks, clicks his pen a few times, and looks at Karen. "I will draft a letter to Dale's office which states he is to be placed on eight weeks of sick leave. Dale and I will meet three times a week. Meanwhile can you get him to a doctor to get prescriptions for some anxiety and depression medicine?"

Karen makes a few notes, holds up a wait-a-minute palm, and looks at Doc. "Which medicine. That makes me nervous."

"We have several good medications available, safe ones. We run into problems with some combinations of drugs. Your primary care provider can insure what we request will not react in a negative way with Dale's other medications. I will write down my recommendations and dosage levels for you. However, your primary care provider will have to write a prescription based on his knowledge of Dale, his other medications and so on. Can you be sure he takes it as prescribed?"

Karen glances at me, and back to Doc. "Yes, Sir. I will."

*I'm such a useless piece of sh' they talk about me like I'm not even here. Crazy boy can't decide about his healthcare.*

Doc says, "Dale let's get you off work long enough for our time together to make a difference. It will take time for these medicines to get in your system as well. I hope by the end of eight weeks you will be able to return to work. However that will not be the end of our journey, it will give us a good start, but only a start.

"You came to see me two months ago Dale. At that time, you were not ready to do real, substantive work. I think you are ready now. Are you ready to begin?"

"Doc I gotta do something, this sh' sucks."

"I understand Dale. Your psyche has been wounded. Think of this as an open wound, or a broken leg. We have to stay off that leg long enough to allow it to heal. Keep the wound clean, and covered so no bacteria can get in throughout your healing process. What we will do now is remove as much stress from your life as we can. I must emphasize the importance you feel no pressure or stress.

"Karen, I can't even have you ask him to take out the trash. It is imperative he feel safe, secure, and protected. Can you work with me on this?

"Yes, Sir." Karen says.

Doc looks back at me. "If your leg were broken, you would not try and run a mile on it. You would not go to Guard Drill would you?"

I look at Karen, and back at Doc.

Karen says, "He broke his leg on a Friday night. Sure enough, he went to drill the next day. Missing drill never crossed his mind."

Doc says, "Really. Dale, to walk or run on a broken leg, would this help or hurt its healing?"

"It'll hurt, could make it worse."

"That's right. To heal we must remove stress and pressure, all external forces. Correct?"

"Yes, Sir."

"This is exactly what your mind your emotions, what Dale needs. You need time without any of this to allow a therapeutic process to begin. You won't be back to who you were in eight weeks. Let us use this time to get a good start. It could be ten or fifteen years before you are fully healed, if ever. You have deep wounds, and to heal will require a lot of work, effort and time. To heal is your only job now. Not your employer, not the army, not even your family. What is good for Dale is now your sole focus. What helps Dale heal. Do you understand?"

*I don't know if I can. I gotta provide for my family, take care of Charlotte, help Josh he's got the same sh'. Be there for Karen, she's still mad I went when I didn't have to.*

I say, "Yes, Sir."

"Are you willing to come see me two or three times a week?"

"Yes, Sir."

Doc looks at Karen. "I'll work on this letter to his employer. Take him to get some lunch. We will have his letter ready shortly. We need to start this afternoon. As of now Dale is under my care and does not need to go back to work."

Karen makes notes, closes her notebook, and places pen and notebook in her purse. "Yes, Sir. We'll go eat. What meds do you recommend?"

"I'll have that for you when you pick up the letter."

Karen stands, purse in hand, "Ok. Thank you, Sir."

We say our goodbyes. Doc encourages us that life will get better. We go to Tres Tamales, a Mexican restaurant, for lunch. After lunch, we request leave at work, see a Doc to get medicine, and avoid people's attempts to put me away as a suicide risk.

My boss supports my sick leave request. She hugs me, almost cries, and says how proud she is I've chosen to take this step. I tell her "whatever my future relationship with the college is. I need this time for me." She wholeheartedly agrees, even tells Karen directly she loves us, is proud of me, and is ready to help us on our journey any way she can.

*Are these rants all in my head, paranoia? She's always been a supportive southern belle type boss. She always cares about people. Who knows?*

*Four hundred forty some odd hours of sick and vacation time on the books. I can provide for my family while I start this mess.*

# 4

*Marital Counseling Number 9*

Anita opens today's session. "What are some goals you two have for our sessions together?"

Karen blurts, "I've got a load of stuff Dale hasn't heard."

Anita says, "Okay, to share more of our emotions. What else?"

"He still doesn't listen to me, or consider my feelings."

Anita clarifies, "So you feel a need to be heard, to be acknowledged."

Quiet to this point, I say, "I have heard, and I have acknowledged. None of this talk will matter. I left again, deployed, and there's no forgiving it."

Karen cries, "I've been supportive. You know I have. Three deployments and then some, I've been supportive through it all."

Anita interjects, "Ok, we'll work on this. Are there other goals for our time together? Dale, how is it you and Josh went over together?"

Karen speaks up, "Josh's always looked up to Dale. When Dale was in California in September of 2009, Josh decided he wanted to go with him to Iraq."

"Wait, to Iraq? I thought you went to Afghanistan."

I say, "It changed to Afghanistan later, at that point, when Josh chose to sign up, our orders were for Iraq."

"Did he call you, just sign up? What happened?"

I breathe deep and stare at Karen.

*Is she gonna tell this one? Great, I get to tell another story.*

\*\*\*

Eighteen of us are in World War II barracks at Camp Roberts California for a two-week training course. I wore a tie-dye t-shirt to travel out here. First night in, I tell the post commander it was my best effort to fit in. She barks, "Not at this base Sergeant First Class."

Third evening here, we stroll to the Post Exchange (PX) to stock up on beer. Here I do not have to hide my alcohol from the kids or Karen. I can drink every night and have no family, work, or anyone question it.

Since we have not yet mobilized, "Big Army" does not care either. Once we get on active duty, we will be under General Order One and cannot drink until we are demobilized.

With my six-pack of chick beer, Light beer with Lime, and a bag of ice in hand, I ease back to my room. Byson, my old friend and our maintenance Platoon Sergeant, and I set up camp in one of two bottom floor offices. Rooms once used for Drill Sergeants or whoever was once in charge.

Our small room has only basic items, two bunks, two wall lockers, and a door we can secure with a padlock. Exterior wood siding visible between bare 2 x 4 show traces of ten or twelve coats of exterior paint through its cracks.

We have one window for "air conditioning"; a large fan in the open bay pulls air through our small alcove. I stow five bottles in Byson's foam cooler and one by my rack.

My cell phone rings. I glance down. Josh's name is on its well-lit screen.

*Crap, gotta go outside to talk, no "privacy" in our tinder box condo.*

Outside I tap accept. "What's up?"

"Dad, I've been thinking. You're gonna MOB sometime next year right?"

*time for more "don't do it because" talk.*

"Yeah, March probly. Why?"

"Is there time for me to go through basic and tech school and go with you?"

*That beer would get this lump outa my throat. Damn.*

I am proud he wants to serve but anxious as well. An internal ethical struggle begins. Father wants to say no and stop his insanity. Sarge wants another good troop with us. My mind races but is unable to reply, as I pace between buildings in sunbaked sand, impatient to have a cold beer.

Josh says, "I haven't talked to Mom yet. You know I've been thinkin' a good while about serving. I figure, why not go with you?"

Shock at this new possibility limits this old army dog to a deep mumble and slow, "Uh… well… I'd have to look into it. Need to call Chapman and Carl."

His excitement blares his response from my phone speaker, "Can you call him and call me back?"

I need to slow us down, for a minute. Dad is still unable to grasp what

Josh proposes.

*What is his reason? Gotta check before we do anything. This is gonna stop if he thinks, "I'm gonna go take care of the old man" or "Mom told me to keep an eye on you."*

"What makes you want to do this?" I stutter into my phone.

"I wanna do my part. I don't wanna join and sit around and never go, ya know? I don't wanna serve and just sit back state-side, doin' nothin', active or guard. I wanna deploy, go to combat, really do my part. Besides, I'm bored out of my mind in college. It's so... I don't know... pointless....." His brief response is well thought out, and certainly rehearsed.

*Old plat Daddy's gotta use caution and wisdom to word his response. I can't discourage a young man's pride in service, but at the same time I visualize Karen's reaction.*

"Understood, Son, to say I am proud of you to consider this is an understatement. Let me make some calls, and I'll call you back."

"Can you get back to me soon? I need to move if I'm gonna do this. There ain't much time."

"Ok, Son, I'll make some calls."

"Thanks, Dad. I really think I need to do this. I'll be waiting for you to call me back."

"Bye, Son."

"Bye, Dad."

I shuffle around our dirt yard to let this sh' sink in.

*Maybe I should have a beer. Now I regret quitting cigarettes ten years ago. I could use a smoke right now. Come on Sarge you're stalling. Call Carl dammit.*

I dial Carl's cell number.

Carl answers in his slow Eeyore/Festus Southern-Mississippi-boy accent, "Yelloooo"

He has been our training NCO since we got back from Iraq in 2005. He is not a computer technician by any means, but he has a heart of gold and an immense determination to prepare our troops to complete this mission.

I ease into it, for my sake as much as for his. "Carl, its Sergeant Sanderford. What's goin' on?"

"Hey, Dale. Y'all doin' okay out there brother?"

"We're good. Barracks sucks, but we're good."

"I'm tellin' ya, we was out there last month... I ain't stayed in that kinda barracks in a long damn time, boy."

I say, "Training's good, staff is professional, it's all good. We'll get what we need."

"Yup, I reckon so...what's up, Dale? What can I do ya for?"

I take a deep breath and blurt, "This is gonna sound crazy, but stick with me here. My son, Josh, wants to drop out of college and go with us."

A pregnant pause allows me to gulp more air. This still has not sunk in. I continue, "Is there time for him to join, finish basic and tech school, and come with us?"

A moan, grunt, a long pause, to scratch his balding head no doubt, and Carl says, "Ahhhh sh'... you serious?" *Harrumph.* "What's Mama say about that?"

"She don't know yet. Josh wanted to check with me first, and we gotta see if it's even possible before freaking her out."

"Well, there'd just barely be time. Basic and tech school is fourteen weeks and you got Christmas exodus. Wait a minute. Lemme get on the computer and see if there's even a school with slots he could get in and finish in time."

I hope for time to think. I stall with, "Wanna call me back?"

I hear Carl pound his keyboard like a woodpecker on a hardwood as he talks.

"Nah... Hold on. I was just in it. This is crazy, Dale. Why's he wanna do this?"

"He's young, like we were once, wants to do his part. I raised a patriot without knowing it."

"I know you're proud he'd even think about this, but.... Damn...That's gonna be hell on your wife, brother! I wouldn't wanna be the one to tell her." His quick mind tries to back his slow mouth out of the pending spouse conversation.

"Come on, dude. I thought you were my friend! Give her a call for me. Break the news to her while I'm out here in Cali, out of arms reach. A real friend would." Most people joke about stressful situations, one way to talk it out without any "mushy" or "touchy-feely" stuff.

"Oh, hell no, I ain't in this one, you on your own, brother. Here we go, it's comin' up. Yep, there's openings in three classes that'd finish in time. He's gonna have to jump on it. By the end-a-the week he's gotta be goin' to Jackson for a physical. He signs up too late and misses these slots and he'll be back here drillin' while we in Iraq."

A hard truth from our training NCO, it would be a lie to tell Josh it is too late or there is not enough time. Josh is nineteen. I cannot stop him. I cannot talk him out of this. Not after he, my daughter, my wife, my boss, even my coworkers, all tried to talk me out of it.

*I gave Josh my reasons via text, voicemail and face-to-face, how can I stop him? Karen's gonna love this.*

Carl's voice derails my thoughts. "Dale, you there, brother?"

All I can push through my desperation to hang up is, "Roger. I'll let him know."

"Tell the recruiter up there to call me, and I'll give him a slot to put him in. You sure you want him to go?"

"We'll see. Thanks, Carl. I'll call you tomorrow. He needs to pray at least overnight before he does anything. This decision has got to be prayed through."

"I hear ya. Tell him to pray hard, and pray for his mama too. Take care, brother."

"Yeah, you too, Carl."

*Gotta be clear and concise talkin' to Josh, best call before I start drinking. Get it over with so I can eat, have a couple... three or four...and get some sleep. Josh's waitin' on you. Just call his ass back.*

I dial his phone, walk, shuffle, and kick through gravel and dirt in California sun, his phone rings.

With only one ring Josh's deep voice answers, "Hello."

"Josh, it's me."

"Hey Dad, I just talked to Mike. He wants to go."

*Hold up now. My own son is one thing, but the only Son of family friends is somethin' else. Mike has been coming to our house since first grade. He is a second Son to us, and brother to Josh. I went over in 05 to help finish this, to keep Josh from going.*

*That sh' did not work. Now we take our children to clean up our mess. Slow it down Sarge. Make 'em think about what they are doing, not everyone comes back.*

I say, "Wait a damn minute. His situation is different. He's got a lease on an apartment, student loans…"

"I know, but he really wants to go with us."

*Breathe deep Sarge, slow and deliberate.*

"Alright, listen up, I called Carl. It is possible to finish training in time to go. You gotta move fast, sign up in a week, two at the most."

This short-term inflexible deadline comforts me. I cling to it.

*These college boys will talk a week, debate, dream and plan, probably won't sign up in time. For once, I'm glad they procrastinate.*

"Okay, do I need to see a recruiter at the unit?"

"I called Chapman, our recruiter. He says you ain't in his district, you'll need to see one closer to home. Chapman knows him. He's gonna call and let him know to take care of you. Get back with me BEFORE you sign anything. There's more to this than joining Cub Scouts."

"Dad.... C'mon.... don't you think I know that?" Josh cuts through my generic warning I give young people before they enlist. "See the recruiter at home—by the cell phone place, right?"

"Yeah, hang on a minute. You need to think and pray overnight. Call me back tomorrow. Okay?"

"You said we gotta move fast, right?"

"Yeah, but let's make sure you're doing what God wants. One night is not much to ask on a decision like this. It took me months to be sure."

"Okay, I'll call you tomorrow"

*Wait a minute. Mike's talkin about…. I need to talk to him. These boys have to think past BS stories of glory and honor.*

"Josh, have Mike call me. I wanna talk to him."

"Dad, you know he almost joined the Marines. He's wanted to do somethin' for a while. He was even workin' out with a Marine recruiter at Bonita."

"I know, but he's moved off to college, got student loans, signed a lease, deposits for power, water, and all. Mike's situation is different from yours. Tell him to call me, and you pray tonight, hard. I've lost friends, not everyone comes back, Son. Call me lunch-time tomorrow, West Coast time."

"Okay. I know. I will. Talk to you tomorrow."

I climb our front steps and close with, "Night, Son."

"Night, Dad."

I rush back to our closet, sit on my rack, stare at graffiti covered walls, my left hand grasps my phone, an open beer in my right. Byson comes in, sits on his rack, looks me over, and says, "What's wrong with you?"

I shrug my shoulders and guzzle half-a-bottle.

*He knows me enough to see something's up. People gotta see it on us, real men don't admit it. We don't volunteer emotional sh'.*

In return for his concern, Byson gets a manly, "Tell ya later."

Byson's son is in. He got back from his first volunteer tour a few months ago. He will not go this time. Duke, a squad leader in second platoon, has a son in our unit who has been back for about a year. Duke has twenty years like me, his wife wants him to go and watch out for their boy.

My head floods with possibilities, thoughts, memories, and fears. I drink and watch a squirrel sneak in the building's entryway.

*All that jumpy little fella wants is a nut, some scraps, something to eat. Lucky dude—bet his son's not going to war with him.*

My extensive and erratic thoughts give way to that rooster ringtone. I grab my phone, finish the beer, and tell Byson, "I'll be back."

"Hello," I answer, as I chase our squirrel friend back outside. I shuffle back to my dirt lot office to pace around and talk to Mike.

"Hi Mr. Dale. It's Mike. Josh told me to call you."

"Mike, yeah, he says you two are thinking about goin' with us."

"Yes, sir."

As I question all recruits I start with, "What makes you want to go?"

"Mr. Dale you know I've wanted to do something in the military for a long time. When Josh told me what he was planning, I was like, dude, that sounds awesome. I mean to serve with one of my best friends and you, Mr. Dale. Knowing we have a mission, not just going to drill or something. That's what I've been looking for."

*What did all those campouts with "Mr. Dale," do to these boys? Have I taught 'em how to answer my questions, or do they honestly want to serve? Have I instilled in them what led me to serve, what leads me to continue?*

A hundred conversations with these boys scroll through my mind.

While I wrestle these thoughts, the question he must have known I would ask fumbles from my mouth, "What do your parents think about this? I mean, you have a lease on an apartment, student loans….You'd have to drop out in during a semester."

Quick and smooth is his reply, same as Josh. "I haven't really, you know, talked to Mom yet, and I know I'd have to leave school. It's… I don't know… seems like what I gotta do. Ya know?"

Mike has a closer walk with God than Josh, or so it seems. When I ask, "Have you prayed about this?" right or wrong, I expect a different response.

"I have a little. I really think this would be good for me…to serve…ya know."

His response is not all I had hoped. At nineteen, both boys need to define themselves and their own beliefs.

I hope for more room for reason with Mike, and continue my questions and "fatherly" advice. "I respect that, but you need to look at all aspects of leaving school. Can you get out of your lease? Will there be penalties at school for leaving? Can you get any of your tuition money back? Check into things and pray some more. I mean really pray this through. Pray about what this will do to your mom too."

Slowly Mike slides another stake in my heart. "I thought about that. It's gonna be tough on her. But I think knowing I'm with you will help her through it."

*Okay, pause, no pressure. Take Mike with us. We have known and gone to church with his parents for years, and he is an only child! They will be devastated if I don't bring him back. This sh' is getting' deep. How do I tell him, "I can't promise you'll come back"? Hell, I can't promise I'll come back. Shut it down and hang up dammit.*

"Pray about it tonight Mike. Call me tomorrow, lunch time out here, okay?"

"Yessir, I will," but discredits my advice with, "But I really think this is what I should do."

Only thing left for "Mr. Dale" to say is, "Okay. I'll pray for you."

*I talked to both of 'em. My wife and Mike's parents are oblivious. Do I call and warn 'em? I know what to do, have a beer, cleanse my head. Wash my brain out.*

"Hey Sar'nt Sanderford, some of us are goin' to town to eat. Wanna go?" Taylor asks as I enter our barracks.

Taylor is my driver out here. My rank got our rental car on my orders. We unanimously agree my eight totaled cars eliminate me as driver.

"Yeah, give me time to take a shower and change."

"We gotta change, too. It'll be a while, say, half an hour?"

"Sounds good."

I walk past Taylor and enter my closet.

*Perfect. Get outta here, get some good food, have a few beers, and forget this sh'. That is just what I need.*

Byson, still on his rack, stares through me with his "what's up" face. Great guy, but I do not want to discuss this a fourth time.

*He's still staring.*

*What the hell, why not spill the beans quick.*

"My son and his best friend are tryin' to drop out of college and deploy with us."

"I didn't even know he was in the Guard."

"He's not, not yet. They hope to get in, and finish basic and tech school before we MOB."

Byson sits up and shuffles to his racks edge, bare feet rest on the bare wood floor. "What's your wife say?"

"Well ole friend, would you call her for me. She don't know."

"You ain't bringin' me in it. That's yo' job. Whatcha fixing to do?"

"Goin' to town, get somethin' to eat. Wanna go?"

"Nah, I'm goin' to the chow hall in a few. Y'all be careful."

\*\*\*

Anita asks, "Did you tell Karen about these discussions?"

"Nope, like the MOB, it wasn't final. They might not go. So far it was all talk."

"He didn't tell me. I sat back here trying to support Charlotte in accepting her Daddy is leaving. I didn't have a clue Josh was even thinkin' about going. He acted like me. Like Dale shouldn't go, I thought he was on my side."

"Karen, how did you feel when you found out?"

"By the time Josh told me I was numb to it all. Nothing left. I knew he had to decide for himself."

"Dale, what happened next?"

"I went back inside, took a sleeping pill, drank a few more beers, and watched a movie on my laptop to clear my head. It did not work. Brain ran all night, got to sleep about zero-two-thirty. Two or three hours sleep is my new normal.

Next day we finished Combat Lifesaver certification with IV sticks in each other."

Anita says, "You actually put IVs in each other."

"Roger. That was part of our training before goin' over. We make it fun though. If you pump your arm just right and yank the tube off, you can spray blood across the room. It freaks instructors out."

"I guess so."

Karen says, "They get a little crazy in their unit."

I shrug my shoulders. "Josh leaves me a voice mail the next morning...."

"Mike and I talked about it. We're gonna see a recruiter tomorrow. I know you're worried and all, but this is somethin' we gotta do."

*Where'd he get that sh'? I have done twenty-four years to keep him from going!*

Our classroom building shades me as I wait for everyone to finish IV sticks. I see Josh's face in my room at Camp Shelby, 2004. He stands frozen, silent and serious beside a bare concrete block wall, efforts to look unemotional and in control fail.

*We shoulda finished. We left our boys a pile-o-sh' to clean up.*

I gaze across California plateau flat land, at a cliff that they say rangers trained on before D-day. Hot wind reminds me of Iraq, a constant hair dryer blowing my face. Smoke and dust flies right to left—no tree, hill, or wall to slow its flight. Details of ranger cliff fade. From my machine gun pit near Khamasiya, in 91 I stare at a horizon blurred by heat waves, oil wells so far away they look like grain silos in Kansas, hours away.

*Desert Shield/Desert Storm, 9-11, Shock and Awe, so many years. So much BS, so much work, friends, good troops, pain, so damn much. Now we're stuck in the mud makin' slow progress. Insurgents halt efforts to rebuild. We improved situations in Iraq with our clear ground, remove bad people, and maintain security of Owesat. Like the Marines in Fallujah. That's what works. That is what locals want, what they ask for. But no. We send our children to fight and die cause we won't do what we must.*

*Stop thinkin' dumbass. Gonna drive yourself crazy. It ain't your job to debate coulda', woulda', shoulda'. You're just a Platoon Sergeant. Take care of your men, train 'em hard, push 'em harder, and try to bring 'em home.*

*Do your job, not politics or theories. Leave that for people eating croissants and drinking cappuccino. Nobody cares what you think anyway. Call Josh back and drive the fu' on.*

I scan the horizon as his phone rings. Scrubby California trees, barren hills, ever-present dust, and hot sun tempt me to watch for Clint Eastwood to top a hill on horseback.

Josh answers, "Hi, Dad."

"Have you talked to your Mom yet?"

"Yessir, she didn't like it much, but she said to do what I had to."

*Karen's self-control is amazing.*

"She's a good woman. This is gonna be tough on her. I'll call her in a minute."

"You should. She don't want me to go, but she don't wanna hold me back."

"Yeah, I know."

*Karen's always supportive, of me, him, our daughter. She's worn out from all the work, hates our time apart, worries day and night. Now she'll worry about husband and son. She tries to understand there are some things a man has to do. I wonder what all she has crammed down inside now.*

*Focus, you're on the phone.*

I ask, "Did you tell her about Mike?"

"Yeah, Dad, she didn't like that at all."

"All right, y'all gonna see the recruiter tomorrow?"

Josh responds, "Yeah. Mike's comin' home tonight so we can go in the morning."

"Don't sign anything without talkin' to me!"

"You think he'd try to screw us?"

I raise my empty hand, palm skyward. "No. But I wanna know what you're doing before something slips you coulda' got."

"Okay, Dad, we'll talk to you first."

\*\*\*

Anita watches for Karen to react. Karen is silent, left hand grasps her notebook, foot taps and she chews a pen in her right hand.

Anita says, "Did he call you back before they joined?"

"No, he didn't. Mike and Josh were signed up before I got back from California, so much for talking to me first."

Her focus on Karen, Anita says, "Karen did you hear concern and questions in Dale's story? Did it sound like he had no concern for you as these decisions were made?"

"I heard it. Doesn't mean much. He still went. But I heard what he said."

"Good session today. We have a start. Please be open with each other, in what you say, and to what you hear. We should not assume to know what someone is saying, what they mean, or be halfhearted in our effort to understand. It's easy to think 'I've heard it before' or 'His or her comments are empty or meaningless.' Be open to who your spouse has been, remember they love you. I mean you're both in here, that says a lot. You both care about this marriage, about each other. Either of you care to say anything else before we close?"

Karen's head-nod reflects my own.

*I'm done talkin; Karen is done; now that is new.*

5

*Therapy Session Number 11*

My right calf bumps Doc's footstool in route to my couch position.
*Why is a maroon pipe pillow and blanket in my seat? I sit there.*
A push rolls Doc's pillow from my space. I fold his small color confused throw and drape it over my armrest, sit, open a blue journal to a blank page and draw a pen from my map case. Top left corner I write "With Doc T" and date time group (DTG), 051700AUG11, opposite it.
*My jackhammer leg is at it again.*
Doc sits to my front, retrieves a notebook and pen from his leather top footstool, scoots back in his matching brown leather chair, and asks, "Dale, how are you today?"
*Here we go same sh', same seat, new journal, his same notebook, and same view out French doors.*
"Same sh' Doc."
"What's on your mind today?"
"Josh."
*There you go Doc, check your pen, again, one more time. Three weeks with that dark brown pen and you still can't get it to write first try. How bad am I? You're s'pose to help me?*
"What about Josh?"
*Making notes already Doc. I ain't said nothin' yet.*
"A lot-o-stuff, memories, emotions, pride, fear, love, anger"
"When you think about your son, are your thoughts of over there, or back here? How is your son?"
"There and here. He's probably drunk. Like most of us after our first trip, he thinks enough alcohol will wash it away."
"Drinking a good bit is he?"

40

Doc crosses right leg over left and repositions his notebook. I cross my arms, leave my pen within to save my journal page, secure between my armrest and left leg.

Doc's right foot draws air circles as mine beats his carpet.

*Why don't his slip-on canvas shoe come off?*

"He drinks daily. Sneaks it in my house, locks his door and drinks; liquor, beer, whatever he can get."

"Do you think it might help him to talk to someone?"

One hand throws a dismissive wave as I say, "He ain't ready to talk, he's twenty-four, won't do it. Thinks he's tough enough, or should be, to deal with it. We beat Hadji, we can beat this too. You know, like my first time in here. I wasn't ready, just came because everybody told me I should."

Arms remain tight across my chest; right hand strokes my gray, two-month unshaven chin.

"I was no use to you then, Dale. No offense, but no progress would be made until you were ready, ready to do some hard work. It is similar with Josh, or anyone. We must choose to seek help. I am not familiar with the term Hadji."

"Over there we call locals Hadji. Muslims use it for someone who's done their pilgrimage to Mecca."

My head snaps right, eyes focus outside, past flower bushes, in time to see a red bird lite atop Doc's crooked baked-clay colored retaining wall.

*All the money shrinks make and he can't get someone to lay block in a straight damn line.*

"That's one reason I didn't wanna go to Medical at Benning. In uniform, I don't let show, or admit my issues. Benning woulda done me no good. I'd been a drunk there, like Josh is here."

"Yes, as we discussed it was likely best you did not go there. You mention several emotions in reference to Josh. Does he know you have more than a father's frustration?"

"Yessir, I often express my pride in him. He and I laugh and tell stories, memories. Like down in Penguin by a marijuana field…"

\*\*\*

Josh's platoon clears a route to our south. My men and I clear for bombs east of Zormat. At the far end of this familiar route an infantry unit, out of Zormat, is building a new Combat Out Post (COP). We are to provide a bomb free path to and from their construction site.

Intel says a pressure plate guru lives in the village three klicks north of the new COP. Word is he's taught most IED emplacers in our Area of Operation (AO) both construction and emplacement.

*Our two-day mission thru his village sucked. Eleven IEDs, several TICs with*

*RPGs, IDF, and small arms. Infantry tried to get Mr. Pressure Plate. As always, he leaves before they get to his house. If we'd a got him our work here would make a difference for troops to come after us.*

Simple mission today clear route Scheibe, again. We pass a local "Taliban observation post" as we call it, an Afghan Army checkpoint. Two of our three platoons report an Afghan troop there photographing us with his phone. We all stop and delete his photos. After we leave, he always gets on his phone. Five klicks past him, "Surprise!" an IED is armed and ready. After multiple reports, they shut down his checkpoint, not that any Afghan army troops are "bad people."

Near the Combat Outpost we turn around, another boring route clearance day, found no IEDs and received no indirect or small arms fire. Hours of drive, search, check, dig, clear, and do over. Seven klicks before the north turn to get home, a text from our Tactical Operation Center pops up on my screen.

One thirty-seven took a hit south of Zormat. A big hit, need help to recover.

*My men are gonna be pissed, get ready for shit-talkin, Sarge. Best tell 'em so they'll shut up before we turn south, instead of north.*

"All VICs, this is One Nine. We been ordered south at Zormat to assist 137 recover. They are unable to recover with one wrecker. All VICs acknowledge."

"Husky One, roger."

"Husky Two, roger."

"One Two Alpha, Aaaand roger."

"One Two Bravo, roger."

"Buff, roger. I copy go help 137 because they can't finish their job."

"One Six, roger."

"Mater, roger that."

"One One, copy, go south at Zormat and help 137 recover. Roger that. Hey, one–nine, you know how far south they is?"

"Roger One One, they're at the sand pit."

"One Nine, this is One One. Roger that, sand pit."

We need more data on their situation before we enter the village. I text Smith as we trudge west.

Smith, or his driver, texts me back:

Husky One hit hard, in three pieces. Recovery VICs stuck in sand.

*Smith is probably barking and pacing around like a bull dog. He hates it when his men do stupid sh'. Top it off another platoon knows his wrecker is stuck. Bet he's cussing so hard he's scaring locals."*

At Zormat, we turn south and take a Papa Bravo (piss brake) before we drop off the paved road. We get radio contact as we enter the village.

"Byson Two Nine, this is Byson One Nine, over."

"Go for Two Nine."

"Two nine, this is One Nine. We are comin' in from Zormat. Whatcha need?"

"One Nine, we need your wrecker and a tractor trailer if you have one with you."

"Roger, Two Nine, we got both. We'll stage at the gas station. I'll come see you on the ground and we'll figure this out."

"Roger that."

"One Nine, out."

"Two Nine, out."

"All VICs this is One Nine, gimme' a halt a hundred meters north of the village. One Two Alpha and I will lead in with Mater and Nine Sixteen. How Copy?"

"Husky One, roger."

"Husky Two, roger."

"One Two Alpha aaaand a roger."

"One Two Bravo, roger."

"Buff, roger."

"One Six, roger."

"Mater, roger that."

"One One, copy, halt a hundred meters afore the village and you, One Two Alpha will lead Mater and Nine Sixteen in."

"Hey there One Nine, this is One One. You want us to follow y'all on in there or just sit out here with our thumb up our butt?"

"This is One Nine, Gimme' Buff and One Six on in with me. We'll turn around at the gas station. One Six and Buff secure the route comin' out and cover Nine Sixteen and Mater at the gas station. Rest-o-y'all turn around and be ready to Charlie Mike, normal order of march. One Two Alpha post up off route southeast of the gas station and cover my ass so I can walk down and see what's up. Nine Sixteen loop it around and park at the station and prep to load. How Copy?"

"Husky One, roger."

"Husky Two, roger."

"One Two Alpha aaaand a roger."

"One Two Bravo, roger."

"Buff roger, Follow you in."

"One Six, roger."

"Mater, roger that."

"One One, copy, I'll stay up here and get us ready to Charlie Mike after you pull 'em out."

"Roger, One Nine, out."

*Nice to have NCOs who can make sh' happen without constant supervision. All I gotta do now is have a Rip-it, smoke, ride in, and dismount to see Smith.*

Our realignment is as smooth as ever; I follow One Two Alpha in. At the gas station, One Two Alpha takes his position. We pull our truck, Lu Lu, forward just shy of the sand pit.

I look to Miller, my driver, and say, "Lemme out here. You turn around and keep security west. RC, tell Miller where you need to be to have a decent sector of fire through these trees."

Miller says, "So now you want me to turn around, sit right here, but not exactly here, I gotta let RC tell me where. Might be back 'ere, up 'ere or even…."

My door open, right leg out, without facing him I say, "Shut the hell up, you know what the fu' I mean. Lemme know if we get a text or anything."

Miller laughs, "All right Sar'nt, we gotcha."

RC yells from up top as I clamber down Lu Lu to sink my boots in loose sand, "Sar'nt you want me to point at way right? What is a sextor? You want me to get a good sextor, what's at is?"

"Do your damn job RC, quit givin' me sh'."

RC's right hand gives me a "go-away" wave. "We good Sar'nt. We ain't let ya down yet have we?"

*You deserve that sh' Sarge. They know what to do, don't micromanage.*

I trudge through deep sand around Lu Lu's front bumper, and down a slope to bypass the blown up bridge. I see Smith past the bridge with Pile. Smith's left pokes Pile's chest as his helmet bounces in rhythm to his operatic mouth movement.

*He is pissed. A good hit and gotta get our help. That is embarrassing.*
*Those are scrubby lookin' flower buds…*
*Ah sh', we had to park right next to this field.*

Smith and I decide to have Mater drag Smith's blown husky a hundred fifty meters north to our tractor trailer. I call Mater forward. He hauls Husky's main body first. Another two trips will get the blown off ends.

I say, "Sar'nt Smith, I'm goin' to the gas station, y'all good"

"We good Sar'nt Sanderford, appreciate it."

"No problem, we'll need you to return the favor one day."

"We would but you know my tractor trailer is still blown the hell up."

"I know. They gonna fix it or what?"

"I don't give a sh'. I'll just call you when I need one."

I shove Smith's shoulder until he stumbles. "Asshole. I'll let ya know when we're loaded up."

Smith laughs with as much vigor as he had instructed troops on our arrival. "Roger that Sar'nt."

Another sand march past blown bridge, up sandy slope, past a village marijuana field, I turn east to the station. Pritchett, my second squad leader, has eight men ready to load and secure today's busted vehicle.

Pritchet supervises our load team. I check security, and standoff to observe.

Miller strolls up, "Sar'nt you know this gas station is freakin' dirty right? Every damn time we get hit down there, people are sittin' out front, right there. No one out front, and it's a easy freakin' day right. You know 'at sh'."

I call Pritchett over. Miller, Pritchett, and I go over to the station owner. Once our interpreter decides to show up, we talk to Mr. Gas Man. He invites us to look around in his store. I send a team in and stay to talk to Gas Man and his nephew by rusty white fuel pumps.

*He probably wants to sell us something. We bought sh' from locals in Iraq, maybe he has some dates. I'd love some bread right now.*

I yell at Miller as he and three others enter. "Miller, look and see if he's got some-o-that pita bread, I'm hungry."

With a thumbs up Miller steps through the door and yells, "Roger Sar'nt, you're buyin' lunch, I gotcha."

*Asshole*

Miller comes back with a fertilizer bag, drops it at my feet, straightens up, lights a smoke, points at the bag and says, "That sh' right there's illegal." He points south toward today's blast hole. "Same sh' we keep getting' blowed the hell up with right down there. This mother f-er's dirty Sar'nt."

I look at Bronson, now on my left. "Get Carson over here to look at this."

Miller and Carson hold certifications to blow in place (BIP) our IED finds. They are not full fledge Explosive Ordnance Disposal (EOD) but they have extensive munitions identification training. Without these two, we would often be stuck in an extended wait for EOD to arrive and handle what we find.

Bronson moves out with a scratchy deep, "Roger Sar'nt."

I look at Miller and see his "I'm pissed, but holding it back" dance; adjust weapon on chest, shrug shoulders twice, tip Kevlar back, drag on smoke, look at Sar'nt Sanderford, look at ground, back at Sergeant Sanderford with a red rooster head cock and open mouth. Once he has done his best to remain quiet, or pumps his words from foot to mouth, he speaks. Like a hydrant hit by a car expletives spew forth between lucid thoughts, hand waves, toke-o-smoke, or finger points in random directions emphasize each sentence fragment.

"Sar'nt whatch'a need Carson for? Don't think I know my sh'? I am freakin' insulted Sar'nt. That's the damn sh' they ain't s'pose to have. That old som-bitch in BIP class up at Bagram showed us that damn symbol, on that bag, right there. Hell, he showed us the damn fertilizer too, case they reuse bags ya know. That's the bad sh' right there. I'd put money on it."

I light a smoke and explain, "Today's Army we gotta be politicians, police detectives, lawyers and soldiers. We gotta be sure. People's careers get cut short when they detain someone they shouldn't have. I get both my BIP guys to ID it and y'all's career is on the line instead of mine."

Miller takes a toke, laughs. "You, Sir, are an asshole Sar'nt Sanderford, sh'. Which part is that right there, lawyer or politician?"

"Detective, how you think they stay on the force? I may be an asshole, but my career keeps goin'."

Bronson's voice to my left announces, "Here's Carson, Sar'nt."

My head turns slightly left to observe Carson's swagger. Weapon inaccessibly slung across his back, helmet cocked back similar to Miller's, boot heels scrape rock and sand with each step. "Whatcha got Sar'nt?"

I kick Miller's bag. "You tell me, you're my BIP guy."

Carson squats by the bag, drops one knee to keep from falling, his pants' ripped crotch open for all to see. He leans the bag left, right, opens it, and allows some of the substance to trickle through his fingers. Straightens up, shuffles back two steps, looks at Miller, and says, "Where'd y'all find it?"

Miller drags on his smoke, then knife points his cigarette hand to the quick stop entrance. "Right in there."

I say, "What is it Carson?"

"Ammonium Nitrate Fertilizer, Sar'nt, no doubt. They ain't s'pose to have it. Guy up at Bagram said they brought in some other fertilizer for 'em when this got outlawed. Same stuff we done found twelve, fifteen times?"

I look at Pritchett and say, "Clean their pockets out, get a grid, makes some notes like back when you were a cop 'n let's take 'em in."

Pritchet steps forward and says, "Roger Sar'nt. Both?"

"Roger, both."

Pritchet is one of several Marines I've worked with in combat. I have yet to have a one disappoint me. He directs men to prepare our suspects.

Josh walks up, points at the pair of garage doors, and asks, "Hey, Dad, anyone check that side?"

*I hope Karen don't find out we are on the ground together. She would be pissed.*

Sergeant Bronson, again to my left, steps to my front, looks from Josh to me and says, "Ain't nobody checked it, Sar'nt, not that I know of."

I hesitate.

*Nothing has happened, yet, an IED, but no small arms, no nasty injuries. Do I want my son out of my sight, my control? Locals know we are gonna take these two. All our troops are busy. What the hell Sarge. 'You want?' Shut up, Mr. Selfish. Josh's here to do a job, he is a troop, like all my men.*

Josh's eagerness to do his duty short circuits my thoughts: "C'mon, Dad, I got this."

In my best command voice I say, "Who's goin' with Sanderford to clear the south end?"

Sergeant Bronson and Specialist Hanson say they will go. The three move out, and discuss entry order in route.

*We have all cleared with three people, even two, but sending my son without at least a four-man-stack? If he get's, sh'....*

Josh glances back as if he leaves to play basketball with a neighbor back home. "We got it, Dad."

My left hand points to dirt to my front; right caresses my weapon. "Report back to me as soon as y'all get out."

Bronson winks his wrinkled left eye and says, "I got 'em, Sar'nt."

Josh faces front, says, "Roger that," and speeds toward the personnel door of the garage.

I watch my son's back, middleman in a shorthanded four-man-stack, enter an old wooden door, and disappear.

*They went in right, and no shots fired, yet.*

I face our detainees by the pumps. Lt. Martin approaches from his vehicle and asks, "Sergeant Sanderford, we gonna detain these guys?"

"Roger Sir."

I watch our men with today's detainees and instruct, "Y'all blindfold 'em and tie their hands in back. Get 'em ready to go. Pritchett got a grid, notes, DTG, descriptions and all that?"

Pritchet says, "Roger Sar'nt."

"Put one in my truck, the other in One Two's." I turn to Lt. "Okay with you, Sir?"

"Yes, Sergeant."

I turn to the open door my men went through, light another smoke, take a long deep drag; see one exit, another, my son third man out, and exhale.

"Hey, give me your gator, Josh."

Josh removes his helmet, stretches his neck gator over his head, and says, "What for?"

"We need a blindfold."

He hands me his gator. "Ok, roger that."

I hand his gator to Staff Sergeant Pritchet.

"Sergeant Pritchet, use this as a blindfold."

"Roger, Sar'nt."

Smith's blown Husky on our tractor trailer, we load a detainee in my truck and our rear vehicle.

I say, "Let's load up, line up, and get the hell out-o-here." My men and Josh's platoon all head for their vehicles.

*Josh and I should get a picture, this is one to remember. IED, Detainees, search of a building. This is a good Father-Son day.*

I wave down Lt. Martin, "Hey, Lt. come here."

Lt. walks toward us. My son stands to my left, I hand Lt. my camera and step closer to Josh.

"Here. Get a shot for me, Sir; it's a great father-son moment."

He laughs, aims my camera and says, "I hear ya, proud Daddy"

"Damn right, Sir, real proud."

That marijuana behind us slips our mind. We enjoy our photo op.

Lt. Martin hands my camera back. I pat Josh's shoulder, and we head to our respective trucks. I stand next to my open door. "Miller, call up and see who's ready to roll. I take a leak, put out my smoke, and climb up Lu Lu's steps to my seat. Inside, I situate the pillow I sit on, secure my seat belt, check my texts, put on my helmet with headset, turn my switch to internal communications and ask, "Who's ready, Miller?"

"We up, Sar'nt, ready to roll."

"Bronson, switch me to 137's freq."

Bronson, in back with our detainee complies, "Roger, there you go, Sar'nt."

"Thanks." I key the radio. "Byson Two Six, this is Byson One Nine, y'all ready? Over."

Josh's Lieutenant responds, "One Nine, this is Two Six, roger."

"Roger Two Six, One Nine, out."

"Two Six, out."

"Switch me back Bronson." I retrieve my smokes from my right sleeve pocket and glance at Miller.

*What's that sh' eating grin about?*

A look out Lu Lu's windshield tells me what Miller's silence does not. "What the hell is on my hood Miller?"

Miller, RC and Bronson's laughter fill our internal communications.

A marijuana plant decorates my hood, right where Little Lu Lu, our porcelain hula dancer, used to be.

*Perfect hood ornament for a Platoon Sergeant. Whatever.*

I key up on our platoon frequency, "Husky One, Husky Two, lead us out."

"Husky One roger."

"Husky Two roger."

A text message arrives as my first two vehicles exit the village.

Hold in place. Brigades are arguing over jurisdiction. You're in 101st AO so they want detainees brought to Sharana. Byson 6 is arguing the point. Hold in place for further orders.

"Bronson, switch me back to second's freq."

"Roger, Sar'nt. There you go, you're on it."

"Roger."

"Byson Two Six, this is Byson One Nine. You get that text from the TOC?"

"This is Byson Two Six, Roger that. Sucks don't it."

"Roger Two Six, let's get everyone north of the village before we stop."

"Roger that One Nine."

"Let me know when your last VIC exits"

"Roger One Nine, will do."

"One Nine, out"

"Two Six, out"

"Switch me back Bronson."

"Got it Sar'nt, you're good."

"Roger."

Miller looks at me, the dirt road, me, left hand pounds his steering wheel, he holds up three of four fingers. "What's up Sar'nt?"

"They want us to take 'em to Sharana."

"What the Fu'? Tonight? That's like eleven hours Sar'nt. It's about freakin' dark."

"I see that sh'. Wait for 'em to finish arguing."

"Whose arguin'?"

"Byson Six and Battalion Six knows how stupid that sh' is."

*They try to send us to Sharana, and I'll tell 'em these bastards got away. Cut 'em loose and go home. Arresting them ain't gonna matter in six months. They'll come back here and start right the hell back up. We ain't goin' to Sharana.*

RC shifts on his pedestal, spins the turret from three O'clock, to five, and says, "Settle in boys, gonna be a long night."

I key up, "Husky One, Husky Two, we are gonna halt north of here. I'll let you know when."

"Husky One, roger."

"Husky Two roger, now is that my just north, your just north or Two Six's just north, One Nine?"

"Husky Two, this is One Nine, I'll tell you when, smart ass."

"Husky Two, roger that."

"One Nine, this is One One. I copy we gonna stop up here in a minute. Uh, can ya tell us what's up there One Nine?"

"One One, higher is debating where we need to take these detainees."

"Is-at-right, uh, One Nine, what options we got?"

"Sharana or Gardez."

"One Nine, Buff here, do I gotta point out Gardez is on the way home boss."

"Not my choice Buff. We're in Sharana's AO. Technically they should handle 'em."

"One Nine, this is One Two Alpha, so twelve hours south, or 30 minutes north to drop 'em on the way home?"

"Roger One Two Alpha, break. All VICs, this is One Nine. Y'all heard what's up, cuss about it on internal coms, keep my net clear."

My demand for radio communications to remain clear offers my men a bit of fun. Jokes allow us to verbalize collective emotions, thoughts, and frustrations. We have to let off steam to maintain control.

Without proper identification of who is transmitting, I hear the following:

Specialist Carson transmits, "Ah, Hell no."

Sergeant French broadcasts, "Dammit we weren't even s'pose to be down here."

Mater radios, "Sh'."

Pritchet, whose call sign is One Three, keys up from the Buffalo, "One Nine, this is One Six, sorry about that hot mic, my bad."

My laugh exhales cigarette smoke across our dashboard.

My right hand raises to my chest switch to key up and we hear, "One Nine, this is One Six, that wasn't us, over."

I key up, "Roger One Six, break, Buff, this is One Nine, nice try, One Nine, out."

Our fight with boredom and frustration continues. Pritchet keys up, "One Six, out."

LT broadcasts, "This is One Six. Y'all quit settin' me up."

We halt in another open flat area. Several men dismount to take a pee break. My patience dwindles. I stare at my computer screen, anxious for our "further orders" to arrive.

RC says, "Sun's 'bout down over 'em mountains."

I glance out my window and watch a beautiful array of colors emanate from a dark yellow globe just visible above grayish brown mountains.

*I love this view. Another good day. No one lost.*

Deep yellow blurs to a dark orange haze as the sun crawls behind cover.

*So damn pretty, lets me shake off today's work before danger surrounds us in total darkness.*

We wait twenty minutes for orders, stationary, a hundred meters north of a dirty village.

LT Martin radios, "One Nine, this is Two Six, we have a crowd gathering back here."

"Two Six, this is One Nine. What they want?"

"One Nine, this is Two Six. Hang on, I'll check."

I light another smoke and wait for Lt. to dismount with his interpreter and chat.

*With his terp, this could take a while. Orders are still not here.*

I take another long drag on my smoke and stare east at a curtain of darkness. Flood lights from our vehicles light our dirt path and fifty short meters to the drape's base. Memory says it is a flat, empty, wasteland beyond the blinds, several kilometers of rock and sand. It is a drastic contrast from bright floodlights up close to an endless veil, which hides unknown activity beyond.

*This stillness is surreal, cannot see goat, bush or bug moving. Reality is a mystery beyond the lights. Hadji, emboldened by darkness, could be two hundred meters out, flipping us off, and we would never know.*

My paranoia surrenders to Lt. Martin's voice from my headset. "One Nine, this is Two Six. They are begging us not to take Daddy and

Grandpa."

"Load up, Two–Six. If they weren't doing bad sh', we wouldn't take 'em."

"Momma's crying, kids crying. Getting to be a pretty big crowd back here, One Nine."

"Just load up, Lt. Let's move north some more."

"Roger."

Miller says, "What the Fu', Sar'nt. Who gives-a-sh' if kids are crying? Remember all 'em cryin' kids in 05?"

"Yeah, I remember. It's Lt's first time with crying kids while he arrests their Dad. Everybody's gotta have a first time."

"He needs to grow a pair and come on," Miller says.

"C'mon, now, you gotta admit he's a good PL."

Specialist Miller begins, "Yeah, no sh' remember—"

I cut Miller off, "I know, I know, drop it. Let's just get home."

A flash of color on my screen signals we have a new text message. Smoke in hand, I say, "Crap, another TOC text," and poke the screen to open it.

Miller says, "What they want? Want us to go back and hug 'em kids?"

I respond to the Tactical Operations Center, and radio Lt. Martin, "Two Six, this is One Nine."

"Go for Two Six."

"Two Six, TOC says continue to hold in place. We gonna get away from your crying friends till we RTB." (Return To Base)

"Yeah, roger."

"One Nine, out."

"Two Six, out."

We halt half a klik north. Lt. Martin sends me a text to ask why we continue to sit in the dark.

*Four klicks outside our AO, clearing for another RCP, again, our blown-up Husky driver's headache gets worse by the minute. It's dark, and we gotta sit here.*

I pass my last message from our Tactical Operation Center along to Lt. Marin:

"Sharana won't send infantry to get your detainees unless you clear the route first. Both RCPs down there are down for maintenance. Battalion, Brigade, and Division Headquarters are arguing about where to take detainees.

*An easy day ruined by political sh'.*

Sun gone, moon off tonight, our floodlights feed the all-consuming darkness. The volume of that constant tone in my head increases in this deafening silence.

*Down to my last four smokes, after this one.*

We count minutes and have a snack. I stare at an unanswered text question, or out the window into the abyss. When darkness reigns, boredom fights paranoia for our attention.

I text the Tactical Operation Center:

Need answer in fifteen minutes or we drop detainees at Gardez and come home. Fuel low can't get to Sharana without refueling. Husky operator's headache worse. delay not helping. Need to RTB ASAP.

Sergeant Knight's return text is one of our favorite and most common intellectual responses to serious questions in combat.

Roger

*What is "roger"? Are you saying: You're Screwed, you don't give a sh' or, the decision makers are gone to chow. What does "Roger" mean?*

I radio Lt. Martin, "Two Six, this is One Nine, over."

"One Nine, this is Two–Six."

"Two Six, we got no decision on detainees yet. How's your Husky driver?"

"One Nine, this is Two Six. We need to get him home. Still no answer?"

"Roger, Two Six, no answer. One Nine, out."

"Two Six, out."

A clock check every minute drags our stagnant progress more than when I used to count grain silos driving across Kansas. Minute count hits thirteen before a text orders my platoon to take detainees to Zormat. Lt. Martin is to take his platoon home to get his operator's head checked.

At Zormat, around Zero-two-hundred, my men do paperwork and sworn statements. A Tactical Human Intelligence Team and Psychological Operations Team (THT and PSYOPS) discuss life's meaning with our detainees. Zero-three-thirty both teams agree Zormat's Afghan Army detachment will hold Mr. Gas Man and his partner until daybreak.

We roll out at zero-seven and take both detainees to the regional detention facility inside Josh's Forward Operating Base.

\*\*\*

Doc says, "So you and your son were together as your platoons arrest suspected insurgents."

"Yessir, a few days later, we hear one got sent up for further questioning. He was a key leader and brother to the top dog down there. The other got released in his village. Locals marched on Zormat to protest and demand their big man back. Even kidnapped and threatened to kill Zormat's mayor. PSYOPS guys said the mayor has close ties to some other insurgent group.

They threaten to kill a person they elected unless we give back a proven insurgent. Win-win for us, keep a bad guy, and locals whack another one. time's about up, ain't it Doc?"

"It is. Thank you for sharing this Dale. Once again the emotions, anxiety, the constant stress of such situations make it clear why we are here, doing this work."

"Another day-o-work Doc, lotta troops had worse."

"Don't belittle your own experiences, Dale. You have had worse yourself. Our focus is on Dale. On what Dale will do with his experiences. Comparison to other people's lives is not only damaging but also impossible. One cannot hope to do such a comparison in an objective way. Neither you nor I know what another person saw, did, or remembers. Can you be sure of any such details for your men?"

"No Sir. I comprehend. I was there. But I can't know every detail in their minds."

"Remember this. Whenever you begin to belittle your own experiences, or think you should be "better," whatever that is, than you are, think on this truth. Can you do that for me Dale? Will you do that for yourself?"

Journal back in map case I close, shoulder it and stand. "I'll do my best Doc."

Doc's notebook plops to his footstool; he grasps both his armrests, and stands. We shake hands. His stumble around his own footstool allows me to open his door and clear the hall before I step out.

I exit and say, "See ya next time, Doc," without a look back. To do so would not allow me to check the corner of the hall, next hall, or that open doorway.

"Ok, take care, Dale. The lady's out front…."

"Roger, I gotcha, Doc. Have a good one."

# 6

Doc Taylor looks up from his damn notebook, fumbles with his pen and says, "Well, Dale, how are we today?"

*Sh' Doc I'm screwed up. How you doing?*

"Doin' okay, Doc."

My cell phone on silent, I stow it in and retrieve a new red journal from my map case, close the case, fold up its frayed shoulder strap, position journal and prop my case against my left ankle.

"What's on your mind?"

Headings for today's fun complete, I look through Doc, and say, "Most times my men."

"What about your men?"

Doc crosses his legs, looks at me, and holds his chin with his pen hand.

I motion to my silent encased phone. "I watch Facebook posts about divorces, alcohol, anger issues. Most of us are havin' a hard time."

"How do you feel toward your men?"

"Responsible. I took 'em over. I brought 'em back. How do I keep 'em safe now? Help with all this sh'?"

"Are such thoughts new you for you?"

"No, Sir. Same ole Plat Daddy sh'. In spite of my screw ups, leaving 'em there, in combat, and everything else, they are still my men."

"Leaving them in combat?"

"You know, when I was medevac'd for stroke symptoms."

I shift on his couch. Doc scribbles and says, "To Germany, is that right?"

"Yeah, Doc, wasted a month while they were still at work."

"Remind me, what was your final diagnosis in Germany?"

54

"They never figured sh' out. A doc at our FOB thought it might-a-been stress, but I told him we hadn't had a truck blown up in three days. After a month in Germany, I got to go back to work."

Doc leans back in his chair, makes eye contact with me and says, "They released you to return to Afghanistan? Without a diagnosis?"

"My neurologist did. Not the shrink, but the neurologist did."

"You saw a psychologist in Germany?"

"Yessir. I thought she released me when I told her I'd take fish oil, and follow up with someone back at work."

"What do you mean, 'you thought she released you?'"

"At Camp Shelby during demob a doc said the Germany shrink put in for me to come to the states for more evaluation and therapy. I told my case worker at Ramstein that the neurologist released me. Guess she couldn't see crazy-boy records, so I went to work."

"Did you follow up with someone at your base in Afghanistan?"

I cross my arms, lean back, take a deep breath and say, "No Sir, no one there full-time. I got back to work and forgot all about it. Stuff to do."

"Going to Germany let your men down?"

"Yessir. While I was in Germany, we had more issues, and Bronson died. I wasn't there for my men."

"How did your men see it?"

"Probly thought I had to go, had no choice. Several saw my confusion, inability to talk and such. Same as usual, but that day it was worse."

"So your men don't hold it against you?"

"No. They respected me; cared about me. A few saw me cry when Doc said I'd get sent out. Cried like a baby when he said I'd end up in Germany and probably back home."

"You cried when told you may be sent home."

"Going home without them meant leaving my men, not doing my job."

"But your men respected you. I would say they still do."

"Yessir, even when I cuss, push hard, yell at 'em, or piss 'em off, they respect me."

"Did you often cuss?"

"No, Sir. Saved it for when I had to make a big impact."

"What do you mean?"

"If you always cuss and yell, emphasis is lost, kind a like threatening to spank a kid but never doin' it. Kid knows you're bluffing, you won't do it. Day before Smith and I saw Mike and Josh in tech. school, I cussed out thirty-six men.

"We were at Fort Leonard Wood to train for a few weeks before mobilization, January 2010. Captain Wayne ordered us to draft an SOP while we were out there. Most of us were more concerned with dinner and drinking than an SOP. Had to wake 'em up. Threw a nice little fit in our evening meeting, cussed, waved my arms, slammed my hand on tables. It got their attention."

\*\*\*

Friday on our way back from class Smith says, "You get a time set up to see your son?"

We are in pre-mob training at Leonard Wood, Mike and Josh are here as well. They got here October, came home for Christmas, and returned to complete Advanced Individual Training (AIT). Most training units frown on parental visits. It disrupts conversion of a teenager into a life taker. It is a tough enough job without unknown outside influences.

"Called his unit five times, nothin' set up yet."

"Let's just go down there and see if we can see 'em."

I shrug my shoulder. "Why not? Let's go at sixteen-hundred tomorrow, Saturday, they'll probly just be cleanin' the barracks."

"Alright then. I'll drive."

"Course you will. Y'all never wanna ride with me."

"Hell no, you wreck cars back home on dry roads. Up here we got freagin' snow!"

"Oh, whatever."

In the hotel's breakfast room, we gather every afternoon and discuss that day's classes. Smith and I make assignments for following days, ask questions, and give safety briefs. No trainer, other unit, nor Big Army has offered us a standard operating procedure, for route clearance. Some generic ones, several years old, but none we are comfortable using. Company standard operating procedures are crucial to get us on the same page. When a vehicle takes a hit and loses radio communication, how do we signal severity of injuries to other vehicles? What is our procedure to recover down vehicles, to clear for secondary bombs and recover personnel?

*Where will I tote my own body bag this time?*

Only one troop, an E-4, put together a list. Specialist Carson gave me a list of what he needs to Identify (ID) and Blow in Place (BIP) IEDs. His list is the only effort aside from general discussions.

We clear Leonard Wood's front gate and head to our hotel, and Sergeant Smith says, "Ain't none of 'em done sh', Sar'nt Sanderford. They ain't serious, think it's a freagin' game."

"I know. They wanna drink, eat, and have a good time every night. No thought for our purpose here."

"Somebody needs to jerk a knot in 'em. Get 'em to start thinkin' about where we're goin'."

I know Smith's answer but we need to agree. "You wanna do it, or you want me to?"

Smith's head snaps right, gazes in my eyes and turns back to the road. A second head spin slings his words from his mouth. "It'd have more impact if it came from you, Sar'nt Sanderford."

Sergeant Smith turns his truck around to face the parking lot exit and parks, second row out, his usual spot.

I open my door, grab my map case and turn to exit his truck. "Alright, let me see what I can do."

We get out and go inside for our meeting. I stand quiet and still opposite the double door entrance, careful to hear thirty men's pre-meeting chatter.

Discussions include dinner options, troops from other units drunk in class, incompetent instructors, drinks for tonight, and a son's birthday party back home. It is hard to hear specifics over redneck laughter.

*Crap, they ain't takin' this serious!*

Troops, humans in general, gain motivation in different ways. However the most reliable motivator in a schoolhouse is anger from leadership, anger at everything and everyone.

*Play it well, Sergeant Sanderford. Wake up time!*

I kick off our meeting, "Listen up. Let's get started. Huskies, what'd y'all do today?"

Sergeant Washburn speaks up, "We went over PMCS, vehicle ops, maintenance, and repair of marking systems, maintenance stuff all day."

"What do we need to know from what you did today?"

"We gotta have good commo with Smith and 'em in the Buffalo. We may want 'em behind us so they can see where we want 'em to dig. There is somethin' new out, it ain't here, but they say it gives a better picture of what's in the ground. We'll get trained on it somewheres else."

Sergeant First Class Smith's brother, Sergeant E-5 type Smith (better known as Tiny) leans forward to see Washburn and expresses our collective frustration. "You'll get that somewhere else. We hear that sh' a lot, 'somewhere else.' My fat ass can't follow you in the Buffalo dude, ain't got a turret, can't cover ya."

*Someone is thinking. He did some thinking back in 05 too.*

Sergeant Taylor blurts out, "He's right. We'd have a huge gap with no gun. Front VIC's be out there all alone."

*There we go. Three people thinking past dinner.*

Washburn jumps in, "Holy sh', he's right. Don't leave my ass out there flappin'. Cover my ass, man."

Lutz, our most sarcastic E-5, joins Washburn's sentiment: "Y'all don't watch the news? Ain't no bad people over 'ere. If ya take a hit and can't move just climb out and ask anybody shootin' to hold fire and wait for someone to come getcha."

I raise my right hand high, like a schoolteacher tries to get third graders to be quiet. "Okay, forward security. Maintenance, make a note: carry spare parts for the marking system and learn how to fix it on the fly."

Sergeant Franks' molasses-paced comment stalls discussion: "We gonna get a list-o-parts from instructors 'is week. I'll make sure they's on it." He turns and looks around, his words flow no faster than his head turns. "If y'all can. Get me a maintenance manual on each-a-y'all's VICs. I'd 'preciate it. They said they'd get 'em to me on a CD, but 'at was two days ago." Franks waves his hands, stares at me and tilts his head left. "So who knows if he'll do it."

I nod to Franks and say, "What's on for tomorrow for y'all?"

"They said we're gonna simulate recovery after a blast. This thing's designed to be blowed up and keep goin'. We'll see," says Lutz.

One after another, we discuss our day, and what's on for tomorrow. I save my "motivation" talk to close us out.

Group talks over I say, "Sergeant Smith and I got intelligence briefings today. Tomorrow we'll discuss tactics."

I share some intelligence data and transition our discussion. "I'm gonna meet with a Platoon Sergeant tonight from Hawaii. He's active duty. They've been training for this mission for like a year and a half. He says they have an SOP we can work from. I'll have it tomorrow so leadership can meet and discuss it after our deal tomorrow night. Now, what have y'all come up with for load plans?"

Everyone looks like I just said we will kill dogs for a year. No one seems to know anything about lists. "We told the NCOs two days ago to get with each group and prepare load plans for what you're training on. Just a list, we'll get into where what goes later. What do you have for me?"

Everyone turns to look at each other with dumb looks, again, as if I asked a high school kids for a volunteer to write on the board. There is no point discussing our request for lists further. It is a good time to give E-4 and below a couple of things, it will help us in coming days. First I will give lower enlisted the benefit of the doubt—my NCO's had not passed on our instructions. This will provide an opportunity for lower enlisted men to impress me by completing a simple list. Second, I won't allow E-4 and below to hear my discussion with their NCOs. This brings two things into play. I can get louder with leadership, and a lack of information about leader discussions breaks down lower enlisted men's comfort.

I say, "E-4 and below, you can leave. Train hard tomorrow, do not drink and drive. We ain't here to get DUIs or have wrecks. Behave and represent the 731st well in all you do. Active duty troops may throw up in class because they drank too much, but you better not let me find out one of you did! Get out."

I bark, "NCOs stand fast."

*Wake up time, push 'em so they'll go back and wake up our troops. If they can't motivate troops to make a list, we'll have a tough time getting our*

*"Leaders" to take troops through a door to echoes of gunfire.*

I pace in silence, our last two Specialists leave, and close the double doors.

My arms wave and pace quickens. "What's up? What do you have for load lists?"

Dumb looks at each other help my anger grow as I prepare my tirade. At a halt, front and center, my hands snap from random waves to finger points and hand gestures.

"Let me get this straight. We have two months to mob. Three months from now, we're in combat, and today you don't think it's important to follow orders? Your troops ain't even heard. Did not know what the hell I was talkin' about! You are about to take these men into battle, and you don't have the balls to interrupt their party time and discuss what to bring on mission. What the hell are you thinking?"

I clinch my lips and fists, pace, and allow my comments to sink in. Silent tension grows.

I take a deep breath to prevent a loss of temper. "Those men want to do a good job, but they'll only do as good a job as you push 'em to do. You have brothers, cousins, and uncles…right here…in this damn unit."

My finger points at people to whom these words apply. "You get to come back, look your nephews and nieces, their kids, in the eye and tell 'em you didn't bring Daddy home alive."

Right hand slams a table, I point at several men before my arms flail and I yell, "You don't have the balls to push 'em, to train hard now. Y'all are scared to take up their freakin' personal time here to get ready so when Joe's leg gets blown the hell off nobody can find a lifesaver bag to stop the bleeding! What the fu' are you thinking? time to step up or take off your damn stripes."

"Only one person came to me with a list. An E-4, a Specialist, did more to prepare for combat in the last few days than my fives and sixes. He never knew I asked for lists. He honestly wants to have what he needs and be ready. You have Specialists out there who care more about survival than you do about bringing 'em home.

"We lost four good men in 05. If you are gonna be this kind a leader, I'll give your damn stripes to someone else. If I have to, I'll put a high speed E-4 in charge of E-6s. I don't care about your ego, your pride, your paycheck, or your friendship. I will complete the mission before us and bring my men home to their wives.

"We have 135 soldiers goin' to combat. We are the only ones to get training on what we'll do. We are here to prepare load plans and an SOP. An SOP that will get us on the same page, so we'll have a frog hair's chance to finish a mission without gettin' someone killed. And you can't drive your troops to do what you're told to. Not that you didn't realize you needed to, not that you couldn't figure out what to do. You were told. How can I trust you to cover the north side in a firefight if you won't even take the initiative to put a list of supplies on a piece of damn paper? How do I know you'll take troops and hit a qal'at if you won't limit his drinkin' time and talk about what you're about to do? What the hell are you doin' here? E-6 and above stand fast, everybody else get the fu' out. I'm done with you."

I lean against the counter, cross my arms, and hear someone say my name. Arm flail kicks in, I point to french doors and yell, "I don't wanna hear sh' out a you. Go out there and look your men in the eye and think about how you don't give a sh' if they come home alive. Have something for me tomorrow, or I'll have E-4's doing your damn job the next day."

Sergeant Smith, our E-6s and me remain.

*Time to fire up my squad leaders.*

"You are my squad leaders. Don't give me those pissed off looks. I don't give a sh' if your pissed! You remember the squad leader you had back in 05 in Iraq. Remember what he did, how he pushed you, what he knew. Your turn dammit! Your old squad leader ain't here. If you don't do for our men what he did for you in Iraq, how can you expect them to perform as well as you did? You say they don't care, they just wanna eat, go bowlin', or whatever. Who's gonna motivate 'em? If you don't get 'em focused and bring out their best who the fu' will. Not just their lives or your lives depend on it, but the lives of soldiers who'll follow us on routes in Iraq."

*Pause and pace for affect.*

*Ok finish it out.*

"If WE do not perform, other soldiers die. I'm done with you. Get out so Smith and I can talk."

Our squad leaders leave with their manliest march to date. Smith stares at me, shakes his head, and tries not to laugh. Doors close, E-6's cross the lobby and turn right toward an elevator.

Smith blurts out, "Where in the hell did that sh' come from, Sergeant Sanderford?"

"What?"

"You're Sergeant Sanderford, calm, level-headed, intelligent, professor-type. They expect me to cuss 'em out, hell, I done it a hundred times, but you? Nobody expects it from you. I've known you for years, and ain't *never* seen you throw a damn fit like that. You scared *me*. I almost went to parade rest, and I *knew* you were gonna do it."

I smile. "You think we got their attention?"

"Are you freagin' kiddin' me? You see their faces? I think half of 'em started sittin' at attention. They didn't know what the hell to do. Couldn't mumble, talk, or do sh'. Eyes were the size of freagin' golf balls. You scared the ever lovin' sh' out of 'em. The squad leaders are pissed. I ain't seen Franklin this mad in his damn life."

"Good. Maybe they'll get to work. We shouldn't have to do this again for a while."

"Oh, hell no. They don't want no more of that sh'. They're scared to damn death. Where did that come from? You don't never do that."

I lean against my counter, by a waffle iron, cross my arms, watch to be sure no troops can see us, smile and say, "I save my fits for when I need 'em. I get a greater effect that way. No one in this room is going to forget tonight for a long time. However, if I throw a fit every day, it's easy to ignore, get used to it. Saving it for a time like this, they don't know what the hell to do. They can't help but pay attention, and they know they did something wrong to make me go off."

Smith chuckles and paces around. "Damn straight. Sh'."

I slide my notebook in and shoulder my map case. "I'm goin' to my room to order a pizza. Y'all won't see me the rest of the night. Gotta seem mad the rest of the day or my theatrics will all be for nothing."

Smith grabs his notebook and turns to exit. "You're good at this sh', Sergeant Sanderford. Crap, I 'bout went to parade rest. You shook me the hell up."

I open one French door for Smith, follow him through, and close it behind us.

"Smith, leaders gotta know how to motivate, rewards, a pat on the back, a quiet word, or short encouraging talk. Sometimes you light a fire. Have a good night. I'll see you tomorrow."

Nervous laughter joins a *pat-pat* sound of Smith's hand on my back.

"All right, Sergeant Sanderford. Go calm down, man. I thought you were gonna have a damn heart attack in there."

I storm to my room, enter in silence, slam the door closed, and called Karen. "How ya doin' Baby?"

*** 

Doc says, "Did this discussion with your troops, you're theatrical fit, have the desired impact?"

"Yessir. Lunchtime next day some troops came to my room with a handful of toy cars and trucks they bought and painted tan. We line our vehicles up on the bed, rearrange 'em, and discuss order of march, tactics, techniques, and procedures. Other troops brought me lists, drawings, and stuff. They got started on it at that point."

"So they were angry, pissed off, but you achieved your desired effect."

"Yup. We remembered why we were there. What was to come, got us focused."

"You mentioned a visit to see your son."

"Yessir...."

***

Smith throws yet another tantrum on our way to see Josh and Mike.

"Look at this sh'! I told my dang brother not to run the heat full blast on the windshield, but no, his all-knowing ass would not freagin' listen. Now I got a freagin' cracked windshield. I wanna whip his dang ass."

"I hear ya. How much you think it's gonna cost?"

"I don't care. If I have to beat the money out of him, he's payin' for it."

"Brotherly love, gotta love it."

"Screw you," he laughs. "So where's his barracks at?"

"Just go like we're goin' to class. I got his building number. It's on the right, just before the theater. Drove by three times already, saw him outside on a pay phone yesterday. He called me, and said the Drill Sergeant on duty let him use the phone to see if I was comin' to visit."

Smith gives me his fixin'-to-cussem look. "I don't know why it's so dang hard to get someone to agree for us to see 'em. They're goin' to combat with us in a couple months. Crap, they need to meet someone from their unit."

"They're both scared sh'-less to meet you."

Smith drags his smoke and spies me out of the corner of his eye. "Why they scared of me?"

"I built you up as an angry Drill-Sergeant type, told 'em how you go off on people, cuss 'em out, and stuff."

He shrugs. "I don't go off unless you're stupid, or do somethin' dumb. Stay in line and we're good."

"That's what scares 'em. They don't know sh', just started basic in November."

"Ah, they'll be alright. I'll just drop your son every time *you* piss me off."

I point to a road on our right, and a single story brick building before it. "I hear ya. Take this right, it's behind that DFAC."

Thirty meters south of a dining facility Smith turns right, toward generic three-story brick barracks. A standard brown sign beside their temporary home displays his unit.

"Yup, there's his unit sign. Park here, we'll go to the far door, by the guidon."

"Roger that."

Smith parks and we step over snow piles toward a mud-stained sidewalk. We clear snow piles, but step in dark black muck before we hit sidewalk. I stomp my feet as we march a long sidewalk to a double door entrance.

"Crap, I feel weird, dude. Last time I was in one of these barracks I was in basic, fifteen years ago. Feel like I'm 'bout to get smoked for some dumb sh'."

"Weird bein' on a training post as an E-7 ain't it?"

"Yeah, I'd like to see my old drill. I'd tie into him and he couldn't say sh'."

"My drills are probably dead. I did basic twenty-four years ago."

Smith shoves my shoulder as we stroll. "You are an old fart, ain't ya?"

"I can still outrun you, little round-ass."

*Wow, been a long time since basic. At least they have nicer buildings; we had World War II barracks back in eighty-six.*

I open a door for Smith. He hesitates and motions me forward. "Oh, hell no. You're goin' first."

"Fine, I got this," I enter like the E-7 I am, pass stairs to the right, door left, and see an open door down a narrow hall to our front. I point to it and elbow Smith. "That's probably the CQ office."

He follows me. I halt at the office door, knock, and surprise todays' Charge of Quarters. An E-6 Drill, looks up from his computer, sees us, and snaps to parade rest. His eyebrows furl inward and his mouth stiffens to exude confidence.

Drill Sergeant Farad's courage kicks in. "What can I do for you, Sergeant First Class?"

"This is Sergeant Smith, I'm Sergeant Sanderford. Two soldiers in your company will deploy to Iraq with us in March. Is it possible to talk with them for a few minutes? They haven't met their Platoon Sergeant."

The young drill remains at parade rest in perfect military bearing. "I will have to call and get approval Sergeant First Class. What are the soldiers' names?"

Smith says, "Douglas and Sanderford."

"Sanderford?" He stares at my nametape, unfurls, and re-furls his eyebrows.

"That's right Sar'nt, he's my son."

He dials his phone, has a brief discussion, hangs up, and returns to parade rest. "Sergeant First Class, I'll call the troops down. You can wait right there in the hall if you like."

I nod. "Roger, appreciate it."

Smith and I back step into the hall, to sit in wooden chairs along the wall. As I lower myself, Smith grabs my arm and pushes me forward. I look at him, he points to a drill sergeant hat, in my chosen chair.

Smith says, "I shoulda let you sat on it. That'd a been hilarious."

"Sanderford, Douglas to the CQ office, now," we hear from the loudspeaker, and again, "Sanderford, Douglas to the CQ office. Sanderford, Douglas to the CQ office, now!"

The professional yet confused Drill Sergeant leans out of his door and reports, "They'll be right down, Sergeant First Class."

Sanderford and Douglas barrel down steps to our right, make eye contact with me, pass us without breaking stride, halt, face the CQ door, and lock up at parade rest.

*This is hilarious, their actually shaking, at parade rest.*

The four of us gather in a small empty bay across the hall from our new drill friend. Both young troops are stiff at parade rest. Smith waits for me to put our boys at ease. I leave it to him.

*He is their Platoon Sergeant after all.*

Josh says, "This is the room they use for people on quarters, Sar'nt."

I pat Smith on the shoulder. "This is Sar'nt Smith, your platoon Sar'nt."

Mike looks at Smith. "N-n-nice to meet you, Sar'nt."

Josh's shaky, deep voice agrees. "Sar'nt."

Smith chuckles. "Y'all ain't gotta be scared of me. Chill out, sh'."

I ask, "Sanderford, why you keep lookin' at my feet?"

"Sar'nt you tracked mud in, we'll probably have to mop it up."

"Welcome to the army, Son. Y'all doin' ok, learning a lot?"

"Yes, Sar'nt," Mike says.

Smith asks, "You guys have any questions? Anything you wanna know, worried about?"

Douglas stares at the fluorescent light above us, Sanderford asks, "What weapons do we need to know the most about Sar'nt?"

Smith says, "Just learn your M-four. I'll get you straight on the rest."

Douglas exhales. "That's good to hear, Sar'nt."

Smith snaps his head left and peers at Sanderford. "Why, did you not do well on crew serves?"

"We only got to shoot like fifteen rounds in 'em, Sar'nt. I don't know them well."

Sanderford adds, "Drill Sar'nt loads it, we fire a few rounds, he clears it, we leave. We don't know crap about any of the crew serves, Sar'nt."

Smith and I look at each other. I shake my head. Smith takes a step back to breathe deep and shake his head.

*I fired a full belt, had to load, unload, clear, disassemble and reassemble the M-60 in basic. Now they just pull the trigger?*

Smith is quick with a response to this revelation. "Your training schedule probly got backed up because-o-the snow. Your drill probly had to make up time somewhere. Don't worry, I'll have you on the Fifty Cal, Mark Nineteen, SAW and Two-Four-Nine more than you want. You'll know those sum bitches for we get overseas."

Our recruits sound off: "Roger that, Sar'nt."

Sanderford asks, "Sar'nt Smith, what will we be doing? What jobs do you think we'll have Sar'nt?"

"Driver, gunner, dismount, you'll get a taste of all of it. We rotate jobs, don't worry about that now. You learn your basic skills, demo, commo, weapons. We'll get you straight on the rest."

My left hand pats Sergeant Smith's shoulder. "Sar'nt Smith has some great troops. I trained some of 'em, and some of our best NCOs. Your team and squad leaders will take you under their wings and be sure you are set for what you gotta do. Don't hesitate to ask questions. It's better to get cussed at for not knowing than to not know it when you need to."

My recruit duet sounds off: "Yes, Sar'nt."

Smith says, "Y'all need anything? From the PX or anything, got what you need?"

My two boys are lock step in unison responses. "Yes, Sar'nt"

I say, "It's good to see y'all. I'm glad we worked out a visit."

Josh says, "You coming to church tomorrow? We get to go to Church on Sundays at the big theater."

"Love to, Son, you know what time it starts? We're off tomorrow."

"I think it starts at ten hundred hours, Sar'nt."

"I'll see y'all there."

Sergeant Smith elbows me. "Sar'nt Sanderford, we probably aught-a-go, let these boys get this nasty ass floor cleaned up."

A stomp of each foot to release more mud on the floor I say, "Yeah this place looks like sh'."

"Dad, you know that was wrong," Josh says.

"It's good for you to clean up after me for a change, Son." I say as I hug him. Mike leans in for a hug as well. I hug him and say, "I'm proud of you boys, real proud."

"Thank you, Sar'nt," Josh says

Mike says, "I appreciate that, Sar'nt Sanderford."

Smith breaks the emotion with a pat on each man's shoulder combined with a handshake. "You just learn all you can here, we got the rest. We got this."

*** 

Doc says, "This sounds like an emotional visit."

"Yessir. Both of 'em got choked up when we hugged. You don't get many hugs in basic, kind a strange when you do. I guess it's even weirder from a man who outranks your Drill."

"I appreciate this glimpse into father-son relationship as you prepare for war. It is enlightening. Anything else you want to discuss today?"

"I got a funny note on Josh's time at Leonard Wood. Josh's cadre had his platoon write a paper to explain why they enlisted. Josh told 'em he joined to deploy with his E-7 Dad. Whenever he messed up after that his Drill would ask, 'What would your father say?' Drills Sergeants are creative people."

"That's funny, Dale. Anything else?"

"No Sir, that's enough sh' for today."

"Alright, Dale. We'll see you back again this week. Just schedule out front on your way out."

I stand, secure my satchel, insert journal and pen, button it, and step toward his door. "Roger, Sir. Have a good one."

From his chair Doc says, "You too, Dale."

*Josh's Journal*

March, 5, 2010   Early days of Mobilization

Sitting around too long makes me think too much. I don't like thinking too much. Home, my ex-girlfriend, my family, what this year has in store for me.

Dad wakes me up at like 0400, though I wanted to sleep in. I wanted to take a nice bath in a bath tub. But for whatever reason during my two weeks home I didn't get many chances to. I had been up most of the night packing. Mike finally left around 0100.

He pulled up my driveway and parked his truck. Wow, time to leave again. It wasn't so bad, I'm used to not being home. Two weeks ago, I graduated from One Station Unit Training (OSUT) at Fort Leonard Wood. Two weeks of good food, friends and family, and all the luxuries at home didn't really spoil me. But I knew I would still miss it like hell.

We packed into my Dad's Blazer and he started the car. We head down the drive and onto Winchester. I watch my home disappear behind a curve. Déjà vu. Here we go again, same ole' sh'. We make good conversation and keep in good spirits on the long ride to the unit. It is definitely weird being around Dad while we are both in uniform. We stop at a convenience store about 30 minutes out.

Dad goes into the bathroom, me and Mike buy food and cold drinks. We come back out, and, as we are pulling out, Dad opens his door and starts throwing up. After a few minutes, he shuts the door and says, "Well that's a good start to our trip."

We laugh together as I ask if he is okay. He says his sinuses get backed up in the morning and make him do that sometimes.

We get to the armory around 0700 and Dad has a leaders' meeting to get to. Me and Mike spend our first few hours standing around looking awkward as the soldiers pile in. I saw guys looking at us, each time they look at my name tape then at my face. I take interest in watching how Dad acts around these men. I want to have something to model myself after, but I realize being myself will get me far enough. We form up a few times and get our baggage packed into some big trucks. "Hey come here, Private." I hear. I turn to see a big guy, E-6 type, his name tape said Donner. I had heard about him, Sergeant Smith and Dad told me he was a bit rough around the edges when they visited us at basic. I turned in my box to SSG Donner and inventoried it, too.

"You think we're going on a vacation or something?" he asks as he sees our TV and X-boxes we packed in the black box Dad let us share. I think it was the one he used back in 2005 in Iraq. Everyone else has a green box.

*Charlotte's Journal April 2010*

Hi. My name is Charlotte Sanderford (although I'm convinced it should be Charlene), and I'm nine years old. When my 21-year-old brother, Josh, heard that Poppa was going off to war, he was all like, "Not without *me* you're not!" and grabbed his buddy Mike and went off to training.

Months passed before I saw Josh again. Finally, me and my parents went off to this military place for the graduation ceremony. When grabbing all the snow I could and throwing it at my Dad or stuffing it down his hood got boring, I decided to just walk back and forth in the snow behind the bushes, pretending I was in a cool forest. After what felt like a *year* of waiting went by, I finally heard marching coming from the street, and soon Josh and Mike and all the graduates were marching by. Excitement was already in the air before they left, so I couldn't imagine what was next.

# 7

*Marital counseling session 12*

I plop on my stiff red chair for another teary-eyed gab session with two women.

*At least the baby doll ain't butt up today.*

Karen is on her love seat, Anita her chair to my three o'clock. Curtains drawn more than last time, picture still crooked, map case by left foot and Anita forces her super encourager smile.

Anita says, "Dale, Karen, how are y'all today?" as she crosses her legs.

*Her smile is hope for an easy hour.*

Karen holds both palms skyward, "Another day of not knowing what's next."

My motionless body accents my soft low voice, "Fine."

Her dismissive glance at me breaks her focus on Karen for just an instant. Anita targets Karen to draw out today's subject. "How is Charlotte?"

"She's glad Daddy's back, doin' good in school, still says 'I like pie' a lot."

"I like pie?"

My right hand waves as if to negate any importance in Karen's comment. "She says it whenever emotions come up on TV, even commercials. She sits silent on the couch, slides her skateboard back and forth with her feet, and blurts it out.'"

"Dale, she's been through a lot. You all have. I'd say not to worry unless it continues for an lengthy period. You've been back, what, four months?"

"Five," Karen says

Anita nods. "It amazes me how people cope. When she says 'I like pie', her emotions may turn off. Verbal words halt or distract from an emotional stimulus. Feel free to schedule an appointment for her. It wouldn't hurt her to get some emotions out."

I stare at Karen and listen to her redundant comment. "One more change for me to deal with. I keep wondering what's next? What else is gonna be different?"

"This deployment took so much from your family. You each have issues to deal with."

My direct tone draws all attention to me. "Yes we do."

Karen's all-your-fault stare gashes my heart. "I knew she'd get hurt. I knew it."

I see tears in her hazel eyes. "We both did, Baby. We both did."

"Oh yeah, we both did. What did you do about it? What can we do now?"

*Awesome. Tears flow down her cheeks. I knew it would be one of those meetings.*

"We prepared Charlotte best we could. Spent time with her, told her we love her. Not much else we coulda' done."

Anita loses her smile, changes to her soft voice and says, "We all need to love Charlotte and, like Dale said, spend time with her. Let her know things are different but you are together. Dale, what are some ways you spent time with her before you left?"

"Before a trip, we all try to make memories with our kids. We don't know if we'll see them again. We want to embrace every moment before we walk away. When it rains, our lake's spillway has a wide, shallow mud hole. Charlotte loves to ride the four-wheeler. Till that point she hadn't played in the mud."

***

In our two-car garage, I look down at my darling. "Charlotte, let's go ride the four-wheeler."

Charlotte kicks sawdust on the floor. "I dunno, Dad, maybe later."

I pull her in for a hug. "Come on. There's a bunch of mud on the spillway."

She leans back, looks up at me, with Josh's mischievous eyes and smirk, and says, "We gonna ride in the mud?"

"Yeah, it'll be a blast."

She shakes her head and stares at our four-wheeler. "Mom's not gonna like it."

"It'll be fine. Put on some old clothes she won't let you go anywhere in."

She looks at me with her cute inquisitive eyes to confirm we will not get in trouble. She is doubtful, but wants to go.

"Are you sure?"

I brush red hair off her forehead wrinkles. "Yeah, let's go. I'll let you drive."

Charlotte sprints inside to change clothes. So fast that I almost miss the faint "Okay" as she slams the laundry room door.

I crank our ride to warm it up. Charlotte returns in a flash.

"Ready, Darlin'?"

"Yup, let's do it, Daddy."

She climbs aboard to my front and grabs the handlebars.

"Hang on, Baby. I'll get us outta the garage. You can drive in a minute"

Her hands fall to her lap. "Yes, Sir."

We back out, ease down our driveway, and turn right toward the spillway. I never drive fast when she is with me, not fast enough for her, anyway. We cruise downhill and pass the dock, hit flat ground, and speed up to enter our muddy playpen.

*There it is, thirty foot wide and forty long, a perfect mud hole.*

I lean left to see her face and say, "You ready, Baby?"

Eyes frozen on water ahead she says, "Daddy, are you sure about this?"

"It's what these are made for. Hang on, it'll be great."

"Okay, but you're answering to Mom, not me."

I punch it. We hit twelve-inch deep water at ten miles an hour. Water splashes wide to our left and right. We glide through. Charlotte's feet rise to stay dry. She learns it is hopeless to do so.

We loop around and hit it again. Faster than our first run. A monsoon of water engulfs us as we slog through muck and mire. Water covers and soaks our shoes, socks, and feet. When we exit, Charlotte decides she is used to it. Two runs and she is ready to drive.

She has more energy than a kid with two funnel cakes. "Daddy, can I drive now?"

"Okay, Baby, but I'm gonna keep my hand on the brake."

Her head turns to look at my hand as she points to it. "The brake slows us down, don't it?"

"I won't use it unless I have to, Darlin'."

Enthusiasm shakes her voice as she looks forward and shouts, "Ready, Daddy?"

"Go for it."

She slams the throttle to its forward limit. We hit water and mud at twenty-five miles an hour. Thank God, its shallow enough we do not go over the handlebars. Water covers us face to foot.

*Yup, she's my little redneck.*

I brake us on the far side. She lets off the gas and laughs hysterically. We turn around, and she floors it again. We skid, laugh, and splash, over half an hour before we go home.

At home we find Karen in throws of busy work. To not think, talk, or worry too much-she cleans house, washes clothes, and does dishes. As we pull up, she throws trash in our blue curb can in the garage. We are soaked, muddy, and ecstatic. Charlotte's laughter ceases when she sees Mom.

My little darlin' still thinks we will get in trouble. I cannot lose my smile, but suppress my laughter. Karen lets me do stupid stuff before I leave. She says, "Be careful," but I know she loves that we spend time together.

Karen grew up in town. She enjoys our rural life but is by no means a "country girl," though part of her wants to be.

Karen's smile bubbles out and negates her forced "mad Mommy" eyes.

I dismount, shake off water, and smile at Karen. "Your turn, Baby."

Karen points to our wet ride. "No, I ain't doin' that."

I glance at Charlotte, still astride our ride, and back at Karen. "Why not, Baby? It's a blast."

"You know I'm not into mud, water, and nastiness."

Both her hands wave for affect as Charlotte says, "It's a lotta fun, Mom. Water goes everywhere."

Karen dismisses our invitation, turns back to the laundry room, enters, and quips, "You two go ahead. I'm not doin' it."

***

I conclude with, "Karen probably thought I should do house work since I wouldn't do any for a year. Instead of sayin' so, she smiled in joy that Charlotte loves adventures with Daddy. Like our lake swims. Karen never joins us, but likes our Daddy-Daughter playtime.

Karen says, "He always spends time with our kids before he leaves, with me too, I guess. Behind all his attention, he still did not care what this would do to her, or to me. All he cared about was going, again, glory, recognition, adventure. All that crap. Meanwhile, I'm stuck, at home, alone, takin' care of a heartbroken nine-year-old Daddy's girl."

Anita asks, "How do you know he didn't care?"

"He went didn't he? He didn't have to, but he did."

Anita looks at me. "Dale, did you imagine effects on your daughter? Were her emotions included in your decision process?"

"Broke my heart, but I can't say so."

Karen interrupts, "You still went. It must not-a-broke your heart too bad."

Anita interrupts Karen, "Why can't you say it broke your heart?"

Arms wave in frustration before I point at Karen, and exclaim, "Every time I say 'I miss you' or 'I love you,' she says that sh'."

My head tips side to side to mock her. I screech, "You still went," slap my leg, and take a deep breath. "Nobody gives a sh' what I felt. What I thought, or dealt with."

Karen says, "That's not true. I work my butt off to be supportive. I'm still here right? I mean you—"

Anita cuts on her calm, counselor voice. "Karen, let's hear from Dale for a minute. Dale, we do care what you went through, and what you felt. Your emotions are as important in this marriage as Karen's are. You two are a team. Y'all are partners."

"Okay. Fine, Karen, remember the tree house?"

"Yeah, I remember. I still don't see why you spent your last few days workin' on it."

"I told you why. You never listened, kept telling me not to, but I did tell you."

Anita says, "Tree house? What's the story on the treehouse?"

"Got back from two weeks at Leonard Wood the end of January 2010. Three Months of four-day drills and two-to-three-week long train up deals were rough on everyone."

I hold out my hand for Karen to acknowledge my understanding. "Especially on Charlotte, and our mob process hadn't even started, wasn't due to till March."

Karen nods agreement.

I raise two right hand fingers toward Anita. "We had two days before goin' to Josh's graduation at Leonard Wood. Josh and I would have two-weeks off before mob."

***

To reassure nine-year-old Charlotte, Karen and I say, "This is the schedule the army has for us. We have to go on time so other men can come home to their little girls. It's now our turn."

Charlotte loves adventures with Daddy. We follow a stream in the woods; take a lake swim, any activity outside is an adventure. She wants a tree house, has for over a year. My commitments to Army and civilian careers have prevented it's construction so far.

I told her months ago I would build one. With no guarantee of my ability to do so when and if I came back, it had to be complete now. In our garage, I sort lumber as Charlotte approaches. Her little feet step from board to board.

She says, "Daddy, what are we doin' with all this wood?"

"We're gonna finish your tree house this weekend, Darlin', like I told you I would."

"Do we have enough wood, Daddy?"

"Yes, Darlin', we got it from Lowe's yesterday. Now we just gotta put it together."

A lifetime of silence follows my answer. Silence is uncomfortable now. With it, one considers, remembers, or contemplates. She is deep in thought, and so am I.

*Lord help me! Where is this conversation going?*

To end our speechless thoughts I say, "I want to finish it before we leave for Iraq, Baby, so you can play with it while we're gone."

Her soft spoken, reluctant reply emphasizes our desire to avoid emotions, "When do you go?"

"We start trainin' in a couple weeks, Darlin', on the fourth of March, it's February now."

"But you just got back. Can't they wait a little while so you can finish my tree house? When will you come back, Daddy?"

My hope to reassure her, and myself, this separation will be smooth has no limit. I describe our schedule for her with emphasis on positive points. "We'll be gone a year, but Josh and I come home to visit for two whole weeks. You and Mom will fly on a plane to come see us for several days in Wisconsin before we go over. That'll be fun. A plane, a new state you haven't been to."

More concern in her voice she says, "You will come back, won't you, Daddy?"

"Yes, Darlin'. I'm planning to come back."

This is the best I can do before a trip. I will not lie to her, but cannot tell full truth either. Josh nor I know if we will come back. Honesty ends her innocence now, to lie may cause more damage later if I do not return. Just like my last trip over, we encourage her as best we can and try to curb her inquisitiveness with vague honesty.

I tell her I love her, Karen and I both love her, God is in control, and Mom will take good care of her. God will protect us as he did me last time.

As I try to reassure her, thoughts of my mortality arise. Will I see her again? No soldier "knows" if they will come back, especially in our line of work. History and current intelligence tells us we should expect twenty to twenty-five percent personnel losses as a unit. Why would I tell my nine-year-old these facts, or Karen? All this sh' rambles through my head as I infer a promise to my little Darlin'. An honest yet vague statement she can comprehend and hold for reassurance over the next year.

To my disdain, she is smart enough to read between the lines of an empty promise. I think she will be a lawyer one day. She ends her board-to-board hop, turns to face me, pushes her curly red hair away from her eye, and over her left ear.

*She's processing my response, great I get a break. Lord please let it work.*

She waits, in silence, for me to be still and look at her. She looks like an adamant schoolteacher. I stop my work, make eye contact with my beautiful young lady, and see a tear in her eye.

In response to my "planning to" answer she whispers, "Alive?"

*Now the dagger is deep in Daddy's heart. Don't cry in front of her, old man. Shut off your emotions! Be who she needs you to be. Your sh' don't matter. Keep it simple.*

"Yes. That's the plan, Darlin'."

Charlotte looks deep in my eyes, listens, and shifts her feet to turn away. Her innocence shatters on the floor next to my hopes to protect it. In silence she walks away as if to say, *I understand you can't promise you'll come home alive, Daddy."*

She disappears into our home.

*Is she protecting me?*

She either won't let me see her cry, or realizes this conversation will not produce what she hungers for.

I step behind the garage and stare in the pine forest.

Memories of Charlotte in 05 flood my mind. Karen told me on the phone in October, "Charlotte told me through her tears last night, 'I don't remember what Daddy smells like.'"

*Why do this to her? Why am I going again? Ah, just get your ass back to work, Sarge, nothing to do now. God said, "Go," and we're goin'. Turn it off and do your job.*

I shuffle back in and stare at piles of wood to reorient my thoughts. One more discussion behind me, lumber before me, I drop my thoughts, and sort lumber.

Wonder if I have enough screws, better check.

\*\*\*

Karen wipes her tears, and nose. "You never told me about that."

"Figured it best not to. You had enough on you."

"Too much on me for too long, I'm tired, tired of all of it."

*Try havin' all that sh' and wondering if your man enough to bring your men home alive.*

Anita shifts her posture forward and cuts to her Miss-super-support voice. "It is a very long road. Y'all are doing so well though. Karen, can you understand why the tree house was so important to Dale?"

"Little better, I guess."

"Let's discuss communication, or lack of it, during pre-deployment. Share with me more on talks with your children, each other. How was your relationship before for this separation? I am naïve about military deployments, how they work, what you do, how you prepare. Walk me through those days."

Karen's tears subside as she shifts to a logistics discussion. "It was different from other times. Back in '91, his first trip, we said goodbye in a parking lot at Bragg. Dale had CQ duty, he had to call everyone in. First Sergeant let me sit in his office a while. Saying goodbye to your husband in front of his First Sergeant, talk about awkward. Dale wasn't Dale in front of him." She looks at me and laughs. "Remember him packing his rucksack?"

My first smile in today's session relaxes my armrest grip. "Yeah, you got tickled and couldn't keep a straight face."

Anita shares an awkward smile. "Got tickled?"

Karen's head shifts side to side. "He packed twenty cartons of cigarettes and one tiny little box of Tide. Forget washing clothes. I gotta smoke!"

Anita says, "Priorities vary."

Karen nods in agreement. "In '04 Dale was at Camp Shelby for five months before goin' over. We had Christmas at home, took him back New Year's Eve, and said goodbye in another parking lot. Driving away from him standing alone in that gravel Josh and I cried, looked at each other, realized how pitiful we looked and started laughing."

"Remember what I wrote on the window at home?"

Karen says, "I don't have to remember, it's still there, 'I Love Y'all.'"

Anita asks, "It's still there?"

Karen says, "Seems weird to wash it off. It's window paint on the inside. Above flowers, Dale and Charlotte planted. They still bloom, by the way."

Karen shakes her head twice and halts it above her left shoulder. "This last one was different. We had to say goodbye like fifty times."

Anita's head snaps back. "Fifty times?"

"Dale trained in California, Missouri, and Camp Shelby, back to Missouri, and Shelby. Their last place was Wisconsin. All on top of months of five day drills at the unit. And, as if those farewells weren't enough, like we hadn't cried enough, Charlotte and I went to Wisconsin for another farewell before they left to go over."

Anita looks at me, "Dale. How did your boss feel about all this? It must have been hard to balance family, work, and military."

"We were blessed. I stopped tryin' to do both at Christmas. I'd only have been there two weeks in February and none in January, so I left at Christmas. Most troops don't get it so good. Guys on hourly wages or making less as soldiers than as civilians caught hell with bills, Christmas, and keeping their families fed our last few months."

Anita says, "Going to war, saying goodbye combined with financial problems, so much stress. Add questions people won't discuss, assumptions, and miscommunication. I'm sure it is an emotional time."

Karen nods her head and pinches her lips. "We were blessed to have it how we did. Goodbyes got tough, real tough for Charlotte. But no goodbye could've been as bad as after Dale's R and R leave in 05."

Anita looks at Karen. "Charlotte would've been how old then, five?"

"Four. We took Dale to the airport. She thought it was another fun day with Daddy. She tagged along everywhere he went in the airport, little hand in his cargo pocket. We told her he was going. She either didn't catch it or didn't want to."

Anita says, "A lot of us ignore things as long as we can if it is gonna hurt."

"Once Daddy went in security and she couldn't go, she lost it. There wasn't a dry eye in the airport. I didn't wanna do that again."

A hand wave to Anita, I interrupt. "I was cryin' on the plane. Even the flight attendant had a hard time giving her safety brief. Charlotte stood in the full-length window of the waiting area. Everyone on the plane could see her screamin' and cryin'."

Anita draws he chin back and tightens her lips, pauses as if to compose herself and says, "How was your visit in Wisconsin?"

Karen says, "Charlotte wrote a family newspaper about it, about hitting a turkey in our rental car, the flight up there. She is so attentive. Remember the newspaper, Dale?"

"Course I do, she made me add pictures. It's still on my computer."

**Family news**
**Everyone knows the most important person in the family is always the father. This is because he owns the house. But the mother is also very important. So I have here a picture of both of them:**

**Funny story of the day;**
**BEWARE OF RAINING TURKEYS! They'll hit your windshield! That's what happened to us. AND IT WAS A RENTAL CAR!!!!!!!!!!!!!!!**
**Well, I guess stuff like that just happens, especially when Dad drives!**

*Josh's journal*

March 8, 2010, Mississippi

We spent the last night before we leave in the armory. "Wake up" is at 0400, *again*. Most of the guys are up all night visiting with their families. Mine left around 1800 the last night. I'm getting used to saying goodbye. Two weeks ago, I graduated my One Station Unit Training (OSUT) at Fort Leonard Wood and bid farewell to all the good friends I made there. But this goodbye is different. This time I'm not the only one saying goodbye. My father is an E-7 Platoon Sergeant in my unit. It was tougher watching him say goodbye than saying it myself. Tougher watching him choose his words as my nine-year-old sister asks him if he will make it home, again.

Mom has been strong to this point. Now I watch her tears fall as he did his best to reassure my sister in a realistic and honest way. "We will see y'all next month - I love y'all," I tell Mom. I didn't want her to hear what my Dad, or Sergeant First Class (Sergeant) Sanderford, is saying to my sister. The company's family support group is sponsoring a bus ride from South Mississippi sometime in April on our four-day pass.

Great, another goodbye. I'm really starting to hate goodbyes. I spend the rest of the night/morning getting to know my new family, the 731st Engineer Mobility Augmentation Company (EN MAC)

Anita asks, "How was she in Wisconsin?"

Karen answers back, "Oh, she did well. She understood more this time. She just wanted to have fun."

I say, "She asked me some questions, how long, that kind a thing. After our change of orders from Iraq to Afghanistan, everyone had questions."

Anita says, "Understandable. Prepare for one thing, it changes, people want as much security and information as possible of the new situation."

Karen chuckles and shifts her head side to side. "We did whatever we could to not talk, went to dinner, Amish country, Mall of America, a boat ride and carriage ride, you know, do stuff instead of stare at each other."

With a thoughtful frown, I nod. "It was a good visit. That weekend was our anniversary. In spite of how busy we tried to be, the final farewell stayed on my mind."

"With it being the last farewell and our anniversary, I wondered if it might be our last," Karen says.

*Tears are off, Baby, don't go into that sh', they'll be back on.*

I look at Anita with confidence. "We didn't talk about it. No need to."

Karen's thoughts are often on Charlotte. "Charlotte realized she could get anything. At stores, the mall, wherever. We'd do anything to keep her happy."

I face Karen and smile. "She played me like a dang fiddle."

*Charlotte's Journal*
April 15, 2010

I have one of the nicest third grade teachers in the world. I was absent for a week because I was going on a trip with Mike's parents and Mom to go meet up with Poppa and Josh for a yearly visit. I'm pretty sure my job as a military kid is one of the hardest parts. Mom's job is crying and being dramatic, I think. I'm not sure what Mr. Douglas's job is as Mike's father, and Mike and Josh and Poppa's job is, to go serve, but the kid's job is hard. Always going places to go see off the military in our family, go see them, or go bring them home, which involves even more drama and crying on the mother's part than when we see them off. So the kid's always going places. And Wisconsin was by far the craziest trip yet....

I sat on the couch in a total-stranger-to-me-but-not-to-Mom-because-she-knows-everybody-on-FaceBook's house. My mom sat beside me as we watched America's Funniest Home Videos on the T.V. in front of the coffee table, which I was having a time forcing myself not to drop my feet on. The coffee table had a small plate of some kind of vanilla wafers with chocolate in the middle of them.

Mr. and Mrs. Hamilton were in the kitchen, chatting with the strangers that they obviously knew. Aside from all I knew would happen that day, I was bored. To. Death! It had been an hour, maybe more, since we had arrived in Mrs. Hamilton's car. I halfheartedly bit into a vanilla wafer sandwich thing. It was kind a flavorless, and you could barely taste the chocolate or the vanilla, which I wasn't convinced was even there. What's up with that? They're actually called vanilla wafers. It's actually in the name! I finished the wafer and stared at the T.V screen, bored. I couldn't take it. "When are we going to leave?" I asked Mom. I don't remember what happened between then and when I was standing in the kitchen beside the small counter, surrounded by adults, who were talking and sipping coffee. Suddenly, the adults realized what time it was, and we were out the door and in the strangers' red car, a tight fit that we had to get used to. I had a window seat and was slightly pushed up against it. Something tells me those kind a cars aren't built for five adults and a little nine-year-old. "I'm bored," I whispered to Mom, who was sitting next to me.

"Here," she said, digging through her purse. She handed me a small box of Tic-Tacs. I chewed a couple, staring out the window.

If there's one thing I don't like, it's boring car rides. Or just anything boring. We *finally* get to the airport, Mom and Mrs. Hamilton thank the strangers as they drive away. I pulled my bag along behind me as we walked over to the two double doors at the entrance.

In the plane, I sat at a window seat beside Mom on the right side of the isle. "Can I do my make-up work?" I asked Mom, reaching down to my book bag, which is actually one of Poppa's camouflage army bags rather than a store-bought.

"Yes, Gladys," she said, not looking up from her boring garden catalog. She always calls me Gladys for some reason, some kind a joke. Poppa calls me Josephine.

By the time I finished my work, I could see Atlanta out the window. Soon, all four of us, Mr. and Mrs. Douglas, Mom, and me, were pulling our luggage along behind us as we walked through the long, black tube that connected the plane to the airport.

Later, we were walking through an airport and one of those fancy airport carts passed us, carrying three people and their luggage. "Can we buy one of those?" I complained, looking from my worn-out legs to Mom. She shook her head and said something boring and confusing about why we couldn't.

I walked alongside the adults, still biting away at the last of my burger. We were walking through another long black tube into the airplane. I wiped my hands on my blue jeans and pulled my DS out of my gray satchel.

I played my Pokémon game as we entered the airplane. "What should I nickname this one?" I asked Mom, even though whenever I ask one of my parents something like that I never really listen. I didn't wait for an answer. "I'll name 'er PE-ancil," I said, typing in a way Josh had made up to say the word pencil. As we took our seats, I had to save quickly and turn off my DS.

"Gladys—" Mom began to warn.

"I'm savin', I'm savin'," I said.

When the plane pulled into the next airport, the four of us emptied out of the plane with the crowd and into the black tube.

Through the long black tube, another plane ride.

Soon, we were walking through the long black tube and into the Wisconsin airport.

We met Poppa at the hotel across town. He had bought me a new cheat code game and I happily slipped it into my DS. While I played the game, Mom had a tearful and dramatic reunion with Poppa. She's so good at her job.

One day in Wisconsin we went out to a store. Poppa found a Pikachu plush toy and bought it for "army purposes." I watched the toy as we walked along through the aisles. I'm not one to play with little-kid plush toys, but there was something about the way the little guy looked up at me. Call me crazy, but I think the doll was smiling at me. Then again, dolls smile at everyone.

Later, we drove to the Mall of America in our rental car. When we got there I could NOT believe my eyes. It. Was. A. Theme. Park. Inside. A. *Building!!!*

One look up at my parents was all it took to say, "*Please!!!!!*"

Worked like a charm. My parents walked me into the giant room, and inside was the biggest theme park I'd ever seen! A big orange sign that hung from the ceiling in the shape of a globe read:

NICKELODEON UNIVERSE

I walked my parents over to the reception booth and the nice lady talked with my nice parents before giving me a paper bracelet. I knew better than to take it off. It was my entrance bracelet. All around us were rides from all sorts of Nick shows; two Sponge Bobs, a Danny Phantom, an Avatar, and more. I was somehow able to convince Mom to ride with me on this huge Sponge Bob roller coaster (which I don't recommend being ridden on a full stomach). But she kept her eyes closed and screamed a little. Ok, a lot. When we got off the ride, Mom said I owed her, but hopefully she's not reading this because it might remind her.

Anyway, after that I jumped around on a Sponge Bob bouncy house and rode lots of other rides before I left. My parents told Josh later to go with me to the Game Stop on the second floor. He agreed and I got a new game for my DS. I had lots of experiences at the Mall of America after all of that, and even got to try Chinese pizza. Don't do it.

Anita says, "Smart girl. Get what you want while Daddy's wrapped around your finger."

"I was so wrapped it wasn't funny. Karen would ask what I wanted to do. I didn't care as long as they were happy. I wanted a few good meals, but we like to eat so I didn't bring it up."

Karen says, "We wanted Dale to enjoy his last few days, Josh too. They both wanted us to not cry. We did a lot of 'what chew wanna do? I dunno, what chew wanna do?' So we let Charlotte pick, she'd speak up."

We get more supportive nods from Anita. "Everyone wants their little girl happy. Did you talk as much before this trip as you had the others?"

Her head shakes in disagreement. Karen says, "Not really. I never agreed it was God's will. Anyway, we'd gone over it all for his other trips. Wasn't much left to say. He was gonna go, leave us, by his own choice. We'd done wills, insurance, bills, and all before, so we just kinda went through the motions."

I shrug. "We spent more time discussing how other people were handling it. Josh, other families, newlyweds, we made no real plans or had deep discussion for ourselves, not for time apart or for afterwards. We'd argued, cried, prayed, said goodbye. By that point, I just wanted to go. Get started. Get it over with."

Karen says, "Yeah. We almost didn't go to Wisconsin. If not for Charlotte, we'd a said goodbye in Mississippi. I wanted her to see Dale as much as she could."

Anita asks, "Regrets about how y'all handled it?"

"I wish I'd been able to be on board like other times. I was done. Dale knew it. He could see it. I told him."

I listen to Karen, face both hands to skyward to my sides and shrug. "In Wisconsin, we laughed, had fun, saw things we hadn't before. Hugged. Said we love each other. What more can you do? However you handle it, it's still goodbye."

Anita says, "Thank y'all for telling me all this. I can't imagine the military life, so many emotions under the surface. Things unsaid or assumed. I understand y'all's silence. What could you say? No matter how you handle it, what you do or don't say, it is still goodbye."

I time check my phone and smile at Karen. "Wanna get lunch?"

"Anita, he always changes subjects like that. A Light switch, 'Bing' new topic."

"Our time is up anyway, Karen. Trust me, I understand husbands at mealtime. They'll schedule you for next week out front. Y'all have a good lunch."

"Okay. Take care, Anita. C'mon, Karen, let's get somethin' to chew on."

I wave over my shoulder, "Bye, Anita."

Karen says, "Bye, Anita, Thanks again."

*Charlotte's Journal*

April 17 2005

When I woke up the last morning of the trip, Poppa and Josh were gone. But, on the counter in their room, was the little Pikachu plush toy from Poppa. I hugged it. "Thank you, Poppa," I thought.

*Josh's Journal*

March, 9, 2010, Duke

I arrived at Fort Duke, Wisconsin, yesterday with the rest of my company. The weather is nicer than expected, but I'm not stupid enough to believe it will stay this way. As we settle into our barracks I can't help thinking it looks like the open barracks from Full Metal Jacket. A long open bay with metal frame bunks on each side of the long "no man's land" aisle for the drill to walk down the middle. The latrine on one end is a lot nicer than the one in the movie. I'm glad I don't have to see Sergeant Donner sitting on the can; that image would not go away. Me and Mike spent most of the first night confined to our racks, sitting around looking awkward.

March 10, 2010, Duke

We wake up and have a company formation around 0500 or so. Me and Douglas stick pretty close because we don't know anybody yet. We go to chow and have a little downtime before our next "hard time." Then it's time to load on a bus and go get our new gear from Central issue facility. Man, this stuff is high speed. I'm used to the Vietnam-era stuff we had at Leonard Wood. I'd better spend some time at the barracks getting acquainted with all this crap. Sergeant Clayton comes over and helps me out piecing together my Improved Outer Tactical Vest (IOTV). He knows a lot from being prior active army and a deployment under his belt. He's real cool, too, 'cause he doesn't mind teaching or showing me how to do something.

We go to some class this second evening here about sexual harassment and basically death-by-PowerPoint type stuff. As an all-male unit, I hope we don't have sexual harassment problems! The Lt. in charge of it all is real cool. He doesn't rant about anything much so we get back to the barracks, and I spend the rest of the night playing Solitaire.

*Dale's Journal*

110600MAR2010     Wisconsin

At Fort Duke now. Josh is nervous about not knowing his job. He is really unsure how he will react when the time comes. Most of the men here are. Josh is just willing to express it. I want to go home too. I don't want to go to war again. Bad things tend to happen in war. It's not fun. This isn't fun. Getting ready seems worse in some ways. This will be a *very* long year. For some reason God brought us here. We must trust he will see us through.

I pray, "Lord give me with the wisdom I need to lead the troops you put in my charge. Help me, Lord! Be with Josh! Give him strength, wisdom and peace. Be with Karen and Charlotte. Give them peace and security. Amen."

*Josh's Journal*

March 24, 2010, Duke

I get up, ready for formation. After we are dismissed and before I could make my way to chow, Sergeant Smith points at me. "Follow me," he says.

I follow him around the left side of the barracks toward the TOC.

"You know what this is about right?"

"Yes, Sergeant"

I've always respected our commander. Captain Joe Wayne was an E-6 before he received his commission. I respect the prior-enlisted officers more than the ROTC or straight OCS guys. We went up the steps into the TOC. Captain Joe Wayne was waiting for us in the orderly room.

"Alright, Sanderford, let's step in my office."

"Yes, Sir."

I follow him in and close the door. Standing there, I worry about what comes next.

"I need a driver. I like your style Sanderford, you're gonna do well in our unit. You've been to college a bit. You dropped out to go to war with us didn't you?"

"Yes, Sir."

"That's good. Good man. Says a lot for your character."

He explains the responsibilities of the position and tells me I'm not getting this opportunity because of my father. He admires my father as a soldier and as a man. He says Dad is a legend in the Mississippi National Guard.

"You have to earn your own name, Josh. You have a good name, and people will recognize it. But you won't get any respect in this unit or any other for what your Daddy did. You gotta earn that on your own. You've made a good start. This is a good chance for you to keep building a reputation as a soldier."

He understands the direction I want to go. I want to stay with my platoon, in the line platoon. I accept the position, shake his hand and go to chow. With a tray of food, I find a table with my platoon, or ex-platoon. I sit down and start eating.

Captain Joe Wayne, my father, and my new Platoon Sergeant, Sergeant Hatfield, sit to our nine o'clock. I look around my table. These men will leave the wire without me in a matter of weeks. I pick up my full tray and cups of Pepsi and head to the trash. One of them mumbles "traitor" as I walk away.

Hurriedly, I throw away my stuff fighting back tears. I've only known and trained with these men three weeks but they are family. I deserted Douglas, my friend, Sergeant Smith, and my platoon.

"What the hell am I doing? Sh'! What the hell am I doing?" I keep asking myself as tears fall. I cry like a girl. I see Sergeant Grossman,

Johansson and Hill leaving as I approach the barracks. I hang my head trying to keep my eyes out of their site. I feel a hand grab my arm.

Sergeant Grossman says, "Sanderford, you okay?"

"I'm good, I'm good."

He can tell I'm lying. He asks two more times before letting go. I go to our latrine upstairs and cry. When Captain Wayne gets back from the dining facility (DFAC) I follow him into the TOC.

"Sir, may I speak to you in your office?"

"Why sure, Josh. I always have time for my driver."

We walk in the office and close the door. Holding back the tears and now anger I have to try and stay with my platoon.

"I can't leave second, Sir."

The redness of my eyes is still present. Obviously, I have been crying, I know he can tell.

"Perfect. That's what I'm looking for. I don't want somebody who wants to leave their platoon. Loyalty. You've got it. Not everybody has commitment like you. Well." *Humph.* "I'll think it over. Come back later tonight. But remember I am the commander. The decision is mine to make."

"Yes, Sir."

I know what that means. I'm moving to Headquarters Platoon. I go on to the range and qualify with my M-4. We return from the range and clean weapons. Another day with my platoon but bitter sweet. I've been thinking all day about seeing the commander again. I know what he'll say, but I keep hoping to stay in second platoon.

After our evening formation and chow I go back to the TOC. Captain Wayne is sitting in the orderly room as I enter the building.

"You're gonna to be my driver."

We talk a short while as he explained what my responsibilities are again. Basically, what I get is to be a representative of the 731st MAC and escort him wherever he goes. He says I'm still a 21 Bravo, and that I would have plenty of opportunities to leave the wire. I feel a little better knowing the decision was never really mine to make.

Back at the barracks everyone in second is supportive and no one has the harsh words I thought were coming. They know I don't want to go. I'm sure they know I cried. Word spreads fast in this company. I'm gonna talk to Dad before I go to sleep.

# 8

*Therapy Session Number 17*

From my corner of Doc's couch, I face him, get out my current journal, stare past flowers and retaining wall at my son.

"What's going on, Dale?"

"Not much. Same ole sh', Doc. Been thinkin' about Josh."

"It is difficult for me to imagine conversations you two shared."

"There was a lot of 'em. Leading your son is…"

My head leans left, lungs fill with air, and mouth constricts their deflation. "Well, it's different from leading other men."

"Do some conversations or events come to mind more often than others?"

"There's so many. Last few days our discussions before we went come up most, two in particular. First one, every soldier wants to have but won't. Regardless of how many times he goes.

"Our fear we're gonna let our buddies, our brothers, our men down. Fear we don't know enough, can't do enough, aren't strong enough, or can't shoot well enough. We build up insecurity from, to us, our obvious weaknesses. Josh shared his with me at Duke."

Pen click, after pen click Doc digs in my head. "What did you say? I am sure you harbored similar thoughts. Your own insecurities about what was to come."

*I knew we'd have to get deep on this one, sh'.*

"Yessir. Good leaders won't show 'em, but we have 'em. Hold it in or push it down. Fears, concerns, and emotions don't matter. Leave it behind, bury it, ignore it, suck it up and drive on. Lead your men. Encourage and motivate your troops to do more than they know they can.

I did share with Josh my concerns on past deployments, tried to encourage him he was well trained. Tell him to train hard and ask questions, never assume he knows a task till he proves to himself he does. You want troops' fear to drive 'em, focus 'em, and keep 'em alert. I reminded Josh no one knows everything, or can do everything. We just practice shoot, move, communicate, our common skills. He has good leaders. Everyone has concerns. We can't know till we go what we'll do under fire, and I'm proud of and praying for him. That's all I could do, right?"

"Dale. You stand there with your son, as you prepare for war, your own concerns in mind and say these things, you encourage him yet deny your own insecurity."

"Yes, Sir."

"Now…Here…In the safety of a quiet office, you question yourself like your son did then, internal debates of your decisions, your leadership. You ask did you do all you could have done, risk yourself for your men often enough. You need to listen to your own advice and apply these principles to yourself. We can all be our own worst critics. Why do you not give yourself as much credit for being human as you have Josh and your men?"

"I'm in charge. Lives depend on me. My men look to me to get 'em home. There's no cryin' in leadership."

"Think about that statement, Dale. Does it not deny your humanity? This standard of leadership is yet another example of your disconnect from your emotions. You require, in yourself, avoidance of your natural fear, and concern.

"Such a separation from emotion combines with horrors of war to injure your mind. Such an injury maintains your disconnect. The injury to your mind brings intrusive thoughts and flashbacks to confound your ability to reconnect with your emotions, with yourself.

"You confess an inability to acknowledge you even have emotions. This division, necessary for survival in combat, is a hindrance back here, in the world, if you will. We must convince your mind, conscious and subconscious, it is okay to feel, to want, to love. This begins with Dale's realization he is safe. Dale has safety and security here. You are safe so you can begin to feel again. Do you see?"

"Yes, Sir, I think so. Like good weapons training. We get to a point double taps are automatic, raise your weapon, double tap, no thought. Muscle memory. Just do, like breathing, farting, or sneezing."

"That's one part of it. Your mind has muscle memory, as you say, a connection of violence to anxiety, fear, and lack of control. Smells, sounds, images and other things can be triggers for you. Their connection to over there can put your mind back where you've been. But you've also trained your mind to ignore and disregard natural human emotion. Emotions you still have from the Stan and new emotions today, here. In combat, emotions can distract. Regardless of their effect on your judgment, one grows to associate emotions with fear and pain. Naturally, our minds do not want pain. Therefore, emotions must go away to prevent pain associated with memories.

"You said two conversations come to mind most. May I ask the other?"

"Conversation about his move from line platoon to commander's driver."

"Can you share that discussion with me?"

\*\*\*

Byson is my roommate again. Sitting on my rack in our room, I get a text.

*So much for down time, what does she want now? Ain't she figured out I can't do nothin' from Wisconsin.*

A space bar tap to pause *Kung Fu Panda*, I pick up my phone and see a text from Josh.

"Can you meet me outside?"

I text back,

"Sure"

He paces in our formation road and motions for me to follow him to the far side. I catch up on a broken up concrete dining facility (DFAC) sidewalk; he stops and spins to face me.

I halt as he turns. "What's up, son?"

My little boy, in uniform, glares at me with taught lips, red eyes, and wrinkled brow. His right index finger pokes my chest. "Did you know?"

"Know what?"

Both Josh's hands raise from his sides as if to taunt me into a fight. "Know about me bein' Commander's driver."

"I didn't know it was nailed down."

"What do you mean 'nailed down'?"

*Whoa now, there's that damn finger again. Boy best ease up.*

*Do not draw Ole Sarge out on you boy, you still ain't met Ole Sarge.*

"Did you do this?"

"No, Son. I didn't."

Specialist Sanderford paces left and right on our narrow concrete walkway, attempts to gain some resemblance of composure. Walks away from me, back toward me, left right, self-control fails him, he halts mid stride, and turns to face me.

*There he is. Josh's back with that look he's given me a thousand times, most often about goin' to church when he don't want to.*

"Did Captain Wayne talk to you?"

"He and I talked yesterday."

"What'd he say?"

"He asked if I wanted you to be his driver. I didn't answer."

"You didn't answer. What exactly did you say, Dad?"

"I said my NCO creed states, 'I will not use my grade or position to attain pleasure, profit, or personal safety.' Therefore, I will not ask that you receive special treatment. You joined to deploy, to do your part. You must serve wherever you're needed."

"What'd Captain Wayne say?"

"He said, 'Alright. I understand. Your son don't wanna move. That's the main reason I want him. He ain't looking to sham out. We go way back Dale, before 05 in Iraq. What do you want me to do?'"

"I told him, 'I will not request special consideration for Josh. He's a troop like all of us.' So Captain Wayne said again, 'I got it.'"

"So you didn't ask for it, but you didn't tell him not to."

"He's the commander, Son. We advise him, guide him away from stupid decisions. In the end, it's his call."

"I wouldn't get this if I wasn't your son, would I?"

"You might. Your new, squared away, motivated, and the reason you joined earned you a lotta respect here. Captain Wayne can't have a goofball driver."

"He told me what I'd be doin'. I looked up online where to walk when I'm with him and stuff. I don't wanna leave second, my brothers, Mike."

"Now you see how I felt in 05."

"05?"

"C'mon, you remember. I got transferred to Battalion from my line platoon. Captain Wayne was my PL before the move. I got moved out of this company, away from these men."

"Oh…yeah. What'd you do?"

"Only thing I could. Made the best of it. Did the job and found any way I could to get off the FOB, especially to go out with these guys."

"But you were an E-7. You could do that. I'm just a specialist. Whose gonna give a sh' what I want?"

"Don't worry. When people are sick, injured, or whatever, you'll fill in. You'll get all you want. Trust me."

"What do I do till then? Every time second platoon goes out and I'm sittin' in an office with my thumb up my ass."

"Make the most of it. Learn all you can. You've thought about bein' an officer. Watch Captain Wayne's leadership style. Learn from him. You'll get an operational perspective your peers may never have."

"I know I can learn from Captain Wayne. But a perspective of my head up his ass ain't gonna teach me sh'."

"I hear ya. Not true, but I hear ya. Don't you be an ass kisser. Do your job. You'll get to see the big picture. Most of your buddies will only see what they have to do, in their truck, on their mission. You'll see what we all do."

"Great perspective, Dad, watchin' a screen in a damn office, ridin' a comfy chair and sipping coffee, while they're in the sh'."

"Oh, you'll be bored out of your damn mind. I was. Learn TOC equipment, radios, forms, decision making, reporting. There's a lot-o-sh' behind the scenes for us to go out and find bombs."

"Now I see why you wanted to stay in the line last time. Mom's glad you moved."

"She doesn't know how often I went out. She don't need to."

"Yeah, I'm learning, learning what not to say to folks back home. This ain't what I thought it'd be. Not what I thought at all."

"You're gonna be fine, Son."

"I know. Just sucks."

"Welcome to the Army. Our actions are for Army needs, unit needs, platoon needs. No longer on what we 'want' or think we 'need.'"

"I know, still sucks."

"You'll get used to it. I'm gonna get a shower, Son. You good?"

"I'm good. Gonna walk around a while. Ain't ready to go back in. In there with men I have to leave right before we go."

"I understand, I cried like a baby when I left these guys. Night, Son. Let me know if you need to talk some more."

"Roger. I will. Goodnight."

*Josh's Journal*

June 11, 2010, Gardez

I'm off work now. In my room listening to music and thinking all about life. I bought some clothes online. I can't wait to be back in some nice civis. Some shoes too. I bought some shoes. I haven't worked out in a while. Since before I went out. I found out last night I will be going out on mission again on the 13th. Possible R.O.N at COP Zormat. It should be fun. We might see some action down Tawagoto. It gets hairy down around Zormat right now. I'm excited to be able to get out on mission again.

This one isn't as high up on the priority list as my last one was, but a mission is a mission. I'll take any one I can get on. Babysitting the TOC 12 hours a day isn't what I joined the army for. But two missions within a week's time isn't bad. Maybe it will elevate me above the "TOC-rat" status.

Doc says, "So Josh moved to an office job. How did you feel about that?"

"Like I told him, he'd get a big picture, all the BS and paperwork that has to be done for us to go out. You always have platoon versus platoon arguments about who's doin' more, who's got it rougher. He saw our efforts to balance work between platoons. It was good for him. I did take security in it. I knew he'd end up goin' out, but for a while it was good to not worry about him."

"Was he safer?"

"Yeah, he was. In our unit, everyone goes out though, off the FOB. We are a family. We all do our part. When a brother is hurt or sick, someone picks up his slack. You gotta go out to do a good job in the TOC, to understand what's goin' on out there."

"So did Josh get out of the office? Did he, how did you put it, 'get all he wanted'?"

My arms uncross, journal drops to the floor beside me, I laugh as I retrieve it. "Oh, hell yeah, two weeks in, he'd got some. He was frustrated by our third week. Within two months, he'd got all he wanted."

"I hear lots of things frustrate one over there. At that point in time was there something specific frustrating him?"

"Yessir. Havin' to go places we knew we'd have issues."

"By issues you mean IEDs?"

"Or small arms, mortars, RPGs, some places are reliable for havin' issues."

"I find myself intrigued by a father-son discussion in such a context. You have an unbelievable bond, one not often seen. Josh sought your advice on his frustrations?"

"Yessir. When we got alone, he'd talk to me. We looked at things different. Experience is a tough teacher. 'Course this trip was different from my others."

"You've mentioned this before. Your tours in Iraq were different times, different missions. Route clearance seems to have a consistently high stress level."

"Yessir. Long days waitin' to see whose truck would get blown up, not 'if' someone would, just who and when."

"And Josh expresses his frustrations to you, as his father and not a platoon sergeant. What could you say?"

"Yessir. After a mission brief to prepare my platoon for another day's work Josh stopped me and…"

***

My platoon will clear route Scheibe, Southern part of our Area of

Operations (AO), tomorrow. We meet on our front porch with cold drinks for a mission brief. Mississippi flag flies above our dusty, camouflage-net-covered wooden porch.

Great place to meet. Benches line two sides between steps. Dark tan paint applied long before our arrival cracks and flakes. An old gray car seat mounted on a wooden box is my throne.

A graffiti covered wooden table supports maps, paperwork, cold drinks, and snacks. Coffee and tobacco decorate gravel below our dirt-engrained 2X4 deck, a thousand cigarette butts from similar meetings lay atop brown rocks. This is home, a comfortable place to sit, meet, or hang out rather than dwell in solitary drab plywood-walled rooms.

Our turnaround point for tomorrow, intersection of Scheibe and Skit, often has mortar fire or IEDs. This ever-changing battlefield requires consistent adjustments in our tactics. Josh, still a TOC-rat, printed satellite photos of the intersection at my request.

My NCOs and I discuss options and ideas. We decide to limit our trucks in the impact area. Our wrecker, rear security, buffalo, and Lt's vehicles will secure an egress. Clearance vehicles will clear through and return. In Lu Lu, we will move north in the impact area to search for Mr. Mortar boy. Front gun trucks will shift south to cover my clearance vehicles and scan for a point of origin (POO) when mortars hit.

Squad leaders and team leaders back brief me to confirm they understand and then go to prep men, trucks, rations, ammo, and water.

Josh listens to our plan. I stow prints in my map case, secure my clipboard, and step down into darkness to trudge through deep gravel to a latrine two buildings away.

I hear Josh's voice call me from behind, "Dad, can I talk to you?"

I halt, turn, and he says, "Printouts work for y'all?"

"Absolutely, they're great. Thanks, Son."

"What are y'all gonna do?"

By flashlight, I act as if he did not hear our half hour brief, and show him our plan.

Josh stares at his prints, my notes, looks up, opens his mouth, closes it, and looks back to his prints.

"What's wrong, Son?"

"I guess you have it figured out."

"We have a plan, till it changes on sight anyway."

"Why y'all goin'? What's the damn point? We get mortars, IEDs. Hell, 128 even had small arms down there. Why would they send you to a place we know we're gonna have problems?"

*Even, you Josh? I still ain't met a troop who never says "they". Sh' I say it too.*

"The route needs cleared. Infantry needs a clear route to get somewhere, a safe route for their missions."

"Why don't they do it?" Josh blurts.

"They don't have the VICs we have, can't take blasts like we can."

Josh shakes his head. "It's stupid to risk lives goin' where you know you'll get shot at."

"That's our job, Son. Someone needs to go there. We do route clearance. You know our motto, 'We clear the way.'"

"But, Dad, you know you're gonna get somethin' tomorrow. Why don't you turn around early? Before you get hit?"

Josh still won't look at me. He stares at paper. I stare down the gravel path, over our perimeter wall, at qal'ats and open desert. "Orders say go to the crossroads. Active army thinks we're a bunch of rag-bag rednecks, but time comes, we do our job."

He shifts and the gravel rumbles under his feet. "We're ordered to clear where we know we'll have problems. No one is even followin' you. You'll be alone. No one would know if you cleared just before there… Just this once, right?"

"My platoon has orders. We'll do 'em."

"I just want you to be careful, Dad."

"We will. I got great men. We'll be fine."

Josh shrugs. "Just don't make no sense."

I pat Josh's shoulder three times. "We ain't paid to make sense of it. We follow orders. Even if we know we'll get hit. If we're scared…it don't matter. That is why we came here. That is what we do. Thanks for the printouts."

"Roger. I still call it a waste of good men. I'll be in the TOC watchin' you on screen. Anything else I can do for you?"

"Nah. Say a prayer for us when we pass Zormat."

"Roger, I will. See ya in the morning."

"Night, Son."

\*\*\*

Doc says, "Your son's concerns seem valid. Obviously, I am a civilian. Were you nervous? From the sound of it, you knew a truck would be blown up; you would receive mortar rounds or small arms fire. Something was going to happen. What were your thoughts as you encouraged your son? And I assume your platoon."

"We knew what was comin', but that's our job. Clear a route, be a decoy, take fire to expose enemy positions, whatever. I had no input on which route to clear when. That's up to higher headquarters based on other units' needs. Was I nervous? Scared? Sure. Be stupid not to be.

"I had freedom of maneuver and tactics within my platoon, made the best decisions possible to bring my brothers home, and put trust in my men to do the same. We never knew when we'd hit a big one.

"Lose someone.

"That's just part of it, we plan best we can, insure cover fire and increase our probability of eliminating a threat. We say a prayer and stay ready to change our plan as situations dictate. It's really kinda simple."

"So you had similar thoughts to those your son expressed?"

"Yes, Sir."

"To whom did you express your own concerns? Who was there for Dale?"

"That's not part of leadership."

"What do you mean? You just told me you had these emotions. Dale had internal struggles. What did you do with them?"

"Me? Go to my room, watch a movie, have some box milk, and a snack. Maybe get on Yahoo with my wife. Have a smoke."

"Did you mention these conversations with Josh to Karen?"

"Oh, hell no. You don't stress the home front over sh' they can't do anything about."

"So to whom were you able to express your own frustrations?"

"I had a lot of great friends in the Stan. I try not to bother folks with my sh', they got their own. Bury it. Be there for the men, the mission, drive on."

"I see. So how did the mission turn out?"

I place my journal on the center couch cushion, re-cross my arms, and inhale until air gets to my toes.

*I don't feel like tellin' a whole damn mission. I'll Reader's Digest it and see if he'll settle for that.*

Through the French doors, I see French's truck as it exits our entry control point.

"We SP'd at zero four hundred so we got to Zormat at day break. Went east and cleared through a set of qal'ats to that open area west of Scheibe and Skit's intersection.

Kids here wave and ask us for water or candy. That old cripple by the third shade tree, north side, is not out today, no one is. An empty village always means, *You won't be bored long.*

Our rear VIC clears the village and egress guards post up. My forward trucks and I continue across a flood prone flat area to rise up past an old dead tree to mortar plateau."

*Charlotte woulda liked to rode a four-wheeler through that mud hole when it flooded.*

We take over-watch positions spread wide across the impact area. Our Clearance VICs clear thru to the intersection.

Four rounds of mortars hit. Don't find any IED's.

Smith fired at Mr. Mortar Man his last trip out there. Obviously, they missed.

Clearance VICs finish, peel off front to back, we follow 'em back through the village. Kids, old crippled dude, everyone is out to wave and ask for water and food.

Doc's head shakes side to side. "How frustrated you must have been. You see locals know what is about to happen, yet say nothing. They do not share information to help you?"

"It's the same everywhere. You learn it's useless to stop and ask questions. All you get is "Insha'Allah" or "We love Americans, no bad people here." They know when we are gonna take fire. They know who's doin' it, but can't help us. Not if they wanna live.

"In Iraq, only one man would help us in Owesat. We called him Abraham. Found him one morning with thirty some odd bullet holes in him. That summer, we arrest over a hundred people from Abraham's village in one raid. Within a week, all the elders wanna to talk. Locals then wanted a voting station, to pave roads, and improve schools. People can't help till the "bad people" are gone. If they try, like Abraham, they get killed when we leave.

"So they signal us by staying inside till the fun's over, whole villages."

Doc says, "It is a hard situation for everyone."

"Course it is. It's a damn war. People in Iraq and the Stan tell me they want democracy, they want a better life. Kids are the same everywhere. Kids want food, safety, fun, a mom, and dad, and hope to skip school. That's what we all want. We all do what we feel we must for our family, our village."

"Are you familiar with Maslow's hierarchy of needs? This implies conceptual morals and other things are not possible until safety, security, and basic needs are met."

"Yessir. Nothing positive could happen until we took ground and held it, like Marines did in Fallujah. We took Owesat, arrested over a hundred bad guys, set up over watch above the village, and controlled who came and went. That safety allowed locals to strive for more than they'd had."

"I see your point, such a dilemma. You have dealt with, sorrow, fear, man's inhumanity to man. We have much more to discuss, Dale. I feel you are making progress. As you consider from this safe place new meanings, possibilities, how you can embrace your post-traumatic stress symptoms, your memories and strive for a new life beyond the wars you've participated in."

*Josh's Journal*

14Jun2010, Gardez

It is 1209 AM. I'm not too sleepy. I had a day today. I stayed up all night and headed out to the VICs at three. After we made sure everything was squared away, we said a prayer. Then we SP'd.

A black route deemed impassable. We knew it'd be a long day. We reached Skit and the roads sucked. Gaps in the roads that were comparable to small canyons or gulleys. We were making little progress and were losing daylight.

One thirty-seven was already past Zormat. Staff Sergeant Franklin passed the husky on what looked to be a heavily-traveled route. We had mine rollers, so I wasn't really worried about it. We led the way a good bit of the time until we saw bypasses in the road.

The husky would get a ping but the Buff wouldn't come up with anything. Some kind of bag the first time. We were approaching a village. It was early afternoon sometime.

Me and Specialist Harper were in the back, Private First Class Cooper in the hatch, Specialist Horshack driving and Staff Sergeant Franklin in the TC seat.

Sergeant Franklin told the husky we would pass because the road again looked heavily traveled. An empty village was to our twelve. We eased our way past the husky.

About twenty meters later I earned my CAB. We hit a pothole then a thundering pop echoed in our RG. The air disappeared and turned into heavy dust. We all began coughing.

"Everybody alright?" I heard Sergeant Franklin ask.

I checked my extremities for movement and checked Harper and shouted, "Yay we're good!" while fighting back a cough.

The blast was right under Franklin but lifted me and Harper from our seats. Our heads hit the ceiling and our ears rang for a minute. The dust disappeared. I saw dirt everywhere and our hood on the ground next to us. Truck parts were everywhere.

As the scene became more visible we began scanning for an ambush. The empty village was to our twelve still. No movement. The wrench element was called forward to get us out. The only things working were our coms. Our sh' was shot.

I watched out the back window for the wrecker. We had dismounts out securing the area. Then to my 10 out the back window no more than twenty meters away, I saw an impact.

It was IDF. I saw Sergeant Richards just to my eight outside our blown VIC turn his head and haul ass. Then about ten seconds later, another impact. This one was further away but still to my ten in a field on our left.

We sent guys to go look for the launch site. The area was open so the job was a tough one. Dismounts went and cleared qal'at. I was getting my first taste of combat.

We had VICs pull around us picking up the pieces of our vehicle when we heard shots. It was sniper fire. We later saw where one round penetrated an RG, Lu-Lu under the driver's door.

Thick rounds. We began taking more small arms in the form of AK's but nobody could tell where it was coming from. We received another round of IDF that impacted even further from the second blast but closer to our dismounts clearing the qal'at.

We continued taking fire until our vehicle was moved from the kill zone. We regrouped there and were told to Charlie Mike back to the FOB.

We got our asses handed to us. The blast is estimated at least sixty pounds HME. I gunned on the way back. We saw villagers appear from nowhere looking and digging around the blast site putting up yellow flags.

Those f-ers knew all along. The head man for the region of Zormat had just been killed from an above assault. They were pissed. We dropped off the VIC at Gardez and learned that 137 had also been hit by the same pressure-plate system, same batteries and all. We have to take this cell out.

Doc says, "Shall we discuss one more conversation with your son? I am sure another stands out, a discussion that defines you and your son's perspectives. You mentioned he got all he wanted. What was that like for you? For him? There together to know, even see, what the other must deal with."

"Yessir, his full package. He was ready to come home a month or two in."

"What do you mean by 'full package'?"

"He got a piece of all they had to offer. IED, small arms, IDF, RPG…a full package."

"This was shortly after you got in country."

"Yessir. Josh was still TOC'n it most of the time. He got out with the other two platoons, not with me. One mission got pretty busy."

"And he came to you about this?"

"Yessir. Next morning he stops me and says, 'Dad we gotta talk.'"

\*\*\*

I halt by the north porch steps, light a smoke, give Josh one, and stow them in my shoulder pocket. "What's up?"

"Dad I'm done. This sh' sucks."

"What're you talkin' about?"

Josh points his cigarette toward our motor pool, takes a drag, and points again. "You know I went out with 128 last night right?"

"Yeah, y'all had some issues."

"Issues, you call IED, small arms and IDF 'issues'?"

Smoke puffs from my mouth with each syllable. "Potato, potahto, hat about it?"

"I am freakin' done, had it all, all of it. How much more do we gotta do?"

"You got your full package ain't ya? You're doin' good, Son."

"Yeah, okay. How much more we gotta do?"

"We just got here." My hand holds his shoulder. "We're not two months in, Son. It's gonna be a long year."

"Yeah, real freakin' long."

Another drag of smoke allows time to drag out or formulate some form of encouragement for this, my young troop. "We're just over a month in, right? We have nine or ten months left. We go home on leave in November, so only eight or nine months of work left."

"'Is it gonna stay this busy?"

"Hard to say, word is winter freezes the ground and slows down IEDs. Gotta wait and see."

"So it could. It could be like this the whole time. Our whole year."

"Could be. We don't have an easy job, just gotta do it."

"Yeah. We gotta. Meanwhile other troops sit on the FOB not goin' out or dealin' with any of this sh'."

"Not all of 'em sit on the FOB. We all got jobs to do. We find bombs; other folks do supply, maintenance, gate guard or whatever. Would you rather have gate guard after goin' out? Come back from a fire fight and stand tower guard for six hours?"

"Ah, hell no. That'd suck."

"Then be glad they're here. Otherwise, we'd do that sh' between findin' bombs."

"I see your point. But damn it's gonna be a long year."

"I know. We ain't bored though, all in how you look at it, Son."

"I don't care how you look at it, IED, IDF with small arms ain't fun."

"Nah, it ain't. But it ain't boring."

"No sh'."

"Get some sleep, Son. You in the TOC tonight?"

"Yes, Sar'nt. Need me to print anything?"

"Yeah. Goin' through the pass, can you do some pictures of the dirty village and the sharp turn north of it?"

"Where Adams almost flipped?"

"No, that's where French almost flipped. Adams was north."

"Oh yeah, that's right. You got some bad drivers, Dad. Nobody else has almost flipped a damn truck."

"Drivers are good. Other platoons don't report stuff."

"Probly so. Night, Dad."

"Night, Son."

***

Doc says, "You did tell him he'd get all he wanted."

"Yessir. The adventure wasn't what he thought."

"Was it that busy all year? Did winter slow things down?"

"We were surge troops, kept it going through winter. IEDs kinda slowed down a bit, but other issues didn't."

"Did your comments impact Josh's perspective of these other soldiers?"

"Some, but it don't change quick. Some of 'em felt bad they weren't going out and we were. That's what their commander told us anyway. A gate guard threatened to whip Bronson's ass one time. We'd been out for a week, finally got back, and this nice, clean little gate guard says that sh'? I was pissed. There are always issues between active army and the guard, just part of the fun."

"Similar to the rivalry between platoons, who does more, gets tougher missions?"

"Yessir, same thing. People put down what others do so they can have pride in themselves, or in what they do."

"This is common, and not just in the military. Do you find you have a problem with civilians now that you are back? Do you look down on others for not going, for not doing their part?"

"Sometimes I do. People here see themselves as so important. Some of 'em…well…what they do has no real meaning. I don't look down on people, not much, except complainers. Not everyone can do what we do. Rather they don't try if their heart's not in it. Hard enough to motivate troops without people who don't wanna serve, don't wanna do their part.

"Some people's jobs are back here. Here they can work, pray, keep our family safe. Like I told Josh, we all have jobs to do."

"True. True. I have never been and I will never go. Through my work with veterans, I'm able to help those who have."

I point a left knife hand at Doc and nod. "If you had the same issues to deal with, it'd be harder for you to help me."

"Exactly, Dale. What did you do about the threat? This soldier who said he'd kick Bronson's ass?"

"Long story short, we had so many trucks damaged or broke we couldn't get everyone home from dropping trucks at maintenance in one trip. Half our trucks ran men home and came back to Josh's FOB for the rest of us. On their way out to come get us is when he said it. Bronson told me what happened when he picked me up. Said, 'Sar'nt I just walked away to tell Captain Wayne what happened and came to get y'all.'

"Like I said Doc, I was pissed. We got to our gate, I got out of my truck, stormed up to the guard shack, and barked, 'What the hell is the problem?' at this young 101st E-4."

"What did the troop say?"

"My finger still in his face he locks up to parade rest, like a good troop, and says, 'I didn't say it Sar'nt. It wasn't me Sar'nt. He lives over there, second barracks, Sar'nt.'"

Doc chuckles. "He didn't want to be blamed for it."

"No, Sir. He backed out quick. I came to my senses, realized the example I was showin' my troops. I said, 'Nobody's gonna threaten to whip my troop's ass. Especially when we been out for a damn week.' I turned around and found seven of my troops backing me up, hoping for a fight. I pushed on shoulders and backs and said 'Move on. Get fuel and reload. Prep the trucks and park 'em."

"And then?"

"My troops moved out and led our VICs to the fuel point. I stormed for the second barracks, thought better of it, and went to our TOC. Captain Wayne had discussed it with their commander, so I tried to let it go, had dinner, and reported on the week's mission."

"Was that the end of it?"

"Yessir, for the most part. That's when a captain from the 101st supply unit on our FOB said his men were jealous we were doin' more than them."

I stow my journal and pen in my map case as I say, "That's enough for today, Doc. I'm gonna go eat."

"I have other appointments, so eat something for me."

"If you insist, I'm goin' to Waffle House before the chiropractor."

"Sounds good. Enjoy your meal, Dale."

"Roger, Sir. See ya next time, Doc."

*Josh Sanderford's Staff Journal, 02 June 2010*

| Time | Event |
|------|-------|
| 2320 | Medium Size Environmental Control Unit in the Tactical Operations Center Stops working |
| 2326 | Sergeant First Class Knight begins looking for remote control for Medium Size Environmental Control Unit |
| 2327 | Sergeant First Class Knight turns red faced angry at not being able to find remote control for Medium Size Environmental Control Unit. |
| 2330 | Sergeant First Class Knight still has not found Medium Size Environmental Control Unit remote control but has broken a chair and two pens in his aggressive process. |
| 2340 | Sergeant First Class Knight call's mayor cell. Reports deficiency in operation of Medium Size Environmental Control Unit. Requests immediate assistance from FOB Maintenance. |
| 2345 | Sergeant First Class Knight call's Mayor Cell. Mayor Cell reports work order must be submitted in triplicate after 0830. A contractual three days for maintenance response follows. |
| 2346 | Sergeant First Class Knight slams phone, leaves Tactical Operations Center slamming the Portal Entry device (door) as he stumbles out. |
| 2350 | Sergeant First Class Knight reenters command post and commands Specialist Sanderford to look for the #$%^@ remote control for Medium Size Environmental Control Unit |
| 2351 | Specialist Sanderford finds remote to Medium Size Environmental Control on Sergeant Knight's desk |
| 2351 | Sergeant First Class Knight, still red faced, sulks and slams, harder than required, himself down in chair with back to Specialist Sanderford. Second chair broken. With questionable balance remains seated with back to Specialist Sanderford dedicated to minimal embarrassment. |
| 2352 | Specialist Sanderford begins Preventive Maintenance Checks and Services on Medium Size Environmental Control Unit (MSECU) though no manual has been issued on the equipment |
| 2353 | Specialist Sanderford confirms Medium Size Environmental Control unit is not working |

| Time | Event |
|------|-------|
| 2354 | Specialist Sanderford replaces batteries in MSECU remote |
| 2355 | MSECU still inoperable, troubleshooting procedures begin |
| 2357 | Specialist Sanderford Removes MSECU Cover Assembly one each |
| 2358 | Cleaning of oxygen intake filter initiated with compressed air container and air flow directional control device (can air with straw) |
| 2400 | Directional Control Device removed to continue oxygen intake filter dust removal processing |
| 2410 | Oxygen Intake Filter particle removal completed. Air Directional Control Device replaced on compressed oxygen canister to facilitate particle removal from Oxygen Intake Cover assembly. |
| 2420 | Specialist Sanderford takes break to prevent exhaustion during maintenance operations |
| 2440 | Specialist Sanderford returns to troubleshooting operations for TOC MSECU |
| 2445 | Particle removal complete Specialist Sanderford re-install's Oxygen Intake Filter and secures Oxygen Intake Cover Assembly on MSECU |
| 2446 | Specialist Sanderford cuts finger on Oxygen Intake Assembly |
| 2450 | Specialist Sanderford still awaiting Combat Life Saver requested from First Platoon |
| 0010 | 30 minute wait for medical support from first platoon is over. Evidently Dad is not sending a Combat Life Saver for my injury, nice to know he cares. Retrieve clear adhesive binding strip from Sergeant Knight's desk. Small manual water removal device from caffeine support area. (Napkin from coffee pot table) TOC Expedient "field" dressing in place (scotch tape and paper towel) Specialist bravely returns to MSECU operator/maintainer duties |
| 0030 | %$^#& Specialist Sanderford takes a break |

| Time | Event |
|------|-------|
| 0038 | Specialist Sanderford hears loud noise from within TOC and rushes to aid of head TOC Rat. On entry of TOC Sergeant First Class Knight is observed laying on floor, partially in overturned chair. Specialist initiates buddy aid. With utmost rudeness, Sergeant First Class Knight refuses treatment and begins self-recovery. |
| 0041 | Sergeant First Class Knight completes recovery process of his person from wooden floor. Kicks chair, which broke earlier, and takes Specialist Sanderford's chair. Orders Specialist Sanderford to take that #$%@^ chair outside. |
| 0055 | Back from chair removal. PMCS and maintenance request forms are completed for damaged chair. Sergeant First Class Knight orders change on all documents from "Damaged" to "Defective." Also orders TOC expedient bandage be replaced with commercially purchased adhesive sanitized TOC dressing (Sponge Bob Band-Aid) |
| 0057 | Replacement of TOC Expedient bandage complete Specialist Sanderford places all used Bandage components and wrappings in unserviceable item disposal receptacle. (trash can) |
| 0115 | Specialist Sanderford feels light headed but continues mission of MSECU repair. No progress. |
| 0130 | Sergeant First Class Knight orders Sanderford to stop #%$^@ with the MSECU and sit the $^&# down |
| 0145 | Sergeant First Class Knight confirms no sworn statements are required for injury sustained during operation MSECU repair. |
| 0150 | MSECU is working. Sergeant First Class Knight fills out documentation to request contract maintenance support for our intermittent MSECU. |
| 0155 | Processing estimated at 3-5 days for maintenance request, two days for diagnosis, if parts are required up to 8 weeks for repair due to remote location of the MSECU on our tiny FOB, FOB location in theatre and transportation issues. Our unit may be required to clear IED's on a route to retrieve repair parts. Another 5-7 day mission. But that's why we are here. |

# 9

*Therapy Session Number 21*

Doc Taylor sits in his chair to my twelve o'clock. "Hello Dale. Nice weather today isn't it?"

"Yeah."

"So what's on your mind today?"

"Been cracking jokes with my men on Facebook."

"You keep up with your soldiers on Facebook?"

"Yessir. We all have issues. Some Facebook posts raise flags, stinkin' thinkin'. I check it a few times a week. Try to get in touch when they don't sound right. Can't take care of 'em anymore. I'm still responsible, though."

"I've noticed you still say 'your men.' Do you feel they have access to what assistance they require?"

"I'm not worth a sh' anymore, but they're still my men. Like sons. I trained 'em, led 'em, brought 'em home, and left 'em on their own. Some troops don't know how to deal with the sh' I put 'em through. I have been where they have been. Our memories match. We've lost two good men since we got home. I don't want to lose another."

"There's a bond among you I will never experience."

"Yessir. No matter how long we go without seein' each other, it's there. We can just sit and enjoy each other's company, without a word."

"These are important relationships for you, and your troops. Do not take such friendships for granted. Your mutual understanding goes beyond what most have, or will ever enjoy. A deep relationship with another human being is not common. I hope you will embrace, and nurture these relationships."

"Yessir. But it's hard to keep track of 'em. Some were attached to us for only one trip, volunteered or volun-told to go. Now they're back with their old unit, or already out, so we never see 'em. Their units may or may not understand. Not all units are the same, or have done similar missions. Mississippi's Adjutant General pointed to me and told one of my banker friends, "These men have been there, experienced everything modern warfare has to offer. If you want to know what combat is like for troops today, talk to him or his men."

"You joked over there? You and your men still do?"

"Yeah, Doc, gotta joke."

"Humor is a good release. Laughter allows one to let out emotions without tears, or words. What do you joke about?"

"In the Stan we joked about everything. Buying a monkey, panic attacks in mountain passes, 'artistic' snowmen, sailing snowball's a hundred meters across a FOB like mortars. You name it, at some point we joked about it, even laughed about IED hits sometimes. Now we tell stories about stupid crap we did, fun stuff, anything to break the monotony."

"Would you share one? We could both use a laugh this afternoon."

"Josh's platoon blasted a song sayin', 'I wish I'd killed more Yankees at Bull Run' on their front porch once. Our XO was duct taped to a bench with a sign on his chest, and leaned against a wall outside for a few hours. My men sprayed silly string on third country nationals who worked our FOB at our Christmas party. There's a lot of 'em…"

"What is the significance of the lyrics 'killed more Yankees'?"

"A new brigade took over half way through our tour. Like most units, they ordered their troops to not associate with us, not to go near our sleep area. They were Yankees, so 'I wish I'd killed more Yankees' seemed to fit."

"Why did so many units disassociate with yours?"

"They were focused on 'nation building.' New folks wanna befriend locals, yadda, yadda, yadda. We were tired of bein' blown up, shot at, and dealing with sh'. We didn't wanna pass out blankets. We weren't there for that. We had blood on our hands. We're combat engineers, not construction."

"Did they just avoid you, or were there times it went further?"

"Sometimes it went further. Threatened to kick our ass, nit-pick our uniforms or mad we hadn't shaved.

Best example was at a FOB down south. We got stuck overnight there a lot. One time their troops and some locals complained about us. Said we were using 'their' internet café, crowding their Hadji mart. One shop owner said Carter, one of my troops, stole some smokes. Some complaints were justified. We are rough men. Panther TOC, their head shed, put us in a parking area under a camera so to watch us on a flat screen day and night.

Two days and nights we slept, laid around, and played soccer under constant surveillance. The battle captain gave orders we could go to one specific latrine, chow, our trucks, and nowhere else. We couldn't sleep in the nice guest house anymore. Had to sleep by our vehicles."

"A unit you worked with?"

"Hell, yeah. We'd got blowed up for 'em."

"How did you and your men react?"

"Normal sh' for us. We always smelled bad, real bad. I told three of my men to use our coffee can bathtub, take a ho-bath and clean up real good. Panther's TOC-rats wanted a show, we gave 'em one."

"Did their observation end?"

"No, Sir. They kept watching. Few days, later they filmed three locals emplace an IED with another camera. Before breakfast, they called me in, watched the video, they gave me the grid, and asked me to go take care of it. Their battle captain said 'higher wouldn't let his artillery shoot 'em for fear of civilian casualties.' Hell Doc, closest qal'at was a klik and a half away. We were pissed. Wouldn't a been civilian casualties at zero-two. Pretty hard to motivate my men, but we found it, blew it up and went home."

"I'm not sure how to respond."

"Respond to what, soldiers believe locals over you, treat you like sh', or after bull sh' for two days they expect you to risk your life for 'em?"

"This unit's behavior to you and your men seems in stark contrast with their expectations. How or why would one not respect men who clear roads, are willing to get blown up, even try to do so for one's own safety?"

"My men are rough, violent men. On base, we focus on repair and refit, then food and fun. Rarely give a sh' about manners or making friends. We offend people."

"That had to piss you off. I am sure you have a story we can laugh at Dale."

*\*\**

We are at Bagram Air Field, fresh in country. I walk back from breakfast and see Sergeants Duke and French in a smoking area with three of our new troops. They all stare at seven blue plastic porta-lets across an open gravel area. We have a nice hard building latrine on the north side of our gravel yard, clamshell sleep tent to the south, and a smoking area east opposite plastic porta-lets.

We share our tent with literally 350 other troops. Porta-lets are here because one nice latrine cannot support us all. I sit atop the picnic table next to my men, light a cigarette and ask, "What's goin' on?"

Sergeant French, picks up gravel to throw, sits straight up, looks at me, and throws a rock. "Nothin' Sar'nt, why would anything be goin' on?"

I blow out smoke as I speak. "First, five of my men are in the break area, all looking in the same direction. Second, two of you don't smoke. Third, we're all bored, there's always paperwork when y'all get bored. Last and most obvious, you said 'nothin' Sar'nt', and asked me why I asked."

French laughs and tosses a rock at a well-used butt can. "C'mon Sar'nt can't we just sit around and relax without you thinkin' we up to somethin'?"

"In my experience, no, you can't."

Duke says, "Sar'nt ain't you sick of these nasty porta-lets?"

"We had the same thing in Iraq, different color, but same thing. What's the deal?"

"Never got this nasty though, Sar'nt."

My gaze shifts from well-used porta-lets, to French, back to the often-overfilled johns. French will not make eye contact. I glance to the far end of our table to our young troops. They look everywhere but at me. "What'd y'all do?"

Laughter erupts from our troops. They continue to avoid my gaze. French holds up his hands as if to say, "who us?" but gives up gestures of innocence.

*He remembers I know him too well.*

French says, "Trainin' Sar'nt. Trainin' locals, them that cleans the toilets, like you taught us to do. A good NCO takes every opportunity to train."

"Anyone gonna get hurt? Already hurt?"

Duke pounds his left backhand to his right palm. "Sar'nt its basic personal hygiene, one person's habits affect all of us. Livin' like this here we gotta work together, right?"

*Who needs correction? Sh'. Why don't they teach hygiene in basic?*

A drag on my smoke to prepare, I frown at Duke. "Who ain't showering? We ain't here to train locals on shower habits. You know they ain't used to havin' a lotta water."

French says, "They smell ain't the problem, Sar'nt."

Moe, Larry, and Curly lose all restraint, laugh, and dance like Pentecostal preachers on Sunday morning. Every word spoken spurs fresh snickers and chuckles. All three move around behind me, away from direct questions and eye contact. I point at one, his mutes his laughter and snaps to parade rest. "You. What's goin' on?"

His scared eyes and jittery jaw turn to French then Duke, back to me.

*He hopes someone will put words in his mouth. Nice, he's still scared of me.*

Duke groans. "Sar'nt I went to the latrine last night afore goin' to bed. Forgot my flashlight but went in and sat down. Again, right there on at damn seat…someone's sh'. Locals stand on each side-o-the toilet and squat. I don't care what they do. But damn if you can't aim, sit your ass down. At least clean your sh' up! Do not leave it for somebody to sit in. Know what I'm sayin', Sar'nt? Ain't right, at's all I'm sayin', at sh' ain't right."

Uncontrolled laughter surrounds us. I fight to control my own. Duke looks down and shakes his head as my laughter joins the choir.

French says, "See Sar'nt. It's like you always say, remedial training must be related to the issue at hand."

"Ok. What'd y'all do?"

Everyone looks back and forth for someone else to speak. Our three stooges behind me among themselves, sporadic glances to my NCO's, and back at each other. Duke and French look back and forth at each other, at their stooges, with an occasional glance to me. Our unseen movie director has followed us here. Hal Roach orders us, in unison, to return our gaze to the toilets.

I take a drag off my smoke, and stare at the toilets. "Someone's 'bout to speak up, what'd y'all do?"

Duke looks at me and takes a deep breath. "Dang it... Fine... got done takin' a shower last night and I says this sh' ain't happenin' again. So I smears Baby oil on both sides of the toilet seat."

I say, "Duke what the hell, now everyone's ass is gonna be greased?"

French holds a calm it down hand to me. "No Sar'nt. Not on the seat, beside the seat, where their feet go to squat."

Our director cues us to replay our "glance back and forth in awkward silence" scene. Troop's nervous eyes contrast my NCOs complacent ones. I light a second smoke, stand, stow the pack in my sleeve pocket, sit down, and laugh. "This should be good."

Everyone joins me. French leans back, crosses his outstretched legs, and folds his arms on his chest. "I don't think it'll work again Sar'nt."

"Again?"

"Yeah, bout zero one last night I heard somethin' bangin', from over at way." Duke's two fingers hold a menthol cigarette and point at the porta lets. "Screamin' and bangin', bangin' and screamin'. time I got out here all's I could see is blue stained rocks by at second blue one. That and blue footprints goin' off at way." He points past the far end of our clamshell tent.

I wave both hands. "Dang it, I always miss the good stuff. He probably told the rest of 'em."

French says, "At's what we figure, hell ain't nothin' else to do so we're hopin' for another performance."

Specialist Smith asks, "Sergeant Sanderford when are we gonna get outta here? Start doin' our damn job?"

I put out my cigarette and field strip its remaining tobacco, stand, throw the butt in our coffee can, and look from troop to eager young troop.

*Don't rush it. It'll come.*

Duke says, "We can stay right here all's I care. If this here is anything like las' time. I likes the way we passin' time right hear. Like it just fine."

French says, "Ain't nobody gettin' hurt doin' this, bored, but not hurt."

I say, "Sept' a local sh' cleaner in the middle of the night."

*Best to enjoy laughs when we can. Gonna stop soon.*

"Don't know, more trainin' here first, gotta re-zero too." My hands slip under my blouse, grasp my pants on both hips, pull them up and slide my thumbs around front, under my belt. "Y'all behave. Get your camera out in case Hadji comes back."

As I walk away Duke says, "Roger Sar'nt." And from French, "Roger that."

*Great NCOs, We need both of 'em.*

\*\*\*

Doc says, "So some poor man had to clean latrines and then fell in."

"Yessir, small price to pay for a day of good morale."

"I see your point."

"Good day, Doc. No tears, snot, or nothin'."

"You know we don't have to go deep every time, only when you're ready."

"I know."

"Have a good one, Dale. Reschedule on your way out."

"Roger, Sir. See ya in a couple days."

"Bye, Dale."

*Josh's Journal*

May 21, 2010, Gardez

Well we're finally here. FOB Alpha. We got one of those spur of the moment flights. I volunteered with a box detail so I rode over in a Black Hawkeye. We got here at night in the dark, but I could tell this was a nice place. I went to the latrine after we settled into transit housing. It had a lot of spacious showers washers and dryers and clean toilets. It's nice here.

I didn't get to my duffel so I had no cover to sleep on. I stayed up the entire night. Hopkins told me I was probably moving over to Commo because our only commo guy, Harper, got his security clearance pulled for something. I guess that's better than being a CO Driver.

I'd like responsibility. I still would rather be out in a line platoon. When the sun came up, we had guys go out on a left seat right seat. I went outside and walked around.

The chow hall has red pleather-like seat covers. It gives the feel of a southern diner. It's not too bad either. This place is so nice. I've only seen one tent. It's also tiny. I can walk completely around the FOB in nine minutes. It has sort of a home feel to it.

I went to the TOC, and the Commo girl there was helpful in teaching me. She is cool. But the rest of them in there are assholes. Typical active army mindset. They think they're tough sh'.

I found out a lot. I will be in charge of keeping communication open between RCPs and the TOC. Sending reports to battalion and everything, It's actually an important job. I was a little disappointed at first about not being put back into a line platoon, but now it feels good having the leadership put trust in me.

There is a downside, however. The shifts are twelve hours. Me and Sergeant Thompson will be the men covering it. 7 to 7 and 7 to 7. That means one of us is the night guy. Since RCPs aren't rolling out at night it's basically TOC - sitting. I don't want that, but I won't be surprised if I get that shift.

Sergeant Thompson has had training on the BFT. Today was the first time I used one. I ran it alone for about ten minutes and did a BFT check with the RCP and sent the hourly coordinate report to Battalion at BAF. I'm starting to get a good idea of how this place works.

Doing twelve-hour shifts will get in the way of getting out to go on missions. Me and Sergeant Thompson will probably become the token TOC rats.

I got a package from Mom today. Holy sh'. Ha-ha. She sent me a birthday hat plates and cups and all kinds of stuff. Ha-ha. I did keep the *pin the tail on the donkey*, though. I thought I could hang that up somewhere if I end up getting a room alone.

I'm going to ask Sergeant Hatfield about that sometime. I got my duffel a few minutes ago. I made my bed and all. Maybe I will sleep good tonight. This weather is starting to get to me. I've been coughing a lot lately.

*Josh's Journal*
  02Jul2010, Gardez
  Once again it's been a while since I've chimed in. Everything's changed. I continued working nights with Sergeant Knight. I kept on smoothly throwing in my desires of going out. I told XO Moore that I'd give him my paycheck for the rest of the year if I could get moved over to Gardez with 137.

A few nights later Captain Joe Wayne was in the TOC talking to me and Sergeant Knight as he usually does before he heads to his quarters for the night (he lives in the back room of the TOC).

Specialist Blart got moved to the TOC from 154. Dad said he kept screwin' up and wouldn't do what he was told on missions. He was pretty adamant in getting him out the platoon.

Blart is a good guy, but he isn't the foot soldier type. I think he will do alright in the TOC. That made five RTO's at that point. Me, Sergeant Thompson, Sergeant Conners, Specialist Harper and of course Specialist Blart.

I was still working twelve hours a day, seven days a week, and having to take turns going out on missions because the other RTO's wanted to go. Me and Blart were the only 21B RTO's. Captain Joe Wayne was casually talking as usual.

I was sitting in the RTO area, working on some pictures or something.

He then said that Sergeant Thompson and Specialist Blart would be doing nights.

I asked him what I would go to and he said, "Ole Sanderford is goin' to Gardez back to 137." I dropped my head and just said, "I appreciate that a lot, Sir."

I would be going over the next day, 01 June, when Captain Joe Wayne would go for a meeting. RCP 128 dropped us off, and I took a three-day pack.

I walked over to the living quarters for 137. I saw our guys out on the picnic tables where they usually hang out. It took around five times telling everybody that I was actually here for them to believe me.

Douglas still thought I was screwin' with him until he heard the Commander say it. Sergeant Smith put me in a room with Franks. I was bummed I wouldn't be in my own room.

The guys were renovating part of the transit housing for some quarters for guys who took the initiative to build it. If I had gotten there a day earlier, I could have claimed a room. I hung out with Douglas and the guys for a while.

I went outside to the porch later. First Sergeant told me that Captain Joe Wayne wants me in his room. The guys built him a room down with the rest of the guys in the transit housing for when he comes over. I was pretty humbled, and happy as hell.

I ran down there and Sergeant Dupre unlocked it for me. Since it was only meant for one-night stays it was the smallest of the rooms. But it had a desk. And best of all I'd be by myself. I really like being alone.

I stayed the night there with my three-day pack. Sergeant Grant asked me how I'd feel about being the driver of the lead RG with mine rollers. I ducked my head and smiled.

Damn. I've already been blown up in a lead RG. They didn't want to throw me in so quick, though. I'd never driven an RG. Especially an RG with mine rollers on the front. This RG had taken a hit already too. Pretty much anytime the husky misses a pressure plate, it's the lead RG that takes the blast. And being that the only thing we have seen so far in our AO are pressure plates, I'm sure I haven't seen my only blast. That sucks. But I'll drive on.

I'm happy to be here. Even though getting hit again is pretty much a freagin' inevitability. I'm not looking forward to that. We ran our mission the second day I was here. Down Tawagoto and Scheibe to CP Banjo. Tawagoto is now a green route for the first time.

Scheibe however sucks. At Banjo there is an intersection where IDF is almost inevitable. COP Zormat is on the intersection of Scheibe and Tawagoto. They have a blimp there that can spot guys putting IED's in. They are also working on building an AFCOP near Banjo.

That caused us to have RCP's going down Scheibe every day to clear it. We rolled out. I was in the Buffalo. We made it to Zormat pretty quick. Around an hour or so. Then we kicked out dismounts with mine detectors in the areas where IED's usually are. We interrogated a few spots and found nothing.

Later on, we got to a spot behind a qal'at on a turn. Specialist Meyer found something. The husky ran over with a GPR and told us to come up and interrogate with the Buff. While we were there, I realized that at this spot the qal'at offered cover from the blimp.

RCP 128 was called to roll out yesterday because the blimp saw a man digging. I knew we would find something. After a few minutes of digging we uncovered a mine with the same three-button pressure plate as always.

We disabled it and Specialist Norton got out to do his first BIP. It was a pretty blast. Decent size. Would have Fu'ed up a vehicle.

We were feeling pretty good at this point. We were almost to CP Banjo and just did our first BIP without EOD. We cleared to the Banjo intersection then began turning around. We saw another element coming our way to deliver stuff to the AFCOP.

We were all feeling pretty good and joking around. I was watching the video Norton had of the BIP and happened to look up.

*Poaawhh.* "Ah hell," I said.

"IDF IDF," I heard through my headset.

About seven seconds later, another one. *Poaawhh.* about twenty meters closer to the road to our twelve.

Then seven seconds later. *Poaawh.* About ten meters from the road.

TC's were coming over the radio telling us to book it. The rounds were hitting around twenty meters in front of the Buffalo at this point.

We should be getting another one here soon, I thought.

*Poaahh.* This one hit the side of the road maybe fifteen meters from the husky. Sergeant Smith came over and said they spotted the guys.

I heard his 240 in the background.

They were returning fire.

As we got closer, we began driving through smoke and dust. Somehow all our VICs got through there and we took no more IDF.

The returning fire was somewhat effective. We continued down the road and made it back to Gardez. We sent some trucks to Alpha, and I picked up my stuff.

Today was a maintenance day. It's around 1030 p.m. now, and I'm getting ready for bed. We roll out tomorrow to go up to RTE Mafi. It is a new route so we don't really know what expect. I am in Sergeant Smith's VIC with Douglas. They didn't change the trip ticket in time for me to be driving tomorrow. I'm not complaining. I'm gonna call it a day.

*Dale's Journal*
191730AUG2011      At home

I was Jumpy at home before I went to get Charlotte, both legs bouncing. Watched *Bully Beat Down* for two hours. I liked seeing bullies get smoked. Josh and I laughed.

Going to pick up Charlotte today I saw small arms from the west. Continuing south, a mortar man at that tennis court. Then three mortar strikes west of the road 200 meters south of me that were 40-50 meters apart. Just prior, I realized I'm choking the steering wheel again. Why am I edgy? Driven that road a hundred times since I've been home. No new houses nor people. Going home, I turn off by that sharp left on road to Alpha where SAF came from towers and IED east side of culvert. Same place dude was killed by 50-cal. ammo can when his RG got flipped by an IED. Coming up drive nervous about kid on phone west side fifty meters out. At Quick Stop nervous going between trucks coming out of store and motor cycle going south as I go north. He should pull over. Will truck come out and T-bone me? All turns on TM Smith, I try to peek around corner and wood line to see what's there. All I see is high ground on east side then drop off on south side with high ground north.

Why did I see stuff this time and other times I don't? Other day on interstate I saw Carters' bridge. Going over bridge by Red Hot truck stop I got nervous. What's on the other side. Hate being exposed on a bridge. What's under me? Carters got killed on that bridge.

Keep seeing dude flying through the air from arty strike in ninety, and the body Brachetti played with on the side of the road. Then body/bones in burning trucks.

Mortars in 05 during the big dig. Sniper fire in Jun-Blatia village. Friends faces, killed in 05.

I wanna sleep on a cot outside. Fresh air, on side of road somewhere. God is drawing me closer, but I am still worried about future. Shaky about working at the college again. Scared of being unable to take care of my family, a failure.

God provides. In His time. He keeps saying to wait, how long? Why not take care of me now? Fix my brain. Prepare me for my old job, or whatever.

I am a failure. A quitter, a man that runs from things that make me nervous or might be an argument. Why am I weak and such a chicken?

Dad never handled confrontation well either. Why not? Cause we are a family of insecure people who see ourselves as less than others? Less strong, less smart, less knowledgeable, less forceful, less professional, less powerful in God. Everything about us we see as failure.

Always sick, always something bad going on. Never celebrate peace and success. Though history should tell me otherwise. Even now I am less of a soldier than others. I am weak and weak-minded. Undetermined and unwilling to suck it up and drive on.

I couldn't do it at the college. I cried going to work. I got sick when I was there and had to deal with customers and instructors. Shook up, sick to my stomach, even threw up.

How can I suck that up and drive on? I have to work through this sh'. All of this crap from being beat down in the fifth grade, to being made fun of in junior high, to not getting back with my platoon in Afghanistan after I was medevac'd.

What do I do with all this crap? I'm a piece of sh'. Can't work, can't play with my daughter, my son loses respect for me as a soldier.

*Sh'* I am ready to go back to the Stan. It's easier to be in combat than living here with a head that don't work and all this emotional BS.

# 10

*Therapy Session Number 27*

Doc Taylor closes his door and sits, as always, to my front. "Hello, Dale. Good to see you. How are you today?"

> *How would you freagin' feel if you ruined your family, let your men down, and walked out on 'em? Now can't even go to work.*

"I'm a depressed failure."

"How so, Dale?"

I close my journal and place it on my stationary left leg. "Lotta sh'. Poor decisions, bad leadership, mistakes, screw ups."

"What have your men said to illicit these emotions?"

"Nothing."

"You perceive you made poor decisions. Yet you consistently strove for the best decisions possible. You have described to me incomplete and incorrect information, time constraints, and ever-changing situations. Decisions under such stress are inherently difficult."

"S'pose' so, but afterward, with knowledge how it coulda' been different, it's hard to look back with."

"Please share one of these with me. A choice you see as an error, you now see as a mistake on your part."

"Our three-day mission on route Mierda…"

\*\*\*

Zero-seven-hundred our first day out, we drop off pavement onto a dirt road in a two and a half klik wide-open area. A narrow gap between dirt wall qal'ats, on the far side, is our first village for today.

Halfway through this flat, dusty plateau a north to south dried up wadi crosses our path. Our trail slopes through both wadi walls to enter, and exit. These crossings are the same everywhere. Steep banks grow taller to enclose our paths as trails descend to a wadi bottom.

My lead vehicle attempts to clear through this first "risky" point at 0900. Halfway up the far side—*kerblam*—he takes a big hit.

*Sh'. That's a huge freakin' blast.*

*Ryan is in there.*

*There goes a tire.*

It is several seconds before my skin compresses to bone. His front tire and rim fly three-hundred meters north, to our three o-clock.

Thunderous radio silent hours seem to pass before Miller, my driver, calls Ryan, "Husky One, you ok?"

No response.

In desperation, we wait for the massive smoke cloud to clear. Perpetual Afghan wind carries dust away as metal hunks and dirt clots impact brush, rock and other vehicles.

Surreal dirt and smoke birth his vehicle.

His AWOL front section abandoned his chassis deep in a blast hole.

"Husky One this is One Nine, can you read me?"

Lungs freeze, arms tingle, and adrenaline throbs in my fingers.

*Ryan*

*Please answer.*

Out his top hatch, I see Ryan wave thumbs up.

French's gunner, McPhee, signals him to get in and secure his hatch. Ryan complies.

My front gun trucks sprint off route north and south to set security. French maneuvers through a wadi wall low point to cover our twelve, far side of our blown truck.

EOD clears for secondary bombs, gathers evidence, and determines it was homemade explosive, thirty or forty pounds. Ryan's AWOL wheel hit it on his far side ascent.

A second smoke lit, pack stashed beside my computer screen and piss bottle. I key my radio. "Mater, this is One Nine, come on up, over."

"Roger that One Nine, Mater's movin'."

Mater follows French's path forward and backs up to Ryan's bare front chassis. Staff Sergeant Pritchet meets me at the blast hole. We pick up mangled chunks of metal, sheered bolts, frayed hoses, and wires. Take pictures for our mission report and consider the year to come.

Half an hour into recovery, Staff Sergeant Pritchet strolls over to me. "Sar'nt Sanderford, this sucks. You see them Hesco baskets right there?"

Pritchet points northwest, across the brush freckled open field, past our men throwing a thermite in Ryan's displaced tire, to a Hesco basket wall. Filled with dirt, they create Afghan Combat Outpost (AFCOP) Tashnob's perimeter, one of many small outposts in our Area of Operation. I step in the blast hole and stare at two of Tashnob's guard towers.

I look at Pritchet. "Yeah, I see it. Saw 'em when we stopped."

Pritchet gives me a hand to climb out. He points down to the hole, at Tashnob, and holds both hands in the air, palms up. "Sar'nt we got hit right here, 'em boys can see us. How in the hell are we s'pose to trust 'em?"

"Just clean this sh' up, we got a long day ahead."

"Roger that. How we gonna keep goin', Sar'nt? Our wrecker's loaded with this sh'."

"Already texted up. We'll figure it out. And Pritchett," I look to Tashnob, our line of vehicles, back to Pritchet, "I'm more worried about havin' only one detection asset for three more days out here."

"Oh sh', Sar'nt. What'd they say about that?"

"Charlie Mike."

Blown up equipment has no effect on mission requirements. Panther, our infantry unit we lead out today, still needs to get somewhere. Like always—clean up, load up, pray up, and Charlie Mike.

Weapon across his back, Pritchett's hands still stretched out to each side. He smiles and steps backwards toward Mater. "Roger Sar'nt Sanderford. Welcome to the Stan."

"Roger. Gonna be a fun week."

"Gonna be a fun year, Sar'nt."

Pritchett turns from me to our men. I check security a third time and walk to my vehicle to check text messages. Pritchet returns to assist and supervise vehicle recovery.

Although we find only one more IED today, it takes twelve hours to make our Rally Over Night (RON) site. We talk to locals in qal'ats beside our site, neighbors for the week.

French parks so McPhee, his gunner, can cover our trail in. Zero-one-hundred McPhee spots some Hadji's with shovels near our trail. Pritchett takes a team up the road a hundred meters, rolls up four locals and brings them to our RON sight for entry in our computer identification system.

French spreads our four new friends several meters apart, faces them away from each other, seats them in the dirt, and supervises troops' efforts to enter them in the system.

I walk around our detainees once, halt to one side of their circle, and pose like MacArthur, and point to the oldest one. "RC get Gray Beard, over here. Mahmud, come here."

RC complies, Mahmud, my interpreter for today, joins us.

*Why do terps stand so damn close? He wanna hold hands or some sh'?*

My left hand points at Gray Beard, my right on my nine millimeter. "Mahmud, ask him why they are in the field so late at night. What are the shovels for?"

Mahmud has a few back and forth loud sentences with Gray Beard.

I stare at his beard, observe his clothes, sandals, and head gear, do my angry face, glance to my truck fifty meters away, and back to Mahmud.

*I'm ready to crash, what the hell, we ain't gonna get sh' out a these guys.*

"Talk to me Mahmud. Don't have a party with him. What'd he say?"

Mahmud's hands grasp his hips with thumbs forward. "They say they cowboys. Take care of sheep. Grow food."

"Cowboys who grow food, tend sheep. What the hell does that mean, Mahmud? What are the shovels for?"

"Him say water plant at night better than day."

RC says, "What the hell is that Sar'nt?"

I take a drag, drop my cigarette, step on it, take a step back from Gray Beard, and look at RC. "In Iraq they use trenches to flow creek water around their crop. Flood it at night and the water soaks in before daybreak. Daytime it'd dry up too quick, probably same sh' here."

"Sar'nt, you ain't gonna buy at sh', are ya Sar'nt?"

"Unless they come up in the computer as a bad guy, ain't sh' we can do."

"This here sh' sucks, Sar'nt, freakin' sucks."

"Take him back over there to wait his turn with French and 'em."

"Roger Sar'nt"

"Mahmud go help French."

"Yes Sergeant."

Over an hour's computer work follows to find none of them are known bad guys. We send Gray Beard and his cowboys home. Squad leaders report on ammo, water, and food. I define and direct my NCOs in guard coordination shift, sectors of fire and sleep positions. We crash, under varied forms of cover, around zero-three-hundred.

Day two begins at zero-six-thirty. We clear west, same narrow route we came out on day one.

Find another IED at zero eight near yesterday's find.

*Good day's start.*

Miller and RC computer check identifications on an eighteen and twenty-two year old near our morning find.

Both young locals say, "No one farm at night," and, "No Taliban live here. Bad people come, cause problem, go away."

*Same sh' as Iraq, "bad people" don't live anywhere, but are everywhere.*

Mutt and Jeff, as I call these two, describe locals who live in several qal'ats, even name most. We like to learn the locals, map their names if possible. Such a list can help catch liars or out-of-towners when we ask their neighbor's name. If Hadji don't know any of his neighbors, he is not a local. Could mean they are one of the "bad people" who cause problems and leave.

We are not here for this kind of work. Our job is route clearance, not infantry stuff. We will be out here three days now and back again later in our tour, it won't hurt to do some data collection as we roll.

Gray Beard, the cowboys nor Mutt and Jeff know who lives in the qal'at with tallest walls. No one knows who lives in them.

> *You have lived two qal'ats away for fifteen years but have no idea who lives there, really?*

We pass this data to Panther and ask if they want us to look into it. They do not. Infantry, on most missions, have specific targets. Often they have no authority to divert from those targets. We continue northwest to clear the snake trail.

We set security in quicker the second night. Motivation comes in the knowledge we have a resupply from Wagoneer in route. They bring us fuel, water, and MREs. Refuel and offload from Wagoneer is quick, but in a rush to get home they run over half our food and water.

> *Yay team, glad we always carry three-day supply.*

Third day we clear northeast to Mamno, find some homemade explosive jugs, a propane tank, and an AT mine, all tied to one pressure plate. EOD thinks it is cool to get something different, as do we. Near dark, we are back at our RON site for a third night under the stars.

I use a stretcher off my vehicle as a cot tonight. Briars kept me awake most of the last two nights. I also wanted to get away from the hundreds of thumb size roly-polies.

> *Like in Saudi, Iraq, and Kuwait, millions of stars in the sky here at night. I guess that's what they mean by Arabian nights.*
> *Beautiful.*

Sunbeams creep in and drench my sleeping bag covered face. A warm glow penetrates my eyelids to wake me at zero-six. Our orders are to move out at ten hundred so I snuggle in to enjoy my first good night's sleep in days. Nice and cool, stretcher is nice and comfortable. I curl up like a dog by a fire, only my nose is exposed from my warm bed.

Miller, who had last guard shift in our truck, yells from RC's gunner hatch, "Sar'nt Sanderford, you up?"

I feel like a kid on Saturday morning. My plan to sleep in interrupted for some stupid sh'. Without a move I bark, "What?"

"Panther's callin' for ya, some sh' about SP bein' pult in."

"What the hell? I'm commin' dammit."

I roll out of bed, in my drawers, slip boots on, shuffle to Lu Lu's steps, open my door, climb up, get in, and key up. "Panther Six, this is Byson One Nine, over."

"Byson One Nine, this is Panther Six, Our little buddies found what they think is an IED. We need EOD up here. I'll text you a grid. Over."

"This is Byson One Nine, I copy suspect IED. Need EOD. You will send grid. Break. I'll let you know when we roll. Over"

"Roger Byson One Nine, see ya in a little while, Panther Six out."

"Byson One Nine, out."

I throw my headset on the dash and look up at Miller. "Call sergeant off the guard. Tell him to get everybody up and get team leaders and above to my truck."

"Roger that, Sar'nt. What the hell, they afraid it's gonna move. We goin' right by 'em to lead everybody home in like three hours."

"Just call him."

I climb down to my bedroom, check my weapon, get dressed, and start to pack up.

"Miller," I shout. "Tell him everybody needs to prep to move."

"Roger Sar'nt"

*Wonder if I jinxed myself sleeping on a stretcher. It ain't as creepy as sleepin' in my body bag in ninety-one. That was creepy.*

*Shut up, Sarge. Pack your sh' and go to work.*

As we lead EOD to the Afghan Armies suspect IED, we find another one. And this one is  thirty feet from our day one and two finds. EOD blows it in place and we Charlie Mike.

Panther screams for us to get there. Nobody likes to babysit an IED for hours. Leaves you in one spot long enough for "Bad People" to maneuver, or run away.

EOD has blown the Afghan Army's IED at eleven-hundred and we prepare to go home.

***

I say, "We got a good laugh waitin' to move out. Two SF guys ask to ride back with us. They live on our FOB. I offer for one to ride in a roller truck and the other in my Buffalo."

Doc says, "How did the two Special Forces men get out there?"

"I dunno. Rode with infantry or ANA, may have been out there for a week for all I know. Anyway, they had no way home. Duke calls up and says they were scared to ride with him. We let him ride in another truck, further back in our formation.

They were good guys to work with, came to see us on the FOB, sat on our front porch, and had a cold drink. Said we were crazy to do route clearance. They always laughed at our loopy ideas to get bombs to go off."

Doc clarifies, "So Special Forces thought you and your men were crazy to do route clearance? They were afraid to ride in, what was it, a roller truck?"

"Yessir. They'd just shake their head at gadgets we made to find bombs, or make 'em blow. I don't think he was scared, just wouldn't get in. Said 'hell no.' Roller trucks try to get bombs to blow up on them instead of follow on troops. SF guy made the right choice. The risk of him bein' blown up wasn't justified. Route clearance ain't his job. To get blown up when he don't have to, that'd be stupid."

Doc asks, "So what about this mission do you see as a mistake?"

"I screwed up. Horne and Pritchet asked to lead out two fire teams the second night. They wanted to over watch where we found IEDs, two days in a row. If I had let 'em, we'd a got at least one bad guy. That sucks."

"Why did you not put out the teams?"

"Gun trucks couldn't cover 'em. Our only way to cover them with a crew serve woulda gave away their positions. Make it a waste of time. Route was too narrow and rough, take too long for us to get to 'em. My dismount commo wasn't worth a sh'. Commo with my teams would be spotty, too risky, with what equipment we had and everything."

"So you didn't do it because it was too risky. You assessed the situation and knew you couldn't accomplish it without unreasonable risk to your men."

"Yessir, our gear, the terrain, shortage of troops, route status. Too many risks I couldn't mitigate."

"Knowing what you know now. With these same variables, what would you do?"

"I'd love to put emplacers under rock piles."

I look down and rub my beard. Gaze out the French doors, past that tall wall qal'at, and down a goat path we call a route.

"All things considered Doc. I'd make the same decision. I brought my men home, all but one. I'd make the same choice."

"So you made the right decision. You are disappointed with the outcome, but the decision was sound."

"Yessir, a missed opportunity, but the right choice. We're route clearance, not infantry. Like the SF guy's choice to not risk bein' blown up, that ain't his job. We aren't equipped for dismount fire teams."

"Do you still believe you made a poor decision, showed inadequate leadership? Or is this a search for ways you could have made a greater impact. Second guessing decisions from an arm chair. Allowing disappointment, emotions, and information you didn't have at the time of your decision to create doubt in your decisions and leadership?"

"Like reporters who second guess cops. They say if, coulda', woulda', shoulda', but the best decisions were probably made. With no threat it's easy to second guess."

"That's right. However, you said, just now, all things considered, you would make the same decision. You realize you may have killed or captured two emplacers. Never the less you would make the same decision, today, you did then."

"I think I would."

"I want you to do something when you start to doubt things you did, decisions you made or what have you. Methodically, consider these things. Use only what information and assets you had at the point in time in question. Ask yourself, would I make the same decision?

"Any other thought processes leave you with more anxiety, questions, and insecurities than you need or deserve. Your men respected you, trusted you, and continued to do so through your year in combat. This speaks to your leadership more than emotional questions of your decisions and leadership.

"How do you think your men feel toward you today?"

"I think they respect me, till recently anyway. Till I broke down and quit on 'em."

"What have they said or done to make you think they no longer respect you?"

"I quit on 'em. I ain't there. I'm on the damn sick, lame, and lazy list."

"Dale, you didn't answer my question. What has even one of your men said or done to show you have lost their adoration, respect or honor"

"They've done nothing. But I know—"

"Stop right there Dale. You assume what your men think. From that you imagine what their expectations of you are. We have discussed this. You do not and cannot know what is in their head, what they think.

"In my years in practice, I find even when a person tries to tell me what is in their head, I rarely get the whole story. Are you making assumptions based on high, even extreme, standards you force on yourself?"

"I see your point. Yes…I'm assuming. They probly still respect me."

"Hold onto this. Just like second-guessing your decisions, do not assume what other's think until you have reasonable information to do so. Not emotion, but facts, reason, logic, Ok?"

"Roger, I'll try. Oh, I brought you a copy of something."

I retrieve two stapled pages from my map case and hold them out to him.

Doc plops his pen on the ever-present notebook and reaches for my documents. "What's this?"

Doc takes the papers, turns to page two, back to page one, and looks at me.

"I had a reporter ride with me one day. This is his article."

"Interesting. Thank you. Shall I read it now or…?"

My left hand brushes air, right secures pen and journal.

"Nah, just look at it whenever. There is a funny story to it though."

I open my map case, insert journal and pen, close and snap it, and stand to leave.

Doc rests the article on his notebook and stands. "A funny story you say?"

"Weston has a quote in there. He says 'third one this week.' He told his mom he never left the FOB. All he did was pull duties in guard towers, sit around, or do supply stuff. He told his Dad the truth, but not Mom. This article got E-mailed around the family support group and his mom saw it. Man, he was in serious trouble with mama."

Doc chuckles and steps left around his footstool. "His decision to not share the whole truth bit him in the butt then."

I clear the threshold of his door, check the hall left then right, check office doors on each end of the hall, and glance back at Doc. "Yes, Sir. Now that's a decision he can rethink."

"I bet he already has."

"Roger that, I'm out Doc."

"Ok, Dale, schedule out front. Wait, they are gone at this point. We ran a bit late again. Well…"

"I'll call 'em tomorrow, like usual. We stay over a lot."

"When discussions go well, I hate to stop. I'd rather be behind schedule and make headway than on schedule and of no help."

"Appreciate it, Doc. See ya next time."

"Ok. Dale. Take care."

*Dale's Journal*

131130DEC13  At home

My parents are riding with us to Hattiesburg, Ms. My niece graduates from USM today. As we travel south on I-59 toward Laurel, I see a helicopter three clicks to our southeast flying south. I look at my wife, then the helicopter. I've seen them before while riding TC (Truck Commander, front passenger) with my wife. Some are flashbacks, not sure this time.

I quietly ask my wife, "You see that chopper right?"

"Yes"

We look at each other and laugh. It's great we're at a point with my flashbacks to laugh about them. I don't judge them to be weakness, a broken mind, or paranoia. They happen and will continue. We might as well get a laugh out of them here and there. No different than when we laughed about bad sh' happening in the Stan.

Like the other day when we discussed Christmas caroling with the church choir. Karen says, "You're not going are you?" She'd like for me to, but riding from house to house with a crowd of people would not be good for me. I like seeing people smile, I enjoy singing, and love Christmas. But I know my limitations. I need to say "no" in such a way she's not as disappointed.

I say, "I don't think that's a great idea. I can see it now. The PTSD sour face Grinch right there on the front row. It'd be like saying 'we are here to bring cheer, *now*, if you don't like it we'll kick in the door and raid your house.' Nah, I think it's best for me to stay home on this one."

Karen laughs and says, "Your probably right."

We aren't giving in nor encouraging my antisocial behavior here. We are, as my shrink says, protecting me from negative effects. Or my Christian counselor says, "Why set yourself up for problems."

# 11

"Dale, I need to step out and get a bottle of water. Can I get you something?" Doc says.

"No Sir. I'm good, Thanks." I enter his door, clear his office, turn left, step to my corner couch seat, sit, get out a journal, and stare at the floor.

Doc returns, sits to my front, swigs his water, and situates that damn notebook in his lap. "What's on your mind today, Dale?"

"My wife, she always asks why I stay in. Why keep going? She doesn't understand."

"Of course she doesn't. She has not been to war. She has been with you in spirit through three deployments, and I believe you are lucky to have her. She is a good, strong woman. Of course, I only met with her a couple of times. I base this on what you share with me. She has dealt with so much. Nevertheless, she has never been on a battlefield, she cannot understand as someone who has been could.

"Have you tried to tell her why you continue?"

My head shifts side to side, eyes glare at him.

*Damn Doc, you don't tell your wife all your sh' from the Stan.*

"I hint at it. Speak to her about him now and then. But I don't know that I've shared all of it."

"You say 'him'. To whom do you refer?"

"A good friend, good Christian. Awesome NCO, technically and tactically. He was our first loss in 05."

"Your demeanor changes as you speak of him. His friendship and he himself hold deep meaning for you."

"Yessir. I wasn't even on mission with him that day. But, yes, Sir. He does."

"And what impact does it have on you that you were not with him? Do you think you should have been?"

My attention is drawn outside. A bird moves his head left and right.

"With him that day," Doc whispers.

*Little Bird says no.*

"On that mission…" Doc's voice trails away.

Little Bird's perch limb shakes, a rose petal falls.

"It goes way beyond that, Doc. I told you I got moved to battalion in 05. Left my line platoon right before we MOB'd for Iraq in 05."

"I remember that. It wasn't your choice, I believe."

"No, Sir. Cried like a little girl. I left my men to be stuck in an office with my thumb up my ass. I had no choice. I fought it, but it was no use. I got moved."

"How does this apply to the loss of your friend?"

"He took my place. It happened in my truck. I have a picture of Charlotte in that driver's seat. Back here, at the armory before…"

*Do I tell him? I'll cry again. Is it time to spill it? I'll look like a cry-baby. Hell, he died. I'm still in one piece. I have no right to cry about this sh'. He died. I was just sittin' in a damn office when he did.*

Doc breaks my chaotic thoughts, "Go on Dale."

"His death saved my life. He died in my place. I'm here, he didn't come home."

"And… So what? What does that mean to you?"

"I started politicking that day to get back to my men. His men. To lead 'em. The Colonel and S3 wouldn't even consider it. That pissed me off even more."

"You wanted to take back your platoon? Knowing that he… Knowing how his first mission went?"

"Yes, Sir."

"Dale. What did that mean to you? What did it make you feel?"

"Sh', guilty as hell."

"Guilty of what?"

My leg stomps like a bull in a rodeo. I put down my journal and say, "I'm guilty of bein' here. Of comin' the fu' home. I ain't paid him back!

"Why should I quit when others have…have done so much more? Why should I get to raise my daughter when they don't?"

My arms snap tight across my chest, right foot is about to crack concrete under Doc's colorful carpet and my unblinking eyes tear. "Why am I here and they aren't? How could I disrespect his memory, his sacrifice, by letting his men, our men, go again without me? How could I turn my back on them? On him? Other friends we lost? On the men who got blown the hell up. I'm sitting here…" I wipe my eyes, "…in one piece and they…sh'. Can't quit, Doc… just can't."

"This is now who you are. It is how you define yourself?"

"I guess so, Doc. I guess so.

"We have exercises to assist us here, to help find new meaning and understanding. Would you like to try one…right here…right now. Let's try talking to this man…the man that took your place, now."

"How the hell can I do that? He ain't here."

"You can bring him here in your imagination."

I stare at my old friend in front of the roses outside. In his faded DCUs, with that pure, honest, real smile on his face. Thin white curtains on doc's tan French doors blur his freckles. "Ok."

Doc pauses to take a breath, and continues, "May I suggest a few questions for you to pose to your friend, to consider with him, your old friend. I know he is not here, but I believe you know what he would answer to the questions you pose. What would he say about what you did after he left in two thousand five?"

In a slow deliberate motion, my head turns to look at Doc, and I strain to return my gaze to my brother in arms, through French doors, between rose bushes and me. I contemplate his gentle nature, direct speech, and his blank face as he considers what to say before he utters a word. I look deep in his eyes and hear his voice. As always, he is direct, articulate, and brief.

My gaze drops to his desert boots and I wipe my tears.

I force my eyes to stare back into those deep dark eyes. "He'd thank me for helping bring his men…most of them, home. He'd appreciate that I did all I could to get 'em back."

Slow deep breathes break Doc's words. "What…do you think… he…would say… about that day?"

My old brother-in-arms' eyes drill my own. I cry. He is happy to see me. Smiles with that touch of 'what the hell are you thinking?' in the left corner of his lips. A look only he can do. Just one look at you and you rethink what you said or did.

Doc asks, "Did he do what he did for glory? To gain respect? To force you to stay in?"

I look at Doc as if he just slapped my sister.

*How could Doc accuse him of that kinda sh'? Hell no.*

Hands shake and wipe my eyes to see my buddy more clearly. But my selfish shame kicks in hard. I cannot look at him.

*I'm such a piece of sh'. He died and I'm a freakin' broke down little baby in a nice cozy office.*

I stare at the floor, Doc's ottoman leg to my two o'clock, see every detail of the dark brown chunk of wood. I force a response. "No, Sir. He did what he did because he had to. We had men on the other side alone, without cover. He took my Humvee through to be sure they were safe. He knew he shouldn't, knew not to go through that gap, but had to, and did.

His troops were over there. My troops were…were in the open…alone. He knew their VIC would bridge pressure plates his Humvee wouldn't. They could cross things he would sink in. But he had to go. Our men needed support. That's when he got hit."

"Is he disappointed it was him instead of you?"

"No, Sir. He'd never back away. Wouldn't ask me to go in his place. He'd go himself. He did."

"Does he expect you to continue in service until you…are…Until you are where he is? Till you've done what he did?"

*Sh'. That's digging deep, Doc. I can't quit. I've not done what he, and others, have. What my other friends have done. But would he expect me to? Did he plan to die? Did he want to? Would he want me to?*

My brief eye contact with Doc brings more shame in my lowly service. Intently, I refocus on the curved ottoman leg and say, "I don't think so. He didn't want to go. None of us do. He'd want me to enjoy life. To enjoy what he gave me. To make the most of my life."

"And what do you think he would say about your having deployed again?"

I peer at my brother's smile…that honest caring gleam in his eye.

*What would he say about my goin' again?*

*He cared for all of us. He honestly cared.*

*What would he say?*

*He wanted to serve our country. To serve us. He was a family man. Wouldn't want my family to go through what his has. He'd want me to raise my daughter and be there for my wife. That's the point of going, of all this sh'.*

*For our families to have a good life, to have their dream, the American dream. We are part of our family's dream. I'm a broke down piece of sh'. For some reason my worthless ass is part of Karen's dream. Charlotte's and Josh's.*

"He'd thank me for watching out for our troops," creeps from my mouth.

I look up at Doc. Through the corner of my right eye, I see my old friend step closer. "He'd pat me on the back."

I turn to my right. His left arm is around my shoulders. I see his tight-lipped smile. The old platoon daddy waits for me to make eye contact. He will not say another word until I look in his eyes.

I both watch and experience as two old Joes lock our gaze. "He'd look me in the eyes…smile…and whisper…'Y'all done good'."

Doc cuts deeper in my soul. "Has all this driven you to take risks you did not have to? Risks your troops could have, or even should have taken but you took instead. Risks you did to protect them?"

"Yessir…It's what we do, first in the door, truck forward in a patrol. Dismount before they do. You can't lead from behind."

"You have both been willing to do and have done for others what he did for you. You cannot blame yourself for the outcome being different. You have taken risks for your men just as he did. Did you have any more control over the outcome than he?"

"No, Sir. Control is a joke in the Stan."

"You took similar risks. From what you have shared with me I can see you've done what he did on several occasions. Yet here you are, not by your own power, not by avoiding risk, not even by sending troops in your place. The fact you have not been killed, the fact you have not given your life, is beyond your control, or that of any man. Why he died, and you haven't, is not within either of your power…"

Doc pauses to cross his legs the opposite direction, takes a deep breathe, and with his soft voice continues, "This fact in consideration…By your own admission that level of control is a fallacy in combat…What do you think your friend, your brother, your comrade would say to you?"

My tears flow like a two-year-old who dropped his ice cream. My brother leans toward me, grasps my shoulder with a firm grip, pulls me toward him, and looks in my eyes…deep to my core.

"He'd say, 'You've done what needed to be done. Thank you for watching out for our men. For leading them through, as I would have.' He'd thank me."

Doc allows me time to ponder. We sit, speechless, in his quiet dim lit office. I stare at my friend, his words echo in my head. Doc is here but remains silent and stationary.

"He'd thank me."

*"He'd thank me."*

"I suggest you share this with Karen. She supports you, tries to understand, and loves you. I am sure she has her own issues to deal with. You have told me you do not share things with her to protect her from dealing with your sh'. Let me point out, Dale. If she is still with you…and you with her….it would be best for you to both understand as much as you can about the other…what the other has gone through. Ultimately, she deals with your sh', she just does not know how to nor what it is. Deeper communication and efforts to understand will allow you to better support each other. To assist each other in the things you must both deal with in this, and future times of your life."

"Yes, Sir. Probably so, might help her see more of my side if I tell her more of what my side is."

"Yes. Yes. Exactly, Karen may never be able to understand the full range of emotions…how this affects your core self. But with this knowledge she can at least attempt to understand, and show compassion rather than continue to question and wonder."

"Yes, Sir. We have a marital session Monday. I should tell her then. Get it out. Get it over with."

"Good. Good. Talk it through. In a session with a counselor may be the best place to open this box if you will. We cannot change where we have been or done. History is what it is. However we can, decide what meaning we draw from it as we move forward. How we cognitively choose to allow it to affect us in the future. This may not end your post-traumatic stress symptoms. You will surely have scars for a period of time, perhaps the rest of your life. Nevertheless, these choices can assist in how you deal with those issues as they come. Has your perspective on your friend's death changed in light of today's discussion?"

"Some. I still wanna serve. But something's different. I don't know. Gotta think on this sh' a while. I'm gonna head out now, time to have a smoke."

"Ok, Dale. Great session today. Thank you for sharing this with me."

"Roger, Sir. Thank you."

*Dale's Journal*

141230JAN2011  Paktya Provence

Captain Wayne and Carl were going to see our Afghan Army Route Clearance Platoon this morning. They like to serve chai when you visit. Josh and I had chai with them today. It was my idea; Josh did not want to go. He said, "I don't need to talk to them folks."

Like always, the Afghans smiled, happy to see us get out of our silver pickup we use on base. The Afghan Lt., Platoon Sergeant and several others were standing outside the barracks, a concrete block building with a concrete floor. Their sheet metal door is open. We see shoes in the hall, beside their individual rooms. They take them off to go in. Makes no sense because there's dirt everywhere here. If they'd sweep the hall they'd have less dirt in the beds. Maybe that's why they don't sweep, only the commander has an actual bed. The rest have mats on the floor. I don't wear my shoes in bed much. Same idea I guess.

Captain Wayne and the Afghan Lieutenant talk for a minute. Captain Wayne and Carl went to their truck. The Platoon Sergeant and his little flunky said "Come, have Chai. You stay."

Captain Wayne and Carl waved them off and said, "No maybe next time, next time."

Captain Wayne looked at his watch and says he's got a meeting to go to. I asked "what meeting?" He told me to shut up.

Guess he's had chai too many times up here and don't wanna waste time when he's got work to do.

Josh and I stayed for chai. We went in the barracks, passed two doors on the left and entered the third, the Platoon Sergeants room. The commander's room/office is across the hall from us, doors closed. The commander is on leave for another week.

We don't take our boots off. Sleep palettes line three walls. Next to a ceiling-height armoire is a small table with his TV and DVD player. Josh sits next to me against the wall facing the TV.

Two Afghan privates sat against the window wall to our right. The platoon sergeant almost lies down on pillows to our left, next to the door. Another young troop came in and Plat Daddy (nickname for Afghan platoon sergeant) points to the armoire and says something in Pashtu or Dari. The young man, I call him Cook Boy, left and came back with a box of milk and made chai.

I got them to put on one of their Pakistani or Indian karate movies. Sound effects of their swings, strikes, and kicks are hilarious. When they turn their head, you hear a swoosh-slap sound.

Cook Boy made the other privates get out the glass cups and snack cakes for us. They served us first, their Platoon Sergeant, and themselves last.

The Platoon Sergeant looked back and forth between Josh and me with a confused look. He concentrated on nametags back and forth and said "your name is same?"

I told him Josh is my Son. His eyes got bigger than golf balls, stroked his beard, looked back and forth between us, then to our other new friends. Says something in Pashto, silence around the room, everyone reflects his back and forth stare at us.

He asked me if Josh was my "real son"

I told him yes.

He said "You bring son here help us? What Momma say?"

"She don't like it much," I said.

Plat Daddy tells me "You have trouble with wife I think. Why you come together?" he asked.

"To help your country have freedom and peace. So you can raise your children to be good strong men like mine."

Looking at Josh he asked, "Why you come with father?"

"I want to serve my country, and I want to help people like my dad does." Josh said

He communicates my and Josh's response in Pashto with the others. They talked about us a while. Platoon Sergeant told me I must be a proud Daddy. Course I am. Josh swelled with pride when I bragged on him.

We snack, drink chai, and chit chat about what it's like here, how many kids they have, that Josh has no wife or child, how old his sons are, how old we are and other stuff. Then my vision got blurry.

I knew another one of my fits was on. My vision closes in around the side, floaters get worse, everything straight ahead is clear but not on the sides. My right arm and hand start going numb then my lips and tongue. It's hard to communicate with these people but it gets even worse with a numb tongue and lips. I gulped my chai to head out before my memory starts to go again. Josh downed his when he saw me turn down mine in seconds. We thanked them for the chai and stood to go.

They kept saying, "Stay, stay, have more chai!"

Josh told them we had to go. I wonder if he knew something was up with me. We left the room, shaking hands all the way out the building. At the truck, I use my left hand to get my keys, unlock the door, and get in. If Josh could drive a standard transmission, I would have had him drive back.

Started the truck with left hand. Couldn't shift with right. Used left hand to drive back, right hand just laid in my lap. Got Josh to get my notebook and pen out of my shoulder pocket, turn to a blank page, and take notes for me.

"Ten-hundred hours having chai with Afghan army, vision blurs, right hand and arm goes to sleep then lips and tongue."

Told him I was having another fit. He offered to drive, but we were halfway back already. We parked at the TOC and I had him take the keys in. I headed to my room, he catches up with me, and says, "Sure you don't need to go to the TMC (Troop Medical Clinic) and get checked out."

I said, "Hell, no. And get sent to Germany again? I've had a few of these since I've been back from there. I'm Okay. Just need to get some rest and I'll be fine. Don't worry about it."

I came to my room and laid down. That familiar sharp pain in the top of my head kicked in before I got to sleep.

Slept a while, woke up starving at 1230, arm still a little numb but lips and mouth are good. Headache continues. Going to lunch now, and I better make sure Josh ain't told nobody.

*Karen's Journal November 2010*

Two weeks for Dale to be home was really hard. There was so much anger in me that we had a difficult time communicating. I was so totally not a part of what was happening in his world and he in mine.

Romantic dinners started out shaky but ended in anger and tears. We had to learn how to communicate again and about the time I expressed my emotions and we came to some like-mindedness it was time for them to go back. *Frustrating.*

Some families choose not to have an R&R together. I get it. I really do. The 05 deployment good bye was *awful?* Charlotte, four years old, crying hysterically in the airport and refused to be consoled or go to the car before saying goodbye.

How do you go through a deployment when it's not your choice? Not well is the answer for most of us. Both husband and wife have to be on board.

I never got on the boat the last deployment.

I was done.

I was beyond it.

I was past it.

It's time for Josh to go to college, Dale to make Dean at work.

It was not time for another deployment.

# 12

*Marital Counseling Number 18*

Anita greets us as we enter her office, "So, how is everyone today? Anything we need to talk about?"

Jackhammer leg engages when I sit in my chair across from Karen, journal tight in hand. "If Karen don't have nothin', I do."

Karen's right palm and outstretched arm offers me the floor. "I don't, please, go ahead."

"Doc told me to share why I'm still in, my motivation to keep serving."

Anita motions to Karen. "Are you ok with this topic, Karen?"

A double handed Pentecostal wave ends with a right hand slap to her lap, and left hand on her armrest. "Oh, I'd love to. I have asked him to tell me for years. I mean twenty years of service and to go again. What about me? What about Charlotte? I'd love to hear…"

Anita's gentle "calm down Karen" hand motion interrupts Karen's monologue. "Yes, you've both shared stories of Charlotte's struggles, stories that break my heart. Dale, what is it that motivates you? Please share your discussion with Doctor Taylor."

"We talked about our first day of missions in 05."

Karen's face goes flush. "When we lost…"

"Yeah."

Karen faces Anita, checks on me twice with sideways looks, and says, "We lost one of Dale's friends their first day of missions. He was a good friend. It was a shock to all of us back here."

"Friend, Christian. One of the best NCOs I have ever known."

Anita says, "What happened?"

I stare through the third square from the right end of Anita's rug, to my one o'clock.

141

*You opened this can, dumb ass, gotta tell the tale now.*

"First day of missions, February of 05, we took over from an active army tanker unit. His Humvee with hillbilly armor gets hit from the bottom with a one-five-five round IED. Hard hit. He was goin' through a cut in a berm to be sure his men had a gun truck with 'em on the far side. So my men wouldn't be open to... Wouldn't be alone. His VIC was different from theirs. The troops' VIC don't activate pressure plates like Humvees do. His Humvee's front left tire did. The charge was offset so the blast centered the truck."

"Sorry to interrupt, Dale. You say 'my troops'."

Karen says, "Dale was pulled from his platoon and put in battalion headquarters right before they MOB'd."

"Dale, was it your choice to move to Battalion? This friend took your place I assume."

Karen says, "Not his choice, not at all. He hated it."

"Yeah, he took my place. He led my men, crossed that berm, took that risk, to protect my men. He died in my place."

Anita says, "Such a difficult day. How did you deal with it?"

"I tried to get my platoon back. Get back to my men."

Anita looks at Karen, "Did you know about this?"

Karen's stare in my eyes shifts from love and concern to a glossed over distraction.

*She don't see me. What is she looking at?*

Karen grunts a soft, "Uh. No"

"Some things you don't tell your wife. I couldn't sit in that damn office all year. Not when my friend sacrificed himself for our men, for my men, for our mission, for me!"

Karen gazes through me. I focus on Anita, and the concern in her eyes.

Anita opens her mouth, closes it, opens again, and says, "Were you able to get back to your men?"

"No. The BC wouldn't listen, told me, 'We need you in the TOC.' Our S3, Colonel Adams, agreed with him. Adams said, 'We need you in here. I'm sorry.'"

Karen says, "I never knew you tried to...why would you do that? You knew how hard a year it was gonna be? With what just happened? All us wives fell apart. Reality hit us in the face. Until then we didn't have to face it. Then we couldn't avoid it anymore."

"You knew how I felt when they pulled me. What that move did to me. How could I sit in that office when they had lost him? I wanted to see his men, our men, through that year."

"I knew his dying hurt you. Your face changes whenever his name comes up. That's what keeps you in?"

"I can't turn my back on my men, on his memory. Can't disrespect his sacrifice and quit."

*Karen sees me now, sees my eyes. Her eyes are still blank. Will she cry? Is this where she says, "you didn't have to go again?" Is her concern for me, is she processing this sh'. Say something woman. I can't read a blank face.*

Anita's gentle voice, full of love and care, breaks our silence. "Dale. Do you have to continue until you do what he did? Must you go on till your family loses you?"

"Doc and I did that 'what would he say if he were here' deal Friday. I look at it a little different now. I have done what he did, the outcome is different, for some reason. I have taken risks for my men, taken 'em with my men. Only God knows why he's gone and I'm here."

"So have you done your part? Are you ready to retire?"

Karen says, "He has no choice now. He's in a medical review. The Army will decide whether he's fit for service or not."

Anita turns to me. "And if you are fit for service, will you keep going?"

"I don't know. My men are still in, but I have done my part. Captain Wayne says it's time for us to let a new generation take over, we've done enough. But now I'd be sending my son. If I quit, he'll go…without me."

Karen says, "Welcome to my world."

"Yeah, I don't know how I'll do on this side-o-the pond."

Anita interjects, "Your son makes his own decisions. He chose to serve, same way you did. You can't protect him forever. He's a grown…"

Karen butts in, "That opens a whole other discussion. Let's leave Josh for another day."

Anita responds, "Fair enough. Karen what are your thoughts on Dale's reason for staying in?"

"I'm gonna have to pray about it. I'm not sure what to think. Glad he told me. It explains his determination to stay in, explains all kinds of stuff. But I'm not sure where it leaves me."

"I love you, Karen. I always have."

"Now that the Army's done with you, now you wanna be here. Since the Army is done with you, it's time to be here for me and Charlotte."

"No, that's not it. And we aren't sure they'll get rid of me. Not yet."

"I just wish you would choose me over the Army, just once."

Mouth open, eyes frozen on her, I sit in dumbfounded silence.

*She's always been there. Even if she didn't agree, like it, or understand, she supported me. What can I say to that sh'? Pick her over the Army 'just once.' All the schools, road marches, jumps, extra drills, missed birthdays and holidays. Have I never picked her over the Army, not even once?*

Anita breaks our silence again. "I think we've gotten a lot out on the table for discussion. Karen you now know why Dale served so long and Dale's in deep thought over your feelings and comments. You two should discuss this privately. Pray together about it. Keep up this open communication. That's a good place to call it a day."

I reach for my map case, stow my journal, and stand up. "Good talk, plenty to think on for next time."

Anita glares back at me as she opens her office door. "Y'all can talk between sessions Dale. You know that right?"

"Oh, I know. We do. Have a good day."

I follow Karen through the door, check the hall left, right, and turn right toward the lobby.

"Bye, Dale. Karen they'll schedule y'all out front."

"Bye, Anita."

Outside I smoke, wait, and consider today's session as Karen schedules next week's.

I open the office building door for her. "Wanna get some lunch, Baby?"

"Mexican?"

"Roger, ole reliable?"

"Okay, you wanna ride together or meet me there?"

I walk Karen to her car, open her door, and hold it as she gets in. "I'll meet you there. That way we don't have to come back and get a car."

"Sounds good. Love you."

I kiss her left cheek. "Love you, too."

In our separate vehicles, we travel to lunch. I park in my end space, next to the road at our favorite restaurant Tres Tamales and spot Josh's truck.

*He always tracks us down at lunch, probably texted with Karen on our way here.*

I exit my vehicle and join Josh on Los Amigos' front porch.

"Hey Josh, what's up?"

We watch Karen pull in and park to our three-o-clock.

"Had class this morning, ain't got nothin' this afternoon."

"How's that goin', back in school?"

"Horrible. They freak out over BS. I do not wanna be there. Have to listen to their cry-baby BS."

Karen approaches, I step past Josh to open Los Amigos' right door. "People here don't know what you know, ain't been where we been, hard for us to relate to 'em."

"Yeah it does, real hard."

I hold the door for Karen and Josh to enter, and follow them in. Spice smells tempt us, as always, to order more than we can eat.

Karen requests a corner booth, to put my back to a wall. Josh sits beside me. We jockey for the best field of view. Karen chuckles at us and sits with her back to the room.

We browse our menus for no reason. We will order our usual.

Josh says, "What're y'all doin' in town?"

I say, "Just met with Anita."

"How's that goin' for you, Dad?"

I scan from bottom to top of my menu and across to the left page. I do not make eye contact. "Made it through another session without cryin' or snottin', guess it's goin' good."

"I hear ya."

"It went good. Your dad finally told me why he keeps in."

Josh says, "Cause of your friend in 05?"

*Ah sh', I told Josh before Karen.*

I say, "Yup. So what are y'all gonna…"

Karen stares at me and blocks my subject change. "You already told Josh and just told me this morning?"

I avoid eye contact. "I…uh…Yes?"

Her angry stare softens, and she quips, "Ok, Dale, enough serious talk for today. Let's eat. I'm ready to laugh about something."

She looks back to her menu; my eyes never left mine.

"Me too, Baby."

"Dad. You never told Mom about…"

I smile and elbow him. "Did Josh and I tell you we saw Wright in Afghanistan?"

Karen smiles and looks up from her menu. "Wright, from Bragg?"

"You remember him, Mom?"

"Yeah your Dad wouldn't let him hold you at WOMACK when you were born. Not till I made him."

"For real, Dad?"

"She don't know all the stuff he dropped at work. We just got you. I didn't want you broke your first day in the world."

Karen says, "Bertrand and Wright came to see us the morning after you were born. They brought us like thirty bucks from your Dad's platoon."

"Good thing they did. Day we brought you home our water got cut off. The bill was just twenty-five dollars but we didn't have it. Not till we got that thirty bucks."

"Y'all were freagin' broke when I was a baby."

"I was a Private First Class. Made like eight-hundred a month with jump pay."

Karen laughs. "We lived in a tiny trailer for two hundred a month. Right before your Dad left for Desert Shield/Desert Storm there was a shooting over a drug deal next door."

Our waiter arrives, recognizes us, and confirms our standard drink orders. We agree, order our regular meals, and continue to devour chips.

Josh drips salsa on our table, takes in an oversized chip, wipes the table, and talks with his mouth full. "Jumping out of planes at Bragg, goin' to combat, and you couldn't afford water. That sucks Dad."

Karen dips a chip in molten cheese. "Remember, Dale. We didn't pay it that day. We brought Josh home on Friday. In my post-partum depression, I cried on the phone with the water company and got our water turned back on."

I nod and swallow a chip. "That's right. We didn't pay till Monday."

"Yup." Karen looks at Josh. "The next day, Saturday morning I woke up and y'all were gone. You slept with us until your Dad left for Iraq. I walk in the living room and there y'all are, on the couch watching cartoons."

My non-chip thumb points at Josh. "I had to start him right."

"So you saw Wright in Afghanistan?"

I wave for more chips. "We were at Bagram waiting for a flight home on leave. Bored out of our minds, our third day there we got called to the flight manifest room. We were all praying we'd get on a manifest."

I sip some sweet tea, and look at Josh. "Musta been a hundred troops in there. We sat, stood or leaned as patient as we could. The admin group up front talked about crap we heard a hundred times. Then this E-7 type speaks up."

Josh holds up both hands in frustration. "They told us the same sh' over and over, and expect us to listen, like we never heard it before."

Karen smiles at Josh and leans her head slight right. "You signed up for it, Josh."

"I know, Mom."

I say, "This E-7 says, 'everyone pass your military ID to the center aisles. We need to check 'em against the dog-gone manifest. As we confirm you're on it we'll call your name to come get your ID.'"

"His voice sounded familiar. I leaned right, toward Josh, to see around this huge head in front of me. A tall black E-7 stands by the podium, left hand on it, right thumb tucked behind his belt, in the front, you know, above his right pocket. Letting go of the podium he put his left hand same as his right. Then I knew."

Karen says, "He stood like that in civilian clothes too, kinda creepy."

"How do y'all remember that? It was back in like 1990."

Forearms on the table, Karen's palms face up. "Josh you know how to recognize people in uniform. How they stand, walk or wave their arms. Y'all all look the same in a crowd."

"I gotcha, my platoon Sar'nt always looks ready to fight."

"Anyway," I break in, "I elbow Josh and said, 'Get outta here.'"

Josh says, "I thought he spotted the list and we weren't on it. I was pissed. I said, 'what?'"

"I pointed at Wright and told Josh, 'That E-7. I know him.'"

Josh leans into the table, and shines his sarcastic grin at Karen. "I assumed he was in the guard. I asked Dad if he was Mississippi Guard."

"I said, 'Nah, I don't know what he's in now. Ain't seen him since 95. You don't recognize him?' Josh tried to get a better look, shrugged and shook his head no."

"'That's Wright.' I said, 'We went to Desert Shield/Desert Storm together. He was weapons maintenance, under Sar'nt. Fella and…"

Josh says, "I called BS right there. I knew he was makin' it up. Dad knew someone everywhere we went in Mississippi. But in Bagram. Come on. I knew he was lying."

"I had to talk Josh into it, I said, 'I'm telling you. That is Wright. He came to see you the morning after you were born at Bragg. We gotta talk to him. He's gonna flip.' I nudged Josh's shoulder to get up and come with me."

Karen says, "Did you get to talk to him?"

Josh says, "We were all supposed to stay out of the way, give 'em time to do their job. But no, not Dad. Wright makes his way through the aisle collecting IDs and Dad steps all over people, to say hello. He liked to a drug me with him."

"Dang right, I reach out to shake his hand. In classic Wright form, he looks up from the ID's with his 'what the hell do you want' look and snaps his right foot back. I said, 'Sar'nt Wright, how you been?'"

"Did he recognize you?"

"Nope, he said, 'Doin' ok' and looked back at the IDs. Probably figured I was trying to use my rank to get on a manifest. So I said, 'you don't remember me?'"

"That's when he looked at my face, name tape, face again and says, 'Professor? Ah sh', what the hell are you doing here?' We do a manly one-arm hug handshake thing.

I told him about our joinin' the guard when we got out in ninety-five. Then I said, 'guess who's with me.' And motioned for Josh to come over. Josh steps up and I said, 'Remember that baby born at Womack?'"

"Wright steps back, and looks at Josh, his name tape, my name tape. He looked back and forth between us, like three times. Made a "rock the Baby" motion with his arms and said, 'This ain't…ah, hell no. What mission you guys doing?'"

Josh grabs my arm and takes over my story. "I said, 'Hello Sar'nt. We're combat engineers. Doin' route clearance south of here in Paktya, on the Pakistan border.'

"Wright shook my hand and said, 'Man it's good to see you. I knew your Dad back at Bragg. We went to Iraq together, first time. You're supposed to be like this tall and he motioned to his knee cap."

I try to re-enter my own story but Josh ignores my open mouth.

"You know me. Mom. I had to ask what he meant when he called Dad professor. He told me, 'Your Daddy could make somethin' out-a-nothin'. He was our MacGyver.'"

An elbow to Josh's ribs allows me to finish our tale. "Wright winked at me and said, 'I gotta get back to work. Don't worry, you two are on the manifest.' I thanked him and we sat down."

Karen says, "So what's he doing now?"

"Not sure. I talked to him after the manifest crap was over. He got out right after we did. Said he was out a couple years. Things weren't workin' out so he got back in. I think he retires soon."

"Dale you should catch up with Bertrand."

"I found him on Facebook. He's Louisiana Guard now."

"New Orleans?"

I shrug my shoulder and tip my head left. "Think so."

Karen looks at Josh. "Josh you know about the Explorer catching on fire coming back from Shelby right?"

Josh freezes with a chip midway to his mouth and stares at Karen. "Wait, on fire? What happened?"

I wave my chip hand. "Not a big deal Josh, just a little fire."

"Your Dad put it out with his soft cap."

"My favorite cap too."

"Come on, Mom, you gotta tell me this one."

"Your Dad was still at Shelby, you already demobed and came home. They wouldn't let him have a car while on active duty…"

"About right, nobody wants Dad to drive."

I shrug as Karen restarts. "A few nights after y'all came back, I was following Dale home from Shelby, bringing the explorer back. I saw a fire under it on the interstate. His car was on fire!"

Josh snaps up his best road-guard-halt hand. "Wait, define 'on fire.'"

My right hand waves as if to shew a fly off our chips. "The transmission had a leak. Some of the fluid got on the muffler, the tail pipe, or somethin'. Once it got hot enough, it flashed and there you go. Not a big a fire."

Karen looks at me and says, "Big enough I see it from my car." She faces Josh and presses on with her drama, "I call and tell your Dad, 'Your car is on fire.' Your Dad, Mr. Master's Degree, Mr. Intellectual said, 'I wondered what that orange glow under my car was!' Like it's no big deal, I'm just gonna die."

"I tell him to get out immediately. He says, 'Maybe if I stay in the car and keep going the flames will go out or at least not get to the gas tank.' I am freaking out at this point. Your Dad's all nonchalant like, 'If I stop, I may not be able to get out before it blows up.'"

Her head shakes side-to-side, palms up again. "All I wanted was for him to get out of the car. Finally he pulls over, jumps out, crawls under the car where the flames are, and put the fire out with his soft cap!"

"Once he puts it out, we're standing on the side of the interstate arguing. He's worried about his favorite cap and all they had been through together. Seriously? I said—using a word you know I never use—'Truck the bam cap.'"

"Then we start laughing. Best stress relief we'd had so far. God brought him home from another deployment and a few days later he almost dies in an explosion, on the interstate, in Mississippi?"

Josh laughs, "What'd y'all do about the car?"

Karen says, "Your Dad wanted to get back in and drive home."

My palm faces up before I reach for a chip. "Fire was out. We were only thirty miles out."

"Did you?" Josh asks.

"I made him get in my car and called a tow truck the next day. I was not having him die in a burning car. Not after waiting all that time for y'all to come home."

Our food arrives and like most American families, our conversation ends.

# 13

*Marital Counseling Number 22*

Karen sits on her couch, at my twelve-o'clock, I in my corner chair. Anita's "artwork" above Karen is still crooked. Books and stuffed animals cover her nude doll, only a foot visible today. Rain on pine straw covered grass in view through open curtains.

Anita seats herself to my three-o'clock, crosses her legs, and then she smiles. "So, how is everyone today? Anything we need to talk about?"

Karen says, "I don't think Dale understands what it is like back here without him."

"Dale, is that a fair statement?"

I note the date-time-group top right corner and close my journal.

*No notes today just listen and shut up.*

"I know they had a lot to deal with. She's basically a single Mom while I'm gone."

Anita says, "How does that statement make you feel Karen. Does that capture what you hope Dale understands?"

*Say more dumb ass. Do not let her say you're dismissive.*

Right hand palm up, left grasps the journal in my lap. "I know that's not all of it. Everyone has a lot to deal with. I watched my troop's trucks get blown up. I have to deal with that. She had issues back here."

Karen says, "I know combat had to be hard, again. And different from the other times. I can't understand what you felt to see that. But I don't think you have tried to understand everything I've gone through."

"I try. I do. I love you, Baby. The tonsils, Jackson, and being

150

followed home. All those piss me off. I wasn't here to protect you, to keep you safe. Or Charlotte."

"I had to deal with those things alone, without my best friend, protector, my security blanket was gone."

Anita says, "Can you tell me about the tonsils? Charlotte's I assume."

*Karen's Journal*

July 2010 AM tonsils

Charlotte had her tonsils removed in July 2010. We debated over waiting till Dale got back but decided to go ahead. She complained frequently of throat pain, snored when she slept and kept an infection most of the time.

It also affected her eating so she was not gaining weight. Thanks to technology, Dale was able to skype with us during most of the day. I was extra careful with her recovery—and some 19 days after surgery she was still taking it easy, eating certain foods and not running around playing.

The week of Vacation Bible School (VBS) is the week she had trouble. I had been at work and my mother-in-law called me and said Charlotte was feeling a bleeding trickle in her throat. Unable to check for myself—she looked and said it looked fine to her.

I called the nurse and she said to put an ice pack on her throat and to keep a check on it. Things were going well but when I got home to get her ready for VBS she was not looking well. So I took the VBS book to church and had the other teacher teach that night. I was going to stay home with her and get her well. She did not feel any more blood trickle and there had been no problems but I knew she needed rest.

When I returned home not ten minutes later – she'd thrown up a huge amount of blood in my bathroom sink and was now cool to the touch and passed out as I carried her to car.

Her skin was gray-looking, and all I could think of was the name of Jesus. I said his name over and over and over with my finger under her nose to make sure she was still breathing. I called the hospital on the way to let them know we were coming and what to expect.

They were waiting for her. I was afraid like I had never experienced before. I found out later her body was responding in a good way to the loss of blood. Slowing down the heart rate to keep her safe, etc.

At the time you think—she's dying. It is your greatest fear as a parent and having Dale gone I was afraid to tell him what had happened. I was responsible for her. He was counting on me to care for her.

I of course told him the first chance I had when he called. He had a right to know. Once I got the courage to tell him, he immediately reassured me he was not upset.

The enemy, satan, attacks you when you are isolated and alone. I believed Dale would be angry with me. He had been gone by now for three months and I felt removed from him.

It is difficult to describe but a person you have known over 20 years can suddenly feel like a stranger when given certain circumstances. The enemy uses these times to hijack you emotionally.

When a couple needs that time together to ward off the attack of the enemy, the best it gets at those times is a phone call. Dale was good at reassuring by phone—think he had learned how and of course had prayed for God to give him the words.

It was a balm to my ache and pain that he did not blame me and I was so grateful she was ok. The pressure to care for your child alone is great and when faced with this type of situation you feel so helpless and so responsible.

They ended up cauterizing her throat. She had a slow bleed all afternoon that she thought was saliva but was actually blood. The doctor came and calmed the staff down. They were ready for emergency surgery but it was not necessary.

Anita, a mother of three, removes her right hand from her mouth and clasps both hands in her lap. "Wow. I can't even imagine my daughter turning pale, passing out, and throwing up blood, mercy."

My eyes drill a red carpet square to my one-o'clock, left of Karen's right foot. "It breaks my heart. Where was I when my Darlin' passed out? Not even there."

Anita points to me and looks at Karen. "Karen, do you hear Dale's emotion? I hear true compassion for you and what you've gone through."

Karen wipes her nose and clears tears from each cheek. "Yeah. I hear it. But that's just one occasion. Morning after morning getting Charlotte to school, going to work, coming home, fixing dinner, going to bed. It all starts over the next day, with no help, no one by my side. I am still married. He should be there for me. I'm there for him."

*There for me? No one was there for me when I was leading a group of men in an ambush. No one understands what I felt leaving my men and going to Germany on the medevac bird. Try spending twenty-eight hours in a truck while dealing with...Screw it. Don't say any of that sh' Dale. Support Karen, today is about her, save your crap for Doc tomorrow.*

My best concerned look on my face I stare in Karen's hazel, wet eyes. "I'm sorry I wasn't there for you. I really am. I am here now. I do all I can now."

"I know you are. I appreciate it. So many times, I wanted you to be here. I wanted you to hold me...you weren't here."

*Three deployments and she is still here. At least we're in marriage counseling instead of divorce court.*

Anita says, "Dale your combat experiences were hard and horrific. Most people here have not and will never have anything similar. Your perspective on what is difficult is different from mine, from Karen's. Do you think sometimes you discount Karen's tough experiences because you compare them to your own?"

*Who don't?*

"Probly do, shouldn't, she's not me."

"Dale, have you told Karen these experiences?"

"We go to war so our wives and children won't have to. I don't tell her much. Why should she deal with the sh' in my head?

Karen says, "I want to be here for you Dale. If you need to talk about something from over there I want you to talk to me."

"I know you do, Karen. I know you do."

Anita curls her lips under in a skeptical frown. "You're not going to are you, Dale?"

"Most of the time, no, I save it for when I'm around my men or seein' my shrink. I do need to be careful comparing 'hard times' here to the Stan. I'll never grasp how she felt going through all that if I do."

"Karen, Dale is going to try to show compassion and not compare your experiences to his. What do you think?"

"I hadn't thought of it that way before. My complaints of taking Charlotte to school every day when he didn't know if he would live through that same day. I need to think about that."

I peer into Karen's eyes, "What happened to you in Jackson, with her tonsils, by any measure they are hard things. It breaks my heart to know you had to deal with so much, alone"

"Thank you for saying that. Thank you, Dale."

Anita says, "What's this about Jackson?"

I stare at Anita, lean back in my chair, and prop my head on my right hand.

*Look to Karen on this one, lady. I ain't sayin' sh'.*

Karen looks at me. I look at her. She tells her story…

\*\*\*

I went to Jackson for my continuing education hours required to work as a Chiropractic assistant. We usually go in April, but in 2010, we went in May. By the time I got Charlotte to school this morning and drove to Jackson, I'm late. Everyone here for the training has gone in the conference room of the hotel.

I see a man entering the building from the rear entrance and I say good morning and walk on to the restroom.

I enter the stall and latch the door. I hear someone coming in behind me but pay no attention to it.

From outside the stall I hear a man describe what he wants to do to me. Such vulgar speech I haven't heard even in the movies. That man from the hall must have followed me in here.

He was sweating and seemed somewhat hyper aware when I said hello to him in the lobby earlier. That's the only way I can describe his behavior. Eyes wide open like on some type of drug.

I stand here in the stall shocked and feeling a fear I have never experienced. Once I realized he wasn't leaving I dialed 911 on my cell phone.

"I need help. I am in the Hilton lobby women's room and a man is in here. He said he is going to do something to me."

They put me in touch with the front desk while waiting for the police. I hung up and called my mother and had her stay on the phone with me until the concierge sent someone to get me.

I keep calling the name of Jesus through what seemed eternity of fearful seconds. God saw to it for the man to walk out of the restroom without another word or action toward me. He had every intention to do what he said he wanted to do. I don't know if I said Jesus' name out loud or not but I know He heard my call and answered by protecting me.

Once downstairs, I called my boss and went to pieces. Shock hit and it took a while to process what happened. The police and management reviewed hallway video and saw him follow me into the restroom.

Once again, an example of what not to share with Dale. I told him but it was a couple of months later, after prayer. He was early into his deployment and I did not want him to stew on this and have it affect him negatively.

He was a Platoon Sergeant and lives depended on him. I was torn because he is my husband and needs to know these things to offer me support, and protection but he needs to be free from distraction about home to protect his men as well by making extremely important decisions every mission, every day.

I really believe the military—especially a branch like the Army - is the third person in a marriage. The soldier is married to the Army too. There is no separation like a civilian job. These guys can't leave the job at 5pm each day and the request for the spouse to understand at times is overwhelming.

You feel like you are the second choice each time. There really is no other way to describe it. Your solider would say you are not second choice, but the feeling remains.

Feelings are a military spouse's worst enemy. We are called to live out what we know and not rely on what we feel. This is easier said than done.

All through the last deployment I struggled with why he would not retire. He saw the toll on us and did it anyway. It was not until he was home and after almost 18 months of counseling that he was finally able to verbalize why he could not retire.

He lost a friend in the 2005 deployment to Iraq to an IED. If his friend gave his life then Dale believed the least he could do was serve until he could no longer serve—either to death or the Army pushing him out.

He was unable to voluntarily walk away when someone he knew gave all. This made perfect sense but the answer did not come until almost two years after the last deployment.

Until that time I had asked repeatedly why he would not retire. He gave me the answer, "I'm praying about it." How are you gonna argue after someone gives that answer?

After time though, it became apparent that the answer was 'I don't want to consider retirement right now.' His actions said this not his words. And this became further reinforcement to my belief when he chose the Army over me. Over our whole family.

Back to the restroom, it was months before I could go to a public restroom without the thought of what had happened in Jackson. When I told Dale finally, he was concerned of course but with it happening a few months earlier, he did not seem as alarmed as I'd feared.

But then again deployed couples do that. Downplay our emotions for the sake of the other person. Once again the military dictates emotional role-playing in your marriage. It is unrelenting so you relent for the sake of the relationship. What's got to give? You do. This is the frustration, insanity of marriage to a soldier.

*\*\*\**

Anita says, "That is so horrific, wow. Do y'all think you each have things you have not told the other? Dale only recently shared about his friend."

Karen says, "In here was the first time he'd told me all of it. I knew about him. I never knew till he opened up in here how deeply it affected him. Drove him to continue—"

Anita raises her hand to Karen. "Horrible things, scary events and most of the emotions attached to them are not out in the open are they? Whatever we call it, we agree you both have things inside the other is unaware of."

I nod.

Karen says, "Yes. We do."

Anita drags on, "We need to keep this in mind, as you approach each other to open up these secrets. If you have not shared an event before, the other person may know nothing about it. I charge both of you to share something, one thing. One thing you know you have not yet shared. This communication will help you understand each other. One ground rule. Y'all gotta listen now. Dale, as Karen shares with you, listen and try to understand. Do not discount it as not that bad, or compare it to combat, or even plan how you're gonna respond. Try to see it from Karen's perspective. Okay?"

Anita watches me nod and looks to Karen. "Karen, when Dale shares with you, I need you to do your best to understand. Not think about his choice to go, or how if he had stayed home it wouldn't have happened. Simply listen to what he is telling you and try to understand."

Karen nods.

"Well y'all have assignments, time's up. Go forth and communicate."

I say, "Ok then," stand and motion for Karen to go first.

Karen says, "Bye, Anita. Thank you," and stands to leave.

*Dale's Journal*

021000SEP2011   At home

Yesterday I had suicidal thoughts, again. Use my field knife behind my collar bone? Drown in the tub or lake? Drive off the hill on TM Smith road? I've had them before but this time I thought "you don't know you won't." I didn't trust myself not to. I got dressed and went to prayer at church. Brother John and others anointment me with oil and prayed for me. I had lunch with Dad, went to see my marital counselor after getting my PT uniform from the house.

Wrong day.

Appointment was Friday.

Went to the chiropractor.

Called the house.

No answer so I went to Bone's house.

Picked up Charlotte, could not trust myself to be alone.

Last night Karen and I talked about it, and called our counselor.

Anita said my actions were right, and I showed I didn't want to hurt myself. Couldn't sleep.

Went to sleep after 0300.

Got out of bed a little after 0900, drank milk watched National Treasure II ate ½ a box of Nutter Butter cookies and had a smoke then went to sleep.

I read the Jehovah Rah extended definition of "Friend" or "my Lord and friend" this morning.

I've been detached, outside myself, all day.

Who am I that He would be my friend?

How can I be a friend with God when I have no true friends on earth?

I alienate myself and keep emotions bottled up.

I kept starting to cry with Karen last night but stopped myself. She kept trying to get me to let it out. So confused, so scared, will I hurt myself, I've been at this for five weeks and I am still a mess.

I'm nervous and scared for our future.

Do I go back to work on the eighth week?

What do I do?

Who am I?

Why am I such a damn mess?

Driving north just past Paul's Grocery on the highway I saw a body on the side of the road. No one cared, we all just drove past it.

When I drive, I'm still uptight and nervous.

South of First Baptist I hit an ambush. Mortars, RPGs, small arms fire from a tennis court, antebellum home, and pine tree wood line. Will I ever learn to stop my mind's made up sh'? End my imaginary blend of two realities, there and here.

How do I find myself without finding God?

Adonai - Father

My image of father growing up was a workaholic that cared more for others than for me. I show love to my children. Both of them.

I gave myself to work and church to the point it interrupted my love for them.

I hold myself to a higher standard than I do my troops.

What is truth?

What is love?

Who is God?

Who am I?

Who does God say I am?

I am not defined by what I've done.

Can we define God that way?

I am not the generic label of husband, or father, or First Sergeant.

Can I understand God through the labels we put on Him?

He is omnipotent and omnipresent.

He can be trusted and confided in.

He forgives better than I forgive myself. He provides. He shepherds.

Can I perceive Him as the omnipresent Platoon Sergeant?

As Plat Daddy, I care for my troops. I expect standards are met in behavior, dress, respect, and performance. All the while I guide, teach and lead them.

On mission and at home I make sure they have rest, refit time, maintenance time, food, water, ammo and security.

I strove to bring them home alive.

God strives for all these things for me.

I strive to build an innate motivation in my troops to want to do what must be done.

God through the Holy Spirit strives to do this in me.

He is the great Provider, Shepherd, Teacher and Leader.

He makes me to walk by still waters and arms me with the truth.

He has issued me a battle uniform to protect me in the spiritual battles.

He expects certain standards be met.

He shows me those standards and holds me accountable to them.

He tells me when I fall short and corrects me.

He expects respect, praise, and obedience. Yet he loves me and, like I did my troops, He listens to my problems and provides assets to help that I would not have on my own.

Like Socrates, he doesn't give me all the answers verbally but guides my thinking to good decisions. Allows and guides my growth in Him. He is the ultimate Plat Daddy.

The greatest friend. The all-knowing technically and tactically proficient

Plat Daddy leading me through the spiritual warfare of this world.

But he goes beyond what I can do for my troops.

Just as I did in combat trying to shape the battlefield and situations for a desired outcome, He controls the entire world to lead me to His desired outcome.

Without submission of my troops, I could do nothing. Without their volunteering and swearing in followed by their dedication to duty, honor, and courage, I could not lead and guide them to victory.

God can accomplish His will without me. I can't without others, I need loyal troops.

I must submit to God for Him to lead me. I must know Him. I must endeavor to become like Christ in order to grow in my life and realize the plan He has for me.

He gives me free will but desires to have me in his platoon. He will not force me to join, but unless I volunteer, I will not have his influence in my life. Unless I complete Basic Training in Him, I cannot be a soldier in His army.

Can I be in His army simply by accepting Him?

I have done that. I cannot be what He wants me to be without my own dedication to service, honor, courage, and the indwelling of the Holy Spirit.

Through that, He and I develop my minute-by-minute, hour-by-hour walk in the Spirit.

In touch with Him, to grow ever closer in love, respect, and submission to Him.

How did I develop into a US Soldier?

In basic I got broke down and built back up in the "who" the Army needed me to be. To walk, talk, dress, and behave as a soldier.

Have I truly allowed myself to be broken down in Christ, to re-socialize, to die to self, and become who I should be in Him?

Next in becoming a soldier, I must continue to adhere to the standard. Measure all behavior against what is right, honorable, and best for the Army.

With Christ, I have not always done this.

To succeed in combat, to continue in the Army, I must strive to Be, Know and Do what good leaders are. What my example is. I must learn battle drills and understand how to employ them. I must be technically and tactically proficient with all weapons, vehicles, and tools provided me.

Same with a soldier for God. We must be tactically proficient with our battle armor of God in shoot, move, and communicate to win the spiritual war in our lives. Without the Holy Spirit in us as our motivation, we will fail. Without our weapons of spiritual warfare, we cannot defend against the evil one and the powers of this dark world.

# 14

Doc exits to get a bottle of water. I get a new black journal from my map case, open the cover and label it "Journal 7, 2011," prepare a page for today's session and wait for Doc's return.

> *This sh' is getting so old, notes with Doc, Anita, outside, in waiting rooms, at home, church, alone. What good are these damn journals, notes, thoughts, and confusion? Still can't work, get pissed off easy, can't sleep. Is all this sh' making a difference?*

Doc returns, sits, and sips his water. "How are you today, Dale?"

"I'm alright."

"What's on your mind?"

"Karen and I had a good marital counseling session yesterday. Course I kept my opinions to myself, wasn't easy."

"What was discussed?"

"My wife wants me to understand how hard her life was, back here. I know she ain't been over. I like it that way. I don't want her to deal with this sh'."

"You've been reminded of your humanity, faced death, you have new perspectives. Do you find yourself measuring things here against things over there?"

> *Don't start that sh' Doc. Anita hit that yesterday.*

"Kinda hard to get upset about sh' back here. I mean, no one's shootin' at me right?"

"True."

"For real, Doc, what back here is so bad you have to cuss people out or flip 'em off?"

Doc looks up, clicks his damn pen again. "You don't flip people off?"

161

"Ok, bad example. I flipped someone off on my way here."

"You did?"

"Yup, then realized what was up and felt stupid."

"What was up?"

"I stop at a red light, some old blonde lady stops next to me and stares, right at me. Just stares and smiles. I'm sick of it. Why does everyone stare at me? Thought maybe I'm being paranoid again. So I kept count of people gawkin' at me, she was number four today. So I flip her off."

"What made you feel stupid?"

"You know my boxer goes like everywhere with me, right. Lucille always hangs her head out the window behind me. I get to watch her lips catch air in my rear view mirror."

"You've mentioned your dog. Wait…"

"Yessir. She smiles at my dog and I flip her off for it."

Doc laughs. "She'll try not to stare now won't she?"

"Probly."

"Tell me about your discussion with Karen."

As Doc taught me, I take a deep cleansing breath, close my journal, and lean back.

*Here we go, another long story.*

"While I was gone she went through a lot, probably stuff she ain't told me. Some of it hard stuff, hard for anyone. Other crap she complains about seems…small, why even talk about it. Just take out the damn trash, ya know, done deal, trash is gone."

"Do you think she considers her 'stuff' as having been as hard as yours?"

"No. That's not it."

"How much of over there do you share with her?"

"Not much. I don't like it in my head, why put it in hers?"

"So she can't compare her hardships to yours."

"No, Sir. I guess she can't."

"Does she tell you her tough times in detail?"

"More than I do, not all of it. She says she did better this time, just wants me to understand, and understand, and understand. Crap, I understand woman. Understand enough anyway."

"She says she got through it better, I wonder what is behind that statement."

"She prayed a lot. Still prays a lot. When she's frustrated or mad that I left, she prays. God helped her with patience. Not completely of course, He helped her with a lot of stuff."

"Did you know she was having a hard time?"

"Yes, Sir. Not details, she wouldn't bother me with full details while I was over. She knew I had to stay focused. Every time I'd say I missed her she'd be sarcastic about my choice to go when I didn't have to."

"This refers to her feelings of betrayal and abandonment?"

"Yes, Sir. I know she had hard sh' to deal with. I know my choice to go caused it. What am I supposed to do now? I'm back, can't work, or be around her or anyone much, but I am back."

"What do you say to her about her experiences?"

"I try to understand, to show I care. Not as much as she does for me, but I do…try."

"How do you feel about her struggles?"

"Some of it pisses me off. Mad about what happened and at myself for not being here. She don't consider it may have been a little hard for me, too."

"Does she belittle what you dealt with?"

"No Sir. She knows it was tough."

"Maybe she needs to see more of that from you. More expressions of love and compassion for her struggles, perhaps she has yet to process some of it."

"Roger, she always needs to talk things out."

"Women tend to talk more than we do."

"Roger, I should work on that. I'll just keep listening, I guess."

"You mentioned things were hard for you. What comes to mind as you say that?"

"She constantly says she had to sleep alone, wake up alone, missed me, no one to snuggle with and all. Hello! I went to bed alone, too! Woke up somewhere in the world without her every time she woke up, here, without me."

"You don't think she considers that?"

"I don't think she gets beyond her pain to consider it. Not yet."

"Your compassion for her struggles, however small they may seem to you, will help her process and move on. Then she will have a greater capacity to consider such emotions in you."

"I need to do more of that. She's a good woman. She's been through a lot."

"It won't be easy. You injury needs time to heal. It is important you not allow other's expectations, even those you love, disrupt your healing. However, your wife is important to you. She has been supportive through your military service and since your return. If you do not work with her on her issues, a detrimental effect on your relationship and therefore on you, is inevitable. While you care for her, I need you to protect yourself from excessive anxiety. Are you able to express to her when you are anxious and need a break?"

"I don't always, sometimes I do."

"How does your wife take it when you do?"

"Better and better. At first, it upset her. Like she said or did something to push me away. She understands better now, still frustrates her, but she goes along with it because she understands."

"What does she understand?"

"That for me to be worth a sh' for her I need time for me. I have to get away from everyone, even her, for 'me time' to be worth a damn to anyone. Biggest part is she starts to understand it is not that she's a nag, clingy, or done something. It's just who I am now. I gotta have 'me' time."

"Please be sure to take your Dale time, before you feel the need. Try to be proactive and take time before your anxiety grows. It is better for you to take breaks from people or conversations than push through when anxiety begins to grow. There haven't been any physical altercations have there?"

"No, Sir. Never have. Almost did once with Josh after my second deployment, well kind-a-did. Nobody got hurt. I realized what I was doing and stopped."

"Good, so nothing since your last deployment."

"No, Sir. I yell, scream, snap, and give ugly looks. Don't know I'm doing it. Nothing physical though."

"I cannot emphasize this enough. You need time for yourself so you can give your wife what you want to give her. It is clear you love her, care for her, and have deep compassion for her troubles, and her emotions. However without time for yourself it could become ever more difficult for you to give her what she needs, and what you desire to give her."

"Yes. Sir. I always do better when I have 'me' time."

"Keep that in mind Dale. Take time for yourself every day, quite often. Do I need to write you a prescription which states I order you to do so?"

"I don't need a note. I can do that."

"Good. I want you to feel free to have time to yourself. It is easy to say you will while you're in here. Will you follow through is the question."

"Yes. Sir. I think I'll go do it now. Go to the park and take a walk in the woods."

"Perfect Dale, peacefulness of nature can be therapeutic. Ok then, have a good walk, Dale."

Journal secure in case, no notes today, I stand and step off to leave.

"Roger, thank you, Sir. Take care."

"And you as well, Dale."

*Josh's Journal*

04Jul2010, Gardez

It's almost midnight now. Today's mission went well...

...I think I had a flashback last night. I was lying here in bed trying to sleep when a pulse went through my head and shook me. I jumped up and started moving body parts. I don't know. It was weird.

Getting blown up wasn't cool but it wasn't too bad of a blast. I don't know what was going on there. I'm gonna get some sleep now. Hopefully I can sleep in.

*Josh's Journal*

05Jul2010, Gardez

We had a mission past CP Banjo today on to Skit. It was my first mission as a driver. Sergeant Smith made the call to put me behind 2-4 to let them lead so I can get used to the routes.

Driving was alright. I didn't hit anything going out there. Gardez was a little challenging because people are running around everywhere and it's a tight squeeze through some parts. I really think eventually I'll hit something.

We made our way down Tawagoto just as we had two days ago. Passed COP Zormat and got onto route Scheibe. We didn't dismount this time. EOD had the great idea to do a simulated IED blast on Skit to try and draw out an attack. Like the fu'ers wouldn't know whether there was an IED put in their front yards or not.

We made it halfway down Scheibe and were told by Hawkeye that the AFCOP they were building at the Scheibe/Skit intersection was taking IDF and small arms. We continued down and made it there, but no fire of any kind was around. The sand got really soft and it was tough driving through some parts.

2-4 got stuck but my vehicle made it through alright. We turned onto Skit after around seven hours of driving. Shortly after, Sergeant Holloway picked up something with his Husky.

The buff went up, interrogated, and found a pressure plate and pressure cooker with thirty pounds of ammonium nitrate HME. EOD did the BIP and we turned around. No hostile response from locals took place so we decided to scratch the high-speed EOD idea. We made it back to our FOB by Gardez without anything happening. The rest of the day we chilled out and sat around.

*Josh's Journal*

06Jul2010, Gardez

I heard Blart moved back to Dad's platoon. It'd suck if they put me back in the TOC.

Today was a maintenance day. Fixed a bunch o sh'. We only have one computer up and operational right now. One went down yesterday. They are the only way we can communicate to the TOC past Gardez. Two computers are required for a mission.

Tomorrow we go over the KG pass. It's a stupid mission. Nothing really happens there. 2-1 got dead-lined too. Our AC is out and that is a six-hour job.

We aren't allowed to roll out without an operational AC. So 2-7 and 2-1 trucks are down. That is mine and Douglas's. Captain Joe Wayne ran to BAF with 128 to pick up their VICs. Hopefully, now that they have those we can get some time off.

I doubt it though. We let XO Moore know we weren't mission capable. One Fifty Four ran us over a short version of the RG for 2-1 to roll in. For some reason, they really want us to go tomorrow.

It's a long-ass drive through mountains and sh'. We don't find IED's there. None have been found that way for a while. The RG they sent had no radio in it, and we don't have anything that will fit in there. We let them know that again, we were not mission capable.

They then made the call that in the morning we would drive to Alpha at 0500 and they would get Harper to look at it. Are you freagin' kidding me. I've learned 137 doesn't get many days off. 154 and 128 have had times when they'd be looking at six maintenance days in a row. It's some BS.

Now in the morning we have to run to Alpha because they pretty much think we are lying to them. Sergeant Grossman's secondary MOS is commo. He knows his sh' better than Hart. Hell, I know commo as well as Hart.

We are all pretty tired and need a day off.

*Josh's Journal*

08Jul2010, Gardez

The mission on the seventh got canceled and rescheduled to the eighth. TOC can't be happy without sending us out somewhere.

Sergeant Smith told me I would be staying back today. So I did.

He said the route was rough and he didn't know what to expect we'd run into. The guys loaded up and left at 0600.

The "mission" was to link up with another RCP to get some trailer and take it up to Alpha. An RG broke down on the way there. 2-1 broke down twice. The husky is dead-lined now.

Sergeant Smith told Captain Wayne that our men are outlasting our equipment. We can't afford to run a mission every other day at this rate or we are going to need new VICs.

We run a mission, get back and one has all kinds of problems. We get half a maintenance day to work on it then we have to run to Alpha for stupid sh'.

We don't have time to fix our VICs. And now we are supposed to run another mission tomorrow somehow. Three RG's and a Husky down because we never have more than a day to work on them.

Things are getting pretty stupid. There's no way we can roll tomorrow. 2-1 has all kinds of problems. 2-7 is still a rolling fire hazard. The mini RG we borrowed broke down today.

We put way too much sh' on these VICs. They can't take it. These VICs are made for blacktop it seems. We really need some days off like 154 and 128 get to fix these things.

They both get five days for maintenance in a row. That is unheard of here. Two in a row is unreal. And they wonder why our sh' breaks down. We're running ten times more missions than anyone else. We all feel that we've been put at a different FOB and worked to death so leadership doesn't have to hear us complain. But this can't go on much longer. Not because our guys can't do it, but because our VICs can't take it. If they really want us to run our sh' to the ground every other day, they'll just have to put up with the consequences of our sh' breaking down. The stress the VICs take every day on these routes is enormous. Thousands of bumps and uneven roads.

*Josh's Journal*
   17Jul2010, Gardez
   Haven't logged in on this for a while now. I'll record what I can think of now. A lot has happened. We did a few missions. Found one IED on Route Skit.

*Josh's Journal*

18Jul2010, Gardez

I'm about to not be able to get on this for a while again. Dad came by today. They had another blast this time on Scheibe. Everyone was fine. We have a….

# 15

Room secure, pillow moved, secure in my spot, journal ready, pen in hand, Doc to my front, in his chair with his damn notebook. Doc opens with his redundant, "Hello, Dale. How are you?"

My head raises, shoulder's shrug, and lungs exhale.

Doc says, "Quite a storm out there today."

"Yes, Sir."

Doc points at my journal. "I see you have your journal. Do you still use the same notebook for your personal thoughts as well as those we share."

"Yes, Sir. With you, alone, with Anita, it's all in here, most of it anyway."

"I am so pleased you continue to journal. This is good for you, Dale. Take time to look back through your notes. A review will aid you to consider how far you have come. Your symptoms of post-traumatic stress remain, and may for some time. We have discussed there is no specific period for healing. Such measures are not conducive to our process, and may impede your progress. That said, I encourage you to celebrate your successes."

"Thank you, Sir, I should do that. We have made progress. I went to sleep early last night, 'bout zero one. If nothing else is, at least that's better."

"Have you considered sharing your journey? Perhaps with your troops, other service members, or service members' loved ones. I believe your personal walk could benefit others. Some people are not able to express their inner thoughts as you have."

"It crossed my mind, maybe a book."

"Yes. It may help others realize they are not alone in their journey. I find a widespread negative perspective toward therapy within the military, and, to a great extent, throughout the United States."

*Who the hell am I to write a self-help book? I can't even work.*

"Maybe I'll type some of it up, Doc. See where it goes."

"Even if you decide not to share with others, to publish, a deep review of your journey may aid you in defining who Dale is today. Not to conform to who you were before, but who Dale is now, and will be moving forward. A new Dale if you will."

"That's a thought, a review of my own, and my family's struggle over the last three years."

"Yes. Absolutely, your family is a large part of your life. What affects you affects them and vice versa. I hope you decide to avail yourself of this opportunity. Now, to today, what's on your mind?"

*There goes ole tippy-tap-tap leg again. Spill it, Dale.*

"Leading my son, over there."

"What do you mean by 'leading' your son'?"

"His platoon Sar'nt went on leave at Christmas, I filled in."

"Do you mean leading him mission or on base?"

"Both. Gotta lead on base to be ready to go out. Josh and I went to dinner one night before a Battalion level mission. That was a weird night."

"Father and son go to dinner, on base I assume

"Yes. Sir. It was great to work with Josh's platoon, a privilege to lead Sar'nt Smith's men. All of them would do what had to be done. They had the best Platoon Leader in our company, a good man to work with."

\*\*\*

Since his first grade year, Karen and I often took Josh and his best friend Mike to dinner at Tres Tamales. Tonight I take Josh to eat at Hadji's restaurant on his Forward Operating Base. Tomorrow we will support a Battalion Level Mission of Afghan National Army (ANA) soldiers. I will ride in a truck near the front of our formation while Josh guns near the rear for Lt. Martin. Josh's first Christmas away from home, my second.

Josh knocks on my door. "Dad, you ready?"

"Roger."

I grab my soft cap to head out and open the door.

Josh stands in our dusty hall with his weapon slung across his back. "Must be nice having a nine mil, gets old haulin' an M-four around."

I pat the nine millimeter, holstered to my right leg. "They take care of us old folks."

We face the exit and step off through our plywood-walled hallway to leave second platoon's main quarters. Sergeant Holloway enters, adjusts his weapon sling, removes his soft cap and stows it in his cargo pocket. "Sar'nt Sanderford, we got coms up. All set for tomorrow."

My focus bounces from Josh, to plywood walls, and to Sergeant Holloway. "Roger, I heard it had a problem."

Sergeant Holloway gives a dismissive wave. "Sh'...yeah, it's up. All's they had to do was replace a couple darn parts. We got her done."

I nod, raise an eyebrow, and ask, "Roger. We're straight then?"

His left hand slides into his pocket to retrieve keys. A confident smile matches his, "Oh yeah, ready to roll, Sar'nt."

"Been to chow, Holloway?"

Holloway unlocks his padlock, un-shoulders his weapon, and eases his door open. We turn sideways to squeeze past. "Yes, Sar'nt. We done did a while ago."

I point at Josh. "We're goin' to Hadji's."

Sergeant Holloway tips his head right, puckers his lips, stops his door from easing completely open, and looks around his door at Josh. "Aw. Ain't that sweet. Daddy takin' his little boy to dinner. Aw."

Josh faces Holloway, opens his mouth, closes his mouth, turns to face a graffiti covered wall, drops his head, and clinches his lips.

Holloway is strong, serious, and direct. However, to horse around he often rolls a troop up in a ball and spanks them like a baby, one of his ways of building comradery.

My right hand slaps Josh's chest twice. "Mamma said to watch out for him. You know how Mammas are."

Josh's head snaps up, back straightens, and sweeps my hand away with a left forearm block. "I can take care of myself."

"I know you can. Let's go."

We exit, cross our porch, ease down three steps in the dark, march through deep gravel, and stroll between a latrine to our right Gardez "castle." Josh's platoon has an office within this castle, a huge qal'at, twenty-five foot tall three foot thick exterior walls, towers on all four corners, a large dark wooden gate for a front entrance and several wooden structures within. Five of our men live in one small structure. Our two Lt's live in tower penthouses of opposite corners.

As we round an Afghan graveyard, our gravel path is more compact. Our pace increases toward the front gate. One hundred meters before the Entry Control Point (ECP) we turn right to enter the Hadji mart. In fun, local national shop owners display hand-painted signs of American stores. Josh leads me past a coffee shop, RadioShack, Walmart, and Blockbuster to Maalik's restaurant.

I open the door for Josh and we step inside.

This is easily the nicest structure on Josh's Forward Operating Base with tile floors, painted plywood walls, and a full-length mirror wall opposite Maalik's counter. A welcome change from our own function focused structures and chow hall tent. His television in the left, back corner plays one of a thousand Hadji DVDs for sale. Bollywood karate movies are hilarious.

We approach Maalik's counter to order, pay, and get our drinks. I review his menu taped to his scratched up Plexiglas counter.

His glass case to our right displays Hookahs, DVDs, sunglasses, and soft drink options. Like folks back home, Maalik never misses a chance to make a sale. Below the mirror wall, across the dining room, a shaggy orange and green "sixties" carpeted stage is littered with pillows. To dine in true Afghan form, you lounge on pillows together.

Joining locals outside the Forward Operating Base for chai, or a meal I have had enough of floor sitting. Even with furniture in the room, we floor sit, and eat from communal dishes. Cool experience but in full battle gear, it is not comfortable.

Most folks call Maalik, an Afghan from Northern Afghanistan, Mike. His long, dark, black hair covers his eyes like a sheep dog. Without a sound, Maalik strolls from his kitchen to take our order, sees Josh, smiles, and says, "Hello my friend."

*How does he walk so quiet in flip-flops?*

Josh stands to my right, ignores the menu, and smiles. "Hey, Maalik. How been?"

"You have not been for a while. I miss you my friend."

Josh says, "I was workin' somewhere else. I'm back now."

"Okay, good to see you. You going to eat?"

"Oh, yeah. I'm hungry"

Maalik sports a full-toothed smile, looks at me, and extends his hand across the counter. "Hello, Sir. How are you? My name is Maalik."

We shake hands. I nod, and return my hand to my right hip under my blouse. "I'm good, hungry, but good."

Josh's right hand points across his chest at me. "You know this is my dad, right?"

"He take care of you here? Or you make him pay for food?"

"No, for real. He's my dad."

The sides of Maalik's smile drop, level with his still exposed teeth, and he looks in my eyes. "You are his father, sir?"

"Yup, I'm his daddy. His mom told me to take him out to dinner, so here we are."

Maalik studies our nametapes and faces. "You are his father?"

"I am."

Josh says, "I told you he was. You don't trust me?"

Maalik steps back, points at me, then Josh, back and forth. "That's crazy. Father and son here to fight for my country."

Maalik steps up to the counter and slaps his left palm on the counter toward Josh. "He is fine man. You should be proud. No problem with him, other people not so much. Your son is good man. You raise good man."

"Thank you. He's a good fella." I look at Josh. "What're you havin'?"

"Special rice, you had it? It is freagin' awesome."

"I have, but I think I'll get beef kabobs tonight." I look up to wait for Maalik to acknowledge my request. He moves hair from his right eye, writes down our order, looks back at me.

I say, "Extra bread?"

"For you, my friend. Yes, Sir, extra bread. To drink?"

Josh says, "Mountain Dew please."

*The chai will have enough caffeine for me tonight.*

"Sprite. While we wait, can I have some chai?"

"Yes, Sir. You like the chai?"

"Yup, real good."

"That will be seventeen dollars, Sir."

I pay. Take my sprite and turn to find a table.

*Wait he didn't include the chai, just drinks and food.*

I turn to his counter. Maalik prepares my chai, hands it to me, and turns to return to his kitchen.

"Maalik, did you include the price of the chai?"

He points to Josh and looks at me. "For his father, free chai, my friend."

"Thank you."

We sit against the back wall to watch TV while we eat. Seven "new to the Stan" troops are at a large center table.

*He's gonna say something negative.*

Less than sixty seconds in our chairs, my son looks at me from across our wobbly table sporting his sarcastic grin. "These new troops talk like they're God's gift to the Army."

"They're young, Son. New. Let 'em talk."

"Come on, Dad. You can tell they ain't left the FOB yet. Listen to 'em."

"I know. We talked about this. Not everyone has the same job. Leave it alone."

"I just think it's funny to hear 'em talk tough about how much work they do, in some office, what shift they gotta pull and what an asshole someone at work is. They come out of their little closet and look at us, National Guard, like we're a lazy piece-o-sh'."

"Look at what you've done. You know the truth. Be proud of what you have done and let it be. Their paperwork supports us, and other troops doin' what we do. At least we don't have to do the paperwork too."

"Dad, you keep sayin' that. But I know it pisses you off to be looked down on like that?"

"Don't matter, let it go. Do not care more about it than they do. 'Sides you don't want SF talkin' sh' about you. Sayin' you don't do sh'."

"They say that?"

"I ain't heard 'em say nothin', just sayin'."

"Oh, roger that."

Maalik arrives with our food, places our orders correctly in front of us, steps back, and clasps his hands over his stomach. "Do you need anything else, my friends?"

Josh says, "Some of your unbelievable hot sauce?"

"Yes." He retrieves a bottle of red sauce, Sriracha I think, and places it on our table. "Anything else?"

"No, thank you," Josh says.

Maalik goes back to work. We enjoy a great dinner. The pita bread, as we call it, is always good. In India, they call it Naan. It is similar to bread locals in Iraq gave us, but without the goat dung flavor.

At my base, they used to cook lamb kebabs on an oblong charcoal grill, like street vendors in Gardez. Maalik does not have any green sauce or crushed red pepper sides like "back home," and no charcoal grill either.

*Wish we still had our Hadji mart. That damn ANA suicide bomber killed...ended a good thing. I miss those smoke flavored kabobs.*

I eat with our interpreters sometimes, but their chow hall food is not as good as those kebabs were, or as good as Maalik's cooking.

Maalik's rice is tremendous, longer grain rice than back home in Mississippi, and spicy with a lot of pepper. He has metal forks and hard plates, much nicer than chow hall dinning. Everything in there goes on a paper plate, runs together, soaks into the plate, and often fights back enough to break my plastic fork.

We eat and watch a movie about some Russian cage fighter dude. Cool movie, ruthless, but cool. I lean back to enjoy my sweet green chai after dinner. His is different from the milk-based chai our Afghan National Army cohorts serve. Maalik comes over to our table. The new troops left while we ate. Josh, Maalik, and I remain.

Maalik stands at the end of our table, his hand on an empty chair. "Mind if I join?"

My left hand motions to his chair, "No, please. How's your business?"

Maalik pulls the chair back, plops in it like a diner waitress who wore the wrong shoes to work. "It is good. They give me hard time when I go to market. They do not want to let me back on base. I try to tell them my job is here. They want us to get off the base for good I think."

Josh says, "I hope not, this is way better food than the chow hall."

I ask, "How long has your restaurant been here?"

"I here two year. Come from Kabul. My father want me do other business. I like this work. I meet people like you. Good people."

I smile, take a sip of chai, and raise my glass to him. "Thank you. We enjoy your food."

"Why more people cannot be friends?"

"Different people, different ideas, different religion, we are all very different people."

Maalik says, "But we want same. We are not so different, Christian and Muslim."

Cup back on the table I face my right palm skyward. "We all want a good job, a safe place for our children, peace."

"Yes, Yes. Many in my country want what you try to give. Americans make good things many places here. I have good job, I miss my children but I have good job. My son goes to good school, expensive. I have good life. People try make us fight. They want go back to way we were before."

I glance at my son, and back at Maalik. "We want you to have a good life. We hope you can have a peaceful place for your families. We do not want to stay here. We want to go home. My son and I want to live a good life in our country. We want to help your people make this country a good place. And keep it safe so many people can have a good life, men, women, and children, keep everyone safe."

"Yes, we thank you. You bring son here, help my country, and keep my son safe. This is good. Other people, they do not want progress. They see new Afghanistan as an American country."

"We don't want your country. We want you to have your own country, to have pride in your people, protect your family, your neighbors. I want to leave and not come back."

"Yes. Yes. But other people. Not Afghan people want keep war. They do not let us be safe. They fight you and other people. We want end of war. I have known war long time. I remember Russians come. They were not like you. They were mean. My family take me to Pakistan when they came. We ran. After they leave, I come back. Come back to my home."

"You remember the Russians coming?"

"Yes, they did not want us to make better. They want only to kill us, want to take over our land."

I am no history buff. I cannot speak to the Russian war here. One valley Josh's platoon spent a week in was nicknamed the "Valley of Death." Dubbed this name when many Russians died fighting Afghanis.

*I guess they had a good coach.*

I say, "The Afghans fought well, Russia couldn't win here."

"No, they had to leave. We make them leave. We need Americans stay now. We are getting better now than we were."

I look from Maalik to my son. "An Iraqi man told me something similar in 05."

Maalik says, "What did he told you?"

"He said 'we are a baby country. We cannot walk on our own yet. If you leave, we will have problems. It would be bad if you leave before we can stand on our own.'"

"Yes. Stay. Help us. Muslim is no different to Christian. Why people fight over religion?"

My son looks at me, lips furled under, eyebrows wrinkle to the center, and head shakes side to side.

*He is scared I will disobey the "no proselytizing" order.*

Big Army discourages us from religion discussions with Afghan people. Orders say not to proselytize. We might offend someone with our religious beliefs. Actually, we got orders not to eat in front of Muslims during Ramadan. Someone with a croissant probably got worried we may offend locals. My terp said, "That's stupid, you are not Muslim."

*If he brings it up, or asks questions, we will see what happens.*

I look back to Maalik. "I am a Christian, you are a Muslim, but we both want this country to do well, to be safe. I want my son to be safe, just like you do."

Maalik nods. "Yes. And you know both come from Abraham. We both want to get to God. We just have different ways to get to him."

A quick sip of chai, my head turns left to right.

*He brought it up.*

"You have to go a little deeper, it gets complicated. We have unresolvable differences on how to get to God."

A hand wave and a mumble, then Maalik leans back in his chair and crosses his legs. "What is difference? I believe in Allah, you believe in God. There is one God, we agree to this. What is different? In your country you believe do this, this, this, to get to God. Here we believe that, that, that. Same God, but he deal different with us."

"Lots of people say this, say Christian, Muslim, and Hindu all serve the same God. We understand him in different ways because of our culture. Some say God shows himself to us so we can understand him in our own way, in our own culture."

Maalik asks, "You do not believe this?"

"We believe many similar things. Our morals, what is right and wrong, treat others well are common to most religions. Christianity and Islam do not center on the same God. Both hold beliefs which make one or the other true. They are mutually exclusive."

Maalik asks, "What do you mean?"

"Our religion says the only way to God is through belief in and relationship with Jesus Christ. If that is true, Islam, Buddhism, Hindu, and other religions cannot be true. None have the same base belief of Jesus as our only way to God."

"We have Jesus in Islam. He was prophet."

"Jesus' truths do not allow us to accept Islam as true. Jesus' teachings do not drive me to want you hurt, to dislike you, or anything. I just disagree with your beliefs."

Maalik says, "Yes you are a friend. We do not argue. We do not fight."

"Yes, my Christian beliefs teach me to love everyone. Not agree with, like or approve their behavior if it is against what Jesus teaches, but disagree in love. Try not to harm anyone. Or even wish them harm."

Maalik says, "Muslim is same, religion of love and compassion, of discipline and learning. It is not about this violence some people try to make it. We have some in Islam that are...fanatic. They want to hurt people. Not most of us. We want good life of peace."

"We've had, and still do, fanatics in the Christian religion. People who use the Bible to do things they should not do."

Maalik motions to the three of us. "Yes and we, we must deal with problems they make. We want safe for son, wife, home, food and happy we want."

"Yes. TV, radio and other things try to make us dislike each other. They want us to fight, to disagree so they can make money or gain power. If more people would have a true relationship with God through Jesus Christ our world would be a much better place."

"Maybe, I believe if less people be fanatic, use religion to do what they want, instead of Allah, would be better place."

"We are alike, aren't we? Thanks for dinner. I hope your son does well in his new school." Josh and I stand, stack our plates and napkins so Maalik won't have to, push our chairs in, and I pick up my Styrofoam cup of chai.

*I'll finish this in my room.*

Maalik stands with us, pats Josh's shoulder, and laughs. "Thank you my friend, good night. I hope your son will do well, too."

"He's done well. I'm a proud dad. Have a good night, Maalik."

Josh says, "Good night Maalik" as we exit.

"Goodnight, my friend. Do not stay away so long."

\*\*\*

Doc Says, "Sounds like a great dinner with polite conversation."

"Yessir. I could get in trouble for what I said, but it was a good conversation. Strange how things work out though."

"What seems strange to you?"

"A month later we were loadin' up to come home. Josh came to my FOB to visit. I went back at my FOB to do First Shirt crap. Anyway, Josh tells me Maalik got kicked off base. The new active army troops found some of the locals were passing intel to the Taliban. We don't think Maalik was, other Hadjis. I might have had a religious discussion with the Taliban. That seems strange."

"How interesting, he sits with you, gives you free tea, calls you friend, compliments your son, and yet may have shared information with your enemy. Information which could have gotten one or both of you killed."

"Yes, Sir. Just part of the game."

Doc offers another gentle hand motion toward me. "Do you find it difficult for you to trust people after such things?"

"Doesn't everyone have trust issues?"

I gaze through his French doors at a rose and listen.

"Our society does not help grow trust. Competitive measures to determine winner and loser categories. However, to have someone betray you this way, to call you friend, and know your son. All the while, work with your enemy. Most of us have never seen such betrayal."

My head turns. I search Doc's eyes. "I guess. We aren't s'pose to let it affect us though, right?"

His pen hand waves palm up. "I see no way it could not affect you. What we need to do is decide how it will do so."

"I guess. How do you come to terms with bad sh'?"

Doc pries, "Like a friend betraying you?"

"Or worse."

Doc furls his brow, looks at his notebook, and back at me. "Can you define worse than betrayal of a self-proclaimed friend in such a way?"

"Not anger, or disappointment, but cruelty of man against man, complete and total cruelty."

"Dale, you have seen man's inhumanity to man. We like to pretend we know all about it. Those who go to war have a perspective on it others will never have. Things you have seen, or even done, which are brutal, some would say evil. It is amazing how far mankind can go to hurt another of his own species."

My hands raise palm up. "Exactly, I know cultures differ, but I see similar attitudes and actions here at home. Right here in our 'advanced' society."

"Anytime it exposes itself can be horrible."

I shrug my shoulders. "Like in 05 when I went with an Iraq army platoon to raid Owesat. Their Platoon Sergeant was in the Iraqi army in Desert Shield/Desert Storm. I fought against him in 91. In 05, I had to trust him to enter a house behind me without shooting me in the back…"

*Again with the stare in my eyes looking for something.*

"That must require a high level of trust, Dale. Were other coalition forces, your own men, nearby?"

I shake my head, stop, and stare at that first qualat we hit that morning, outside, behind the rose. "Most of the day no, they weren't. Not within several hundred meters through the village."

His right hand goes palm up this time. "So you really did have to trust this Iraqi platoon. Led by a man you once fought against, with your life no less. I ask again, how did you trust him?"

I see myself, south side of number one qal'at. Sergeant Fathal and two others lined up with me in a four-man stack west of the entrance. Number one man kicks the door, gunfire starts, we all rush in. "I didn't. Sometimes you just say a prayer, and go in the door, screamin' women, cryin' children, AK fire, just say, 'Lord Help', and go."

The movie screen through Doc's French doors blocks my view of the roses with a new scene. Images of children, women, qal'ats, and river road by the Euphrates.

My private review slows, and pauses on that little girl, that day.

*Was she his daughter or granddaughter? Was the fat lady in all black his wife?*

Doc circles his pen hand three times toward me. "Please continue."

\*\*\*

Our Battalion Commander assigns me to work with an Iraqi platoon to raid Owesat, a village thirty-five miles southwest of Baghdad in Al Anbar province. Sergeant Fathal, my Iraqi army counterpart, and I prepare his troops for tomorrow's mission with door entry battle drills.

Between iterations of our drill six or eight Iraqi troops, tell me not to trust the long beard fella. In private conversation, each makes a similar statement. "He is not Iraqi, he foreign fighter," or "He come from other country. Careful, might shoot you out there if he can."

We gather Fathal's platoon together for a group photo, I print a copy for Sergeant Fathal. He and I have a strange bond, Ole Sarge to Ole Sarge.

His medic, my closest thing to an interpreter for the day, writes everyone's name by his face. Long Beard wears goggles and a ski mask in our photo.

*He didn't have that on before the photo, or after?*

Names written in blue ink, I walk to the Tactical Operation Center, copy the photo for Fathal, give the original to Captain Campton and report their warning.

I point at Ski Mask Boy, insure Captain Compton observes him, and end our conversation, "If I don't come back, find this guy."

We roll into Owesat at zero-three-thirty, dismount, and hit target qal'ats. Detain a few and, like every other day after a raid, search for weapons caches with mine detectors.

In our sector of Owesat, it is a slow day. I walk over to see what our troops found buried in an old man's yard. Guy had three one-five-five artillery rounds stashed beside his house.

We take the one military age male there to the street and search his buildings, and find no real intelligence, propaganda, or weapons. As always, his wife cries and screams as we search out buildings.

I told Medic Boy to stay beside me, he has, I look at him and point to the main house. "What's up with "Madam?"

He looks at the house, back at me, I point at her, he prances to the house, and her. Fathal, his troops, and I clear the old man's sheds.

I exit our last "shed with a bed" and see Medic Boy in route from the house. He stops, hands upside down on his hips, nose a few short inches from my own. "Madam want talk man in charge".

Fathal looks at me after the medic tells him more in Iraqi than his broken English enables him to tell me.

*This is your freagin' country dude, why look at me?*

I pat Fathal's shoulder, step toward the house, and pull him along. "Let's go see what she wants."

I lead Fathal and Medic Boy between green trees, along a short levee trail of Old Man's garden, and up a short dirt incline to the front door. I stop a few feet from Mrs. Screamer Lady, fake interpreter to my right, Sergeant Fathal, and a few of his troops shuffle in sand several steps away to my left.

*Great, now I get to talk to another cryin' woman through a mediocre terp. This will be great.*

She stands there, cries and whales, leads five or six children around her in a unison cry, scream, hold each other floor show.

*Go ahead lady, say some "He good man, No Al Qaeda, good man. Do nothing. We love Americans." Gimme' a new song, change it up woman.*

I point at her, look at Medic Boy and elbow him. "What's she want?"

No one says a word. I cannot look away from the children, the woman. My hand rests on my M-4 pistol grip. I say again, slower, "What does she want?"

A slapstick director commands our huddle, Medic Boy looks at me, I point at the lady, in shock, he looks over at Fathal, Fathal looks at me to avoid Medic Boy, and diverts his gaze when I look at him, Medic Boy wrinkles his unibrow and looks back at me, then to Mrs. Screamer Lady.

*C'mon dude you been my terp all day. Ask her dammit.*

We are not to "shame" locals or the Iraqi National Guard. To yell at him would make me lose my interpreter. Poor embarrassed fella would go pout in his ambulance.

In Iraqi he asks, she answers, the girl under her left arm cries louder, says something, and clutches Mom's waist with both arms. Screamer Lady's hands wave like an irate Italian woman. She and Medic Boy talk back and forth, she screams, they talk.

I elbow Medic Boy's ribs, again. "What'd she say? I'm right here. Talk to me, don't just talk to her. What'd she say?"

"She say give girl for Mr."

"Do what? What's she talking about?"

"You give Mr., you take girl. She young. Girl is…um…virgin."

I look at Fathal. He avoids my gaze. Mumbles to his troops, who all walk away, he steps toward the road.

*Does he think I'll...?*

*Why'd he send his troops to river road?*

Fathal looks at me but still does not make eye contact.

*Don't wanna be part of it, but you think I will. You saying 'Go-ahead American.'*
*This girl is like a year older than Charlotte, what the...fu' this sh'. I'm out.*

I turn toward River Road, step off, and grunt. "La, La."

Mrs. Screamer jabbers, pushes the pre-teen off her hip and toward me. The girl fights to clutch Mom. All the children stare at me and wait for an answer. Screamer Lady talks to Medic Boy, her words flow faster than a pissed off Puerto Rican, waves her arms, and pushes the girl away.

"La, La," I say.

I turn away to go check on our detainee, Medic Boy touches my left arm and sticks his over grown nose in my face. A fly strolls across his thick brow above his left eye. "We should give him back. He is old. She need man."

"We're done here. Tell her to stay in the house."

Sergeant Fathal tells me, "You leave man, you get girl. You keep."

The girl understands. Her dark eyes flow streams of tears down both dirt-caked cheeks as she fights to hold onto, to stay with, Mom.

I say, "La, La."

Mom begs, cries, yanks my arm, the girl screams and tries to hide behind Mom's hip. I say again "La, La" and pull away.

I step off to River Road, where I find her husband zip cuffed, on his knees, and in tears.

*Sh', tears every f'in where.*

I swig some water and wait for US troops with a detainee truck to pick him up. Fathal's commander rides past me in his white S-10 pickup.

*Perfect.*

His driver parks on River Road to my right, detainee kneels to my left. Captain Fat Boy gets out and shuffles toward us, passes me, draws his pistol, and mumbles in Arabic.

*He's walking to the detainee.*

I step forward.

He presses his pistol barrel to our detainee's forehead.

I command, "La, La."

Old Man's forehead skin wraps around Captain Fat Boy's pistol barrel, sweat runs over its front sight. Commander Fat Boy pushes his weapon to force our detainee's head up and back.

I grab Captain Fat Boy's arm. "We ain't doin' this. Awgaf, la, la."

My grip on his firing arm tightens. I pull his arm, and pistol, away from Old Man's head.

He faces me.

I stare in his dark eyes. "La...La...No."

He stares through me, and sweats like a fat cowboy toe to toe with Josey Wales.

*You gonna shoot me?*

He is frozen.

Our eyes drill into the other's mind.

My firing hand lowers to my weapon.

He holsters his, turns, mumbles and shuffles back to his ride.

*Probably thinks grumbling scares me, old fat piece-o-sh'.*

Medic Boy steps into my personal space, his bad breath and body odor permeate my nostrils. He leans still closer to my ear and whispers, "You shame Capitan in front of men. You should not stop him."

Left index finger in Medic Boy's face, right hand grips my M-4, anger shakes both finger and voice. "I don't give a sh' who I shamed. We ain't doin' that sh'. Not while I'm here."

*There he goes back to his ambulance. Fun's over anyway, good time to shame him and lose my terp.*

***

Doc says, "Such a horrific event, to witness such depths of human suffering. How far one will go to maintain what one considers normal. How do you tie this to here, to the United States?"

"What's the difference between killing a man on his knees and a group of people beating another human being? All this sh' goin' on in the states riots, revenge beatings, looting. Different weapons but the same mentality, here, the same inhumanity is in it all"

"Once we experience the depths of despair, man's inhumanity to man, pure cruelty without remorse one is more sensitive to it, can sense it." Doc leans forward, the leather of his chair making noise beneath him. "Recognize it more readily. You have seen how far one man will go to harm another, for no reason but his being of another sect or religion. I am sorry you had to witness that. I sense, however, it is building a compassion for others in you. These experiences, the things you've seen and done, are creating within you a true empathy for those being treated unfairly."

"Some. His dark eyes with no remorse, concern for his reputation over the life of another man. Fathal's absolute complacence to this little girl, to her father is no different than our violent divisions here in America?"

"You make an interesting correlation. How do you see either coming about in our social structure, our beliefs? All men have the capacity for horrible things. Veterans must deal with it, even within themselves. Why do you think some go so far and others do not?"

"Scope creep."

"What do you mean by scope creep?"

"In projects we have to work hard to define our scope of work. To fix a specific problem, organize certain tools, or make a specific task simpler. As a project begins, like at home, we see other things close by, or affected by today's focus. Without strict discipline, the scope of a day's project expands, sometimes to an unmanageable level. You know the old 'as long as we're here we might as well…' saying. Same thing happens in human morality. Allow a little of this, a little of that. Next thing you know morals are out the window and we aren't sure how we got there."

"So you see this as a societal pattern," Doc says with a thoughtful look. "To continue down a path of complacency until we cannot determine our path, how or why we have redefined our morality."

"Or even what morality is. Once gone we have no benchmark to come back. Political correctness pushes us to accept what we once would not. Now it seems most have no moral compass. 'Whatever's good for you.' or 'I don't believe in what you do, but if it's good for you, fine.' All that crap. Is there no definitive right and wrong?"

Doc says, "Having done the things you've shared with me. Experiencing, and witnessing atrocities, injuries, and death. It is natural you have these questions. In combat, one may be required to redefine right and wrong to survive. Just because you come home, those definitions do not automatically reset. Our minds are not so easily swayed from combat morals to our old back-in-the-world morals."

"It goes further. Yes, we come home confused, but society has no answer. People tell us 'what is right for you is your reality.' This is useless to us. I see dead bodies on the side of the road near my house. What the hell do I know about reality, or even morality?" I ask but don't wait for an answer. "How can I define right and wrong without a reference? No absolute truth. As we go down the 'good for you good for me' road where will we stop? Or why would we stop with no common truth to stop us. Why question people bein' violent, addicted to sh' or dysfunctional when we deny any common measure of right and wrong?"

"I see your point. How would you define free will? Man's free will is a large part of what you describe."

"Absolutely. God gave us free will. No man should take it away, not me, you, anyone. However, what guides our will? Our upbringing, what people teach us? As we make choices, what do we use to measure which of our desires to satisfy?" I eye the red squared carpet and ask, "Is there common ground there? A teacher at my daughter's school said a parent called and cussed her out for sending a note home about little Johnny not doing his homework. Daddy cussed her out and said it's her job to teach and not to bother him again. What the hell is that? What does little Johnny learn from dear ole Dad? How will it affect Johnny's future decisions?"

"Someone cussed out a teacher for an attempt to gain parental involvement?" Doc shakes his head.

"Yes, Sir. You'd be surprised. So what is that parent listening to as they make a freewill choice to exercise their freedom of speech on a teacher? What drives them to choose an uninvolved parental plan? According to our society, no one should tell him how to raise his kid. All opinions are equal. If the saying 'nothing is absolute' is true why does gravity work everywhere? If physical laws are true everywhere, why not moral or even spiritual?"

Doc's hand leaves his chin, and turns palm up beside his cheek. "I'd say gravity works everywhere as far as we know. Or do we perceive gravity working and cannot see otherwise because of blinders on our conceptual image of this world?"

My right hand waves skyward and slaps down on the couch center cushion. "Well, if you go there we can throw everything out."

*What's with the nod, Doc? Are you frustrated with me? You're the one that thinks weird sh' about gravity.*

Doc stops his nod, resituates in his chair, and swaps positions to right leg over left. "It gets complicated as we discuss morality. Who defines it? Most religions share common morals. However, do those apply to unbelievers, to atheists? If so, who decides what applies and what does not? Whose morals are absolute, your morals, mine, or whose? How do we determine this? Aside from a dictator, no one has authority to determine absolute morality. It seems questions never end but only bring more questions."

"Look, Doc. The questions are there if we weigh all opinions equally. Is God's opinion not weightier than mine?"

Doc says, "To that I must ask, who's God?"

"And there we are again. There is no single truth, just opinion and theory. My head hurts. I think we've done enough for today."

"Ok. Dale, reschedule out front. Great talk, as always. I enjoy the way you blend this journey with spiritual questions."

"I don't see a separation. I have P-Tids" I nod and hand gesture to offer clarity, "PTSD." I am created in His image. How will the two coexist within me?"

"You have a spiritual foundation. Investigate what this means to you. You are in the midst of many questions as most combat veterans are. To have a foundation on which you can build is a good thing for you. You need absolutes, wisdom, and answers you can use to rebuild yourself as you embrace who you are today. Focus on this for next time. We must stop now. I would love to continue this discussion."

"I'll think on it. Where does that leave people like my son? Troops who throw out or question the beliefs they grew up with. Or those who have never heard or listened to the gospel? On what do they build? See my point? Next time I guess, have a good one, Doc."

"And you as well, Dale."

*Karen's Journal 25 December 2014*

Christmas Day 2010 - Dale is due home around February of next year. I am tired and mad. Christmas stinks and I really thought about taking Charlotte skiing somewhere because being at home for Christmas without the guys is just wrong and frankly stupid. All of this was preventable. We volunteered to have Christmas a month early so others could be home with their families for Christmas. It's ok to be the nice guy but on Christmas Eve and day, you wanna question being the good guy. Visiting extended family without your own family is depressing.

Anyway, we head home Christmas day from my mom's and are on highway 145 and pass a guy preparing to turn to the right to the next highway. I guess he had an issue with that because instead of turning right he decides to follow us. I did not think so at first but 25 minutes later, avoiding our house and riding all around the community, it's clear he wants to do something about it. Really? Get over yourself dude!

So I drive back to town and call my mom who suggests I drive to the police department and let them discuss it with him. Once we got into downtown he turned off.

So here's the dilemma...do you tell Dale? What can he do? But I'm mad, aggravated, and sick of it—sick of him being gone all the time. Of having to take on a crisis or scary situation alone. I shouldn't have to be in the situation to start with, right? [I can't remember if I mentioned it to him till he got home or not.]

# 16

Room clear, French doors secure, I post to corner seat, and prepare my journal. Doc returns with another damn bottle of water. "Dale, how are you today?"

"I'm fine."

He sits, prepares a blank page, clicks his pen three times, leans back, and crosses his bony legs. "Do you still see images?"

"Saw one on the way here, thought a truck was gonna T-bone me at a red light."

"I'm sorry, what do you mean by T-bone you?"

"Nail you from the side. Center your car with their bumper, hard, and fast. Like a T-bone."

"I see. And what was your reaction?"

"Saw it, hit the gas, braced for impact, realized I was bein' stupid again."

"Being stupid is not a good way to describe it. Your subconscious attempts to protect you. To keep you safe from threats, both real and perceived. Predictive images based on current surroundings and feasible threats. You have, through experience, trained your mind to consider risks other's do not. Such possibilities may never enter another person's minds. How you react to these is our work's focus.

"I urge you to judge yourself less for these intrusive thoughts. Observe the thoughts and your surroundings. Ask why you see a specific image, in a certain circumstance. Ask yourself if there are common cues. Search for cues which induce intrusive thoughts. Once you identify these, you may adjust your environment to minimize specific situations, smells, sounds, or images. This will allow you to embrace your PTSD symptoms. These adjustments are one, of many, methods to live your new life."

"Yes, Sir. You said that before. I calm down quicker when I try to figure out where the images are coming from, or why. Did I take my meds? Am I anxious? Did I see, smell, or hear something? I think being around people increases it all."

"Dale from what you have told me, I agree. Prolonged exposure to other people is an issue for you. Are you still able to give yourself permission to be away from everyone? Do you say no to activities before your anxiety grows?"

"I have good days and bad days. Part of me still says, 'a good husband and father would be there for this.' Like Charlotte's Veterans Day program at school. I feel like a jerk if I don't go. They play patriotic songs, show pictures, and of course, there is a crowd. What kind of Dad doesn't go to their kid's Veterans Day program?"

"Listen to yourself Dale. You measure yourself by what others may think, or say. Rather than use these unhealthy metrics, please focus on what Dale needs, or wants. If you want to support your daughter, and other veterans, at such an event, make a conscious choice to prepare in advance. Take extra time to yourself prior to the event. Afterwards as well, even if you do not yet feel a need to. You will provide greater support and love to your family if you take care of yourself."

"That's what the shrinks at Shelby told me, at demob."

"At demob?"

"When we got back to the states we demobilized at Camp Shelby. Medical checks, head checks a lotta stuff."

"If you don't mind I'd like to hear about your demobilization process."

"We had as much stress at demob as we did getting ready to go over."

***

Near midnight, we arrive at Camp Shelby to demobilize (demob). First Army orders us to be back at zero-seven for our first set of briefings. After months away, we only get a few hours with family.

Thanks to General Farley, we did not have to be back until zero-nine. As we expect with our troops, two arrive late. Our men do an unbelievable job in combat, on field maneuvers, but with any time off, someone will mess up.

We go through generic demobilization briefings. Big Army plans to demobilize us in three to five days, and send us home.

Leave combat and a week later we are off the payroll. On our own to try to live our old life, go back to work, play with our kids, and take out the trash. As if none of us brought a problem home. Army does not care if we did, neither do we. Big Army wants us off their payroll and we want off General Order One so we can drink all this out of our heads.

Demob is always the same. Show up, sit, or stand in lines for people to check your ears, eyes, teeth, yadda, yadda, yadda. Briefings complete at twelve-hundred and twenty troops sprint to be first in line. These troops will go through medical and psychological screenings and say "I'm fine, no problems" so they can get home to their wives, children and beer. No one wants to be here. We have been gone a year and our families are an hour drive away. One thought drives us at demob, "I made it home, I'll be fine if you'll just let me out of here."

We rush our paperwork through station, after station, after monotonous station. A laundry list of check this and fill out that. Once we have a signature, initials, or stamp in each box on our sheet we go to final check out to get our DD214 and go *home.*

A nurse screens us in building one and sends anyone he suspects has "issues" to Behavioral Health. Half of us win tickets for head checks.

My second trip to Psycho, our second day back, seems to duplicate my wasted time yesterday. Sit here all morning, get lunch, return, and park in my same back row, end chair. I had been back from lunch ten minutes when I witness another indication we have a long road ahead.

*Bang!*

The daycare's north side doors, on my left, fly open and slam into their respective walls. Staff Sergeant Rollins barges in, marches through, and slams his two-inch thick medical file on the counter, kicks a flimsy temporary wall to his right, and wails, "Excuse me!"

Specialist Johansson, the receptionist, snaps his head left, eyes open wide, stands up and faces Rollins. He stutters in an attempt to get off the phone, holds up a finger to signal Rollins to wait, and jerks his body tense when Rollins yells, "Ah, *hell* no. I ain't waitin'. Y'all mother f-ers don't know what the hell you're doin', It's freakin' time for me to get home to my wife and kids. Get off the damn phone and get somebody out here to sign off on my damn paperwork right freakin' now."

Johansson hangs up and whispers, "One moment Sar'nt," and rushes to "the back" for help.

In the waiting room we all relate to Rollins' behavior. He is a great troop, awesome NCO, and found bombs well. He has lost patience. Seventy-two hours ago, we were in Afghanistan, now we have done enough paperwork to kill half the trees in Mississippi. Throughout our once silent room some laugh, some never flinch, I glance over, see who it is, and focus back to a talk show on TV.

*He's just gotta let it out, he'll be all right.*

Specialist Johansson returns with two head docs. Both shrinks try soft discussion with Rollins.

*Yeah right, cuddly sh' ain't gonna work, he's just warming up.*

Both Docs escort Rollins to the inner sanctum of Brain Descramblers-

R-Us. Rollins pulls away from Doc Thompson's gentle touch on his shoulder, clears the threshold, and yells, "These people can't get their damn act together! I'd be fine if y'all would finish my freakin' paperwork and lemme get the hell out-o-here."

I catch him outside after his back room visit. "Rollins, I don't think throwin' a fit is how you convince Doc Thompson you're ready to go home, man."

"I know Sar'nt Sanderford, I know. But damn they wanna send me to Benning. Hell, I made it back lemme go home."

"I understand, believe me, but you'll be home in a day or so and get on with your life. Just play along then you can start gettin' ready for our next trip over."

"Alright Sar'nt, I just need to get away from these stupid sons-a-bitches."

"Take a break. Come back in an hour or so. Chill out man."

"Roger that, Sar'nt."

Rollins heads toward our orderly room. I stuff my smoke in the butt can and head back to my seat, to wait. An hour later, Johansson announces, "Sergeant First Class Sanderford." I go in, scan the open room, doors left, and right, a copy machine on the far wall, no change from yesterday.

A skinny little woman waves me to her door. I enter, check her room, and sit as far from the door as I can. We chit chat about our unit, our mission, how many men have been seen in here, and their common issues.

Mrs. Walton says, "We were notified about your unit a week ago. Once we heard what you all went through, it was clear we would need plenty of time open when you all arrived. We have never done this, but we set aside three full days with no appointments for other units. We want to focus on your unit, and your issues."

*"No sh' lady. Wait, I bet she tells every unit that to make 'em think she cares."*

She reads my medical file to pull my record up on her computer, looks through paperwork, medical records, and plays on her computer more. Her forehead wrinkles, eyes glance at me, at my file, her screen, and again from the top. I cannot see her screen.

*Lady, if you're confused, how you gonna help me?*

She looks at her screen, at me, back to her screen. "Sar'nt. Sanderford…um…" Click, click, another glance at me, back to her screen. "This says you were to return to the states in October of last year for psychiatric evaluation and treatment."

"Yes, Ma'am. I was medevac'd to Germany for stroke-like symptoms in September last year. They never found the problem so I talked my case worker and providers into lettin' me go back to work."

"Why?"

"My son and my men were still there. I would not come back here, take it easy, and chill out while they were at work. It was hard enough to leave 'em when I got medevac'd. I was not comin' back to the states without 'em. I would have been a basket case. Besides they never figured out what my problem was in Germany, after a full month, I figured they wouldn't back here either."

She stares at her computer. Her right index finger taps the screen and slides right, as if to lead her eyes through complicated text. As her hand hits her lap, she peers sideways at me. As if to say, 'poor old Sergeant cannot understand.'

She dumbs it down for me, "But your Psychiatric provider in Germany said you had acute stress issues and required further evaluation and treatment."

"Yes, Ma'am, she did. I told her I'd see a chaplain in country, talk to someone there till I came home, and I'd follow up at demob."

"Did you see someone in country?"

"No, Ma'am. We didn't have a permanent chaplain at our FOB. Only stress counselor was at my son's FOB. I was over there workin' with his platoon some. I went to see him once, social worker type I think, was a day we had six troops go see him. They got freaked out over a suicide bomber in our Hadji mart."

"And why did you not follow up?"

"Cause, they might have sent me back to Germany. My men were at work. At work is where I had to be."

"But Psychology in Germany never released you to return to theater."

"She said she'd let me go back if I'd take some fish oil and follow up in country. So I went back"

"No. There is nothing in here to release you back to theater. The last note entered refers you to the states. How did you get back in country?"

I shrug my shoulders and hold both hands up in frustration. "Hell I thought she released me. Maybe caseworkers can't see crazy boy files. I told my caseworker I got released, she did my paper work, and I went back."

She types, clicks her mouse a hundred times, my leg tap accelerates with every click.

*I'm ready to get outta this touchy feely daycare and do the next thing. C'mon woman, what are you typing? Check a box on my sheet already.*

She starts on me again, "So how do you feel now? What types of experiences did you have in country? Do you have trouble sleeping?"

*Blah, blah, blah. Same fifty-some-odd questions we all answer 500 times.*

*Who had the bright idea 'If someone's losin' it put 'em through this ginormous pile-o-stupid questions.' Real smart.*

An hour of cuddle fun and she pushes me off on two other people. She scheduled a brain function check, come back to see her, discuss my brain check, and see some other shrink.

*This is gonna take three more days.*

Josh turns twenty-one next week, and is ready to get home and drink. He falls in with our speed demons, is done, and home in four days. Like most, he has sleep problems and other issues. He's bought into Old Joe's "I just need to get home, away from stupid people who ask "how does this make you feel," have a few beers, and rinse out my head" philosophy.

Four days out of Afghanistan and Josh is home on leave. Old Sarge still has Thyroid nodules to get measured, hernia looked at and brain scans to redo.

I watch my men go home, a few each day. Back to the shrink's office after a second brain scan/function check and visits to three other docs. Today I get to meet with two shrinks at the same time, Captain Cho and Mrs. Walton.

*Scared to meet with me alone, lady? I bet its Rollins' fault.*

Captain Cho opens, "Sar'nt Sanderford, you been through so much. I cannot imagine. Your whole unit has been through a lot. We need to refer you to Warrior Transition Unit. You need more evaluation and treatment. We hope you will go. The Army needs to investigate these 'fits' and help you with emotional and mental condition, too."

*Why does everyone wanna send me to Benning? Karen says Josh's not doin' good, she needs my help. How in God's name can I help him when my head don't work, my brain is broke.*

*How can I help anyone from Benning?*

*I'm done with this trip. If I go to a WTU, I'll be there at least six months, and they'll probably force me out of the army.*

"Ma'am, I'd prefer to go home, my wife needs help with our son."

Captain Cho looks to her counterpart. "Your son is in poor healt'?"

Walton gives me a momentary glance and stares at Captain Cho. "His son was in Afghanistan with him, Captain."

Her enlarged eyes glare at me. "Your son, he go with you?"

"Yes, Ma'am, he dropped out of college, joined our unit, did basic and tech school, and went with us."

"How is he?"

I give a dismissive left hand wave, inhale, glace down, and lean back in my chair. "Don't sleep, drinks every day, won't talk to people more than five minutes, normal stuff after a first deployment."

"It's normal." Captain Cho's back straightens, eyes bulge, and head nods side to side. "This is not normal. May be common, Sergeant, but we should not call this normal. Sergeant Sanderford, wouldn't you be more help to him, to your wife, if you go to WTU and take care of yourself first?"

"Probably so Ma'am, but he needs help now. My wife needs help now. I need to go home. I'll work on my stuff there."

Captain Cho looks at Mrs. Walton, Mrs. Walton at Captain Cho, both look back at me.

*Dammit, this slapstick director follows me everywhere. Sign off on my paper, lady.*

Captain Cho nods on her third glance at Mrs. Walton, who nods back. "We must refer you to WTU."

Both sweet little ladies look at me. Captain Cho continues, "I understand you desire to help family. However, you need time to fix yourself. Sergeant Sanderford need to take care of Sergeant Sanderford to be able to take care of family."

"Do I have a choice, Ma'am?"

"You can deny it. We can discuss your options. It will limit your treatment methods. Please consider taking time to heal on active duty, Sergeant."

"Can I think about it overnight?"

"Yes, Sergeant. We will prepare paperwork. You call you wife, think about it, come back tomorrow, meet with us and we finish."

"Yes, Ma'am."

Back at our orderly room, Carl and Captain Wayne encourage me to go to a WTU.

Carl says, "You broke on the army dime. Army ought a fix you."

Captain Wayne says, "If it takes you a year at Benning, make the Army find out what's wrong with you—what those fits are."

*At Benning, I can drink. No one will know. That would be nice. Take my time to transition back to civilian life. Maybe they will find out what is wrong.*

Friday morning, day five in the states, I go back to the shrink shop and agree to go to a Warrior Transition Unit.

Captain Shrink lady says, "I am so glad you are doing this. You have been through so much. It will be best for you to be better when you get home to wife and daughter."

Paperwork transfers me out of my unit and into a medical hold company to process and move to a Warrior Transition Unit. I move into a barracks with eight of my troops until we go either home or to a Warrior Transition Unit.

*Twenty-five years in the military about to be First Sergeant I get to bunk with the troops. Yay, great way to help us get better, neither they nor I will relax in here.*

All moved into an open bay barracks, several troops join me, a few NCOs as well. time to call Karen and let her know I'll be transferred to Benning.

I walk outside, up a grass hill to the hardball road, shuffle in roadside dirt, light a smoke, and debate what to say.

*She won't like this sh' at all. Just get it over with ya piece-o-sh'.*

I dial her cell number, hear it ring, and hope she will not answer. She does.

"Hello"

"Hi, Baby, how are you?"

"Doing ok. I'm ready for you to come home."

"Well, we need to talk about that."

"What? We need to talk about what?"

"They're sending me to Benning for evaluation and treatment."

"Don't you have a choice? You said yesterday you had a choice."

"I do. But it might be the best thing for me."

*Yeah, much better, won't have to deal with civilians, be able to drink and not have any responsibility for anyone.*

Painful silent seconds feel like hours. I hear her breathe.

*She is pissed.*

"What about what I want, what about your daughter? Josh is not doing well here. You are just gonna leave me here to deal with him, alone? You're choosing to leave, again."

"What's up with Josh now?"

"He's not the same; stays upstairs or goes up the hill to his friend's house. He drinks too much, won't talk to me, can't be around me, or anyone. Gets mad quick. I hear him at four in the morning, gettin' food in the kitchen. He never sleeps. I need you here to help. And your daughter needs you too."

"I need to find out what these fits are. And the shrink lady's mad I went back to Afghanistan from Germany."

"Do what you want. That's what you're gonna do anyway."

"Karen, you there?"

I look at my phone, screen says, "Call ended."

***

Doc's right outstretched arm displays a road guard palm at me. "Did your wife hang up on you?"

"Yes, Sir. Sure did. She has never hung up on me. I was like, 'Crap! What do I do now? Josh's gonna be an alcoholic, Karen don't know what to do, Charlotte keeps asking why Josh's home and Daddy ain't.' I wanted a damn drink that night."

"Did a drink, or was it two, help?"

"I didn't have one. We were still on General Order One, not allowed to have alcohol. Some folks cheat, but I don't. Too much of a geeky old army guy, I guess."

"You face a decision at this point. Go to Fort Benning or come home. As the behavioral health provider said, perhaps you could do more for your family after you took care of yourself."

"Maybe but at Benning, I'd a dove in the bottle. Drinking was my first thought about going there. time to myself, no-body watching. I would a beat myself up for shirking responsibility. Karen needed me, Josh needed me, and I needed my life back. I needed to get back to work. My civilian job had been without me over a year, if I didn't go back soon they'd realize they don't want my old ass. Benning was an option to get time for me. I at least wanted to know about my fits.

Took a while, but I quit whining and sucked it up. Decided to go home and help Karen. time to quit being selfish and get back to the world, to my job, to bein' a Dad."

"And how did behavioral health take your decision?"

"I went to the shrink shop to see Mrs. Walton the next morning. She had my paperwork for Benning ready. Without a hello or anything I said, 'I need to demob and go home.'

She asked what changed my mind, tried to talk me into getting healthier before goin' home. She was nice about it. My family needed me, so I was goin' home. Benning wasn't for me."

"You mentioned you'd be drinking a lot if you went there."

"There's more to it Doc. In uniform you can't cry, snivel or spill all your sh' out like I have with you. Be a sniveling cry-baby First Sergeant? Hell no. I'd bury it and say whatever they wanted to hear. Can't show all this crap and lead soldiers."

"Do you see this as an emotional requirement you place on yourself? Is this thought process taught in the Army?"

"Both. I had this First Sergeant once; he had issues, pulled a knife on me once. Other senior NCOs cussin' all the time, pissed off about little sh'. Not the best way to build comradery, trust, or confidence in your men."

"You cussed troops, showed your own anger."

"Only when it served a purpose, uncontrolled anger or emotion in leadership will either shake troops' confidence, or spread the same emotions through them all."

"Would you have had troops at Benning?"

"We had several men sent there. One died there. I wouldn't a done this work there."

"I see. You say one of your troops died there."

"Yes, Sir."

"I'm so sorry, Dale."

"Roger, we lost some after 05. Since we got back this time, we've lost two."

I close my journal and stow it, secure the map case flap, check to my left and right, and scoot forward to the couch edge.

"You have lost two men in your first year back."

My hands clasp between my legs, knees apart, map case on my shoulder, feet flat on Doc's floor. I am ready to go.

"Roger, time to go, Doc. I'm gonna go have a smoke."

I stand and step off for the door. Doc drops his notebook, shifts in his chair, and stands as I open his door. I do not look back.

"Dale, would you care to have a smoke and come back in?"

I clear his threshold, look left, right, left and right again, and continue to my right.

"No, Sir. I'm done for today."

Doc must have made the doorway and leaned into the hall. I hear, "Alright. Dale. Thank you for sharing with me. I realize it is very difficult for you."

I make a left, check the next hall, pause, and glance back at him.

"Roger, Sir. See ya next time."

I step off.

"Bye, Dale."

# 17

*Therapy Session Number 51*

Doc Taylor closes his door, shuffles around the footstool, and says, "Sorry for our late start today. I have been a bit behind since this morning."

"No big deal, Doc. I got nothin' to do."

"What do you have on your mind today?"

"Had more flashbacks—one time Karen and Josh were with me."

"Tell me about your flashback with Karen and Josh, Dale."

"We were on our way home from dinner, at the fish camp. Karen drives, I'm in the TC seat, and Josh's sits in back, behind Karen. (Truck Commander, front passenger seat)

"I point to this Black Hawk in a hard bank, and say 'chopper ten-o-clock, two klicks.'

"Karen looks at me, where I point and back at me. 'I don't see anything.'

"I look back at Josh, and he says, 'Ain't no chopper, Dad.'

"I told 'em. 'She's gone. It was in a hard bank. Like she's takin' a shot or quick landing. Y'all missed it.'"

Doc says, "Was there a helicopter, Dale?"

"No, Sir. Couldn't have been, ain't no Black Hawk anywhere near here. Even if there were, there's no reason for it to bank so hard, over civilian land, where they'd been logging, near Bedford."

Doc puts down his pen, looks at me, and leans back. "Remember our view of post-traumatic stress symptoms as an injury. Some connections in your mind are not the same as before."

"Yes, Sir. I do."

"Also, your subconscious uses such images to warn you, remind you of threats or possibilities which may hurt you. Anxiety, stress, frustration, or some other trigger may initiate such a process. Can you think of any trigger present before or during the helicopter episode? Were you upset or see something that reminded you of over there?"

"We drove thirty minutes to have dinner with Josh, his girlfriend, and her parents. My first time to meet them."

"Sufficed to say you were on edge. A long drive, new people and situations could cause you anxiety."

"Yes, Sir."

"How is Josh?"

"He tries to wash the Stan out with alcohol, women, and video games. You know, ignore it, have fun, stay busy, and move forward."

"Does this method work for him?"

"No more than it does any of us. Most often it leaves troops with divorce, and alcoholism. We don't wanna be around people so we either go antisocial or over compensate by being super outgoing, life of the party, makes it all worse. Most of us get to the point we can't cover it up before we'll ask for help. Till we can't do it anymore, like me, we suck it up and drive on."

"You are correct, Dale. No one can force Josh, or any veteran, to open up to help. One must be ready, in search of it. To force it on someone often creates more anxiety, stress and can make symptoms worse. You have done well. You have grown. You now embrace your injury as an opportunity for growth. Post-traumatic stress is unlike other injuries. It does not have a time limit, nor a prescribed method of treatment. We have techniques, but as a therapist, all I can do is provide information about what PTSD is and how it affects you and guide you to develop your own treatment. If Josh is still, as you say, sucking it up and driving on; he is not ready to face his issues, his trauma which caused them, or what he must do to thrive."

"I hope he faces it quicker than I did. I drove on until I couldn't face people, function, or make simple decisions. I don't even try to pay with exact change anymore. The person behind the counter gets paid to count change, let 'em do it."

"You don't like to count change."

"It pisses me off to stare at coins in my hand and not be able to figure out how to make forty-seven cents. I stare at it and nothing clicks. Can't figure it out, quicker to let them do it, they do it all day, their job not mine."

"Do you see this as a post-traumatic stress issue or from your multiple concussions?"

"I dunno, you saw the TBI tests, it says my brain don't function like it used to. What difference does it make, P-tids or TBI? It is what it is, and it ain't gettin' better. So I'll let cashiers count change, or Karen."

"Have you told your wife about this?"

"Yes, Sir. Before I did, she was mad at me every day. Now she sees stuff like paperwork or paying bills different. When I face things my brain won't figure out, I get pissed off. See myself as a sick, lame, lazy, loser. My flashbacks and stuff get worse. Screw that, best for her to handle that stuff. I don't need to get pissed off because of a few coins."

"You have a great wife. Her effort to understand and support you is a testament to her love and devotion to you, and to her maturity as a person. Not everyone has a wife willing to put up with such changes. Nor is every marriage open to honest discussion of these issues. You are truly blessed to have her."

"Hell, yeah. She's awesome. Lots of troops, after every trip, get a divorce. Half my squad got a one after our first trip back in ninety/ninety-one. Not everyone is willing to push through all this sh' and get to open, honest talk. Half of us, like my son, think we gotta be strong, not share sh', to share admits weakness. Our wives wanna figure out what's up, figure us out, but have no idea what's in our head. Assumptions and confusion frustrates, disappoints, pisses off, and grows resentment, in them and us. Put that sh' on a pile of unresolved emotions from when we left or while we were gone and it seems ones sole option is to leave. Our wives, and we, just want it to stop. We need it to stop. Nobody wants to fuss and fight all the time. Some spouses never get half-a-chance to understand."

"Why do you think couples do not understand, or get to a place they can work together?"

"Many people never get past their own emotions to hear what their spouse has inside. Others never express it. They figure their spouse won't or don't wanna understand. Either way it starts a downward spiral."

Doc says, "Most people fill in gaps of information with assumptions. Many individuals have a surface or generic definition of post-traumatic stress disorder. It is impersonal and often drives assumptions one is weak, broken, or inferior to others. Some spouses and families derive erroneous assumptions their soldier no longer loves them, or other similar, negative misconceptions. This is a logical assumption when a soldier withdrawals and seems distant. Even the soldier does not know why. It is great you and your wife talk through so many emotions and struggles. You have a rare marriage."

"I don't think it's so much a rare marriage as it is our dedication to it. Like my devotion to duty, we commit to each other no matter what. She's taught me to express more than I ever thought I would. She won't leave sh' alone till we talk it through, all the way through I mean. It takes both of us being open though. Neither of us can do it alone. We scheduled marital counseling before I even left the Stan. I need this time with you to be able to work with her. I think it takes both, ya know. Course she has to wait for me to take a break from talkin' sometimes. Like you do, I gotta be free to go have a smoke, or come back the next day."

"That is insightful, Dale. You expressed it perfectly. We must work on ourselves, to become all we can, and be capable of the hard work required in a relationship. This break time is an important realization for you. Hold onto this. Insure you take time for yourself, for you to heal and grow. Do not sacrifice yourself to do for her or anyone else. If you will do for Dale, do what Dale needs, then you can grow into what Karen needs Dale to be. Your time alone, no one's demands on you, or placing expectations on yourself of what you assume they want from you. This is vital for you to heal. You have given so much for others, in service to mission, and your men. You must make room for yourself. You are as important as anyone else in your life."

"Yes, Sir. I'm learning."

"To turn away from our natural impulse is not healthy. You have done this for years. Soldiers are required to do so for mission's sake."

"True, I can't be concerned with my own interests and focus on the task at hand."

Doc says, "Many believe Scripture says we must bring thoughts into submission and discipline yourself. However, it is to bring one in control, not into punishment. The shame of Adam and Eve caused them to hide from God. We fear his wrath but actually, he loves us where we are. Few people are able to embrace whom they are, as made by God, and know he loves us. Assumption before Jesus came was God is mad at us.

*Why you stop, Doc? Waiting for me to argue?*

His pen hand makes a 'gun' and points at his temple. "Often we have a problem believing God loves us. It seems he holds a gun to our head and says 'If you believe I love you I won't pull the trigger.'

*I've had troops do that, Doc, not funny.*

My attention shifts to the rose. I listen to Doc's philosophical sermon.

He says. "Humans cannot believe Jesus' simplistic concepts and have turned back to sacrificial methods of gaining forgiveness. In these methods, one must sacrifice in order for God to forgive. Aztecs, Hebrews and others condition their believers to fear a vengeful, wrathful God."

*Wake up Dale, he stopped. He thinks 'religion is just a set of man-made rules, and all religions are equally valid.*

I look back to Doc and nod in agreement. "I see what you mean everyone's got a list of do's and don'ts, rules and regulations."

"You must make your spirituality your own, ask questions anew, and gain ownership of it yourself rather than just accept what you've been taught," Doc says.

My head jerks right, eyes focus outside.

*There's a bee on the rose. Is Doc saying 'maw and pa said it but it ain't true?*

In my peripheral vision, I see Doc nod forward, back, forward, and back. "Open new ground within, remove the weeds, and receive truth. Your hope for healing is through spiritual transformation, brought about in deep personal interaction between Dale and God. Exodus 20 says only God can do this. We all have to 'Find Him' and Him alone.

*Bye bee. Wait he's going to another rose.*

Doc's rocking chair head stops. "Dale, true love is a spontaneous move of the heart not a stagnant set of rules. Seeking and finding is a loop, not a task. Continuous seeking with an openness to learn, staying a spiritual child. A child does not drive a stake in the ground and say this is truth. He continues to grow making more and more discoveries. You see, Dale, if we hold tight to a revelation or absolute truth we assume we completely understand an infinite God. This type of certainty, of definition inhibits further growth. We are no longer open to new, deeper perspectives or information."

I watch Mr. Bee squeeze into a third rose.

*Wait a minute, Doc. Question everything. Is nothing fact? If I find an answer; question it too? Is there one answer? Are there no universal truths? Do you mean all truth is to be questioned, analyzed, and any may be valid "for me"? Hold up, saying "there is no one truth" is a damn "one truth" ain't it? Sh'.*

"I can see that. People who decide they 'know' something don't allow themselves to question what they've decided is fact. Makes sense."

"You said it a more succinct way than I, but yes," Doc says with a small smile. "As to the religious rule set, I find a prohibition of something most often increases our desire for it. Guilt over having that unclean thing brings fear of a vengeful God."

*When's the last time you questioned that, Doc? Maybe God wants us free, not addicted to sh' that hurts.*

"Let us return to Post-traumatic stress before we go." Doc looks down at his notebook. "At times when an arm is injured, a deep cut, doctors leave the wound open to heal from the inside out. If the skin were to heal before the underlying tissue there may be infectious germs trapped within. If this occurs, we must open it, treat the infection, remove germs, and re-mend the outer layer. Post-traumatic stress disorder is an injury. We must draw out pain, inner turmoil, and emotional infection to have any hope to heal the Dale within. When we act as if our emotional, intellectual, and spiritual lives are healthy, but have not dealt with inner infection; internal issues remain. Such buried infection will, at some point, grow to affect external layers of our being."

*Ain't that why I am here, Doc. I got too much sh' inside?*

I nod. "Like tryin' to fix a septic system with all the sh' still in the tank."

"Okay, that is a new analogy. For proper function, one must deal with any sh' inside. However, we cannot expect any tank, in service for decades, to be immaculate. We will not eat from said tanks internal wall. No matter how hard we try, we cannot get rid of its pungent odor and traces of what was once inside.

"This is how it is with post-traumatic stress. I do not wish to give you the impression we can remove all effects of your life's experiences. Nothing we do here, or anyone does, can remove injury, memories of things you have seen and done. History remains and resultant injuries will leave scars. Like the cut on an arm, we talked about. It may heal and regain much of its function, but it will never be as it was. You seem to grasp this."

"Yes, Sir. Stuff from Desert Shield/Desert Storm still bothers me, ain't gone. That was what, twenty some odd years ago?"

"Right, we need to go deep, very deep inside Dale. See what we need to clean out, gain new perspectives on, or think through to a new truth. We cannot rid ourselves of traumatic experiences. In meticulous fashion, we can decide how our past will affect us in the future. This is a slow process. Some try to accomplish all this in aggressive long sessions, to bring to mind experiences one may not be ready to deal with. I find this method less successful for long-term gains. In our sessions, we discuss and deal with what you are ready to. What you bring up, what repeats in your intrusive thoughts or flashbacks. You are safe here. You are in control of our conversation. You may leave or change subjects at any time. I hope I have made this clear to you."

"Yes, Sir. You have."

"Would you care to discuss another topic today?"

"Am I ready to work? Can I go back and be any better than I was?"

*My boss never answered my question 'am I capable of doing this job now?' I asked her that before starting this sh' with Doc. Am I any better or just relaxed because I got drugs and ain't been at work? Am I worth anything to anyone? Maybe I shoulda just stayed in the Stan. I wonder if I can go back.*

In his calm voice Doc says, "For you to focus on this is not healthy. I will let you know when you are ready. Trust me to make such determinations. A camera cannot take a picture of itself without a mirror. Place all anxiety of readiness or progress measures on me. You have no choice. You cannot return to work until I release you to do so. Just focus on yourself."

*Again with the 'you're too damn crazy to know your crazy.'*

"I understand, Doc. But my eight week sick leave runs out next week."

"The date may be near. However, you are not ready. A return to work now could cause you to regress. Possibly even beyond where you were before these eight weeks. I cannot, in good conscience, release you until your mental state is solidified and robust. You have made strides, learned skills, talked about memories, gained perspectives on both post-traumatic stress disorder, and the events, which led you to have it. Nevertheless, your current stability is fragile. We cannot risk further damage or reduction in your progress. We just cannot. I, and your wife, need to protect you and allow you to continue your process."

*I went to war to protect her, my kids, and you. Now I am so broke I have to be nursed. Calm down, Dale. You know there is truth in it. You cannot do what you did before. Not now. Not ever?*

"Will I heal?"

"I'm afraid I can't answer such a question, Dale. Have you healed? I would say yes, to a degree. Will you heal completely? No one knows. Nor does anyone know how long it will take, if it happens. You may heal in months, or fifteen years. On the other hand, you may learn to cope and live a new, different life. You know you will not be who you were. We cannot flip a switch and be back to years ago as if you were never in combat. Your very deep injuries remain. Any healing process requires time, effort and most of all prevention of additional stress. Added stress in your life now will not only prolong your process, but could take you back to square one, right where we began."

*Like running on a broke leg. I didn't do that. Maybe I shouldn't "think" on a broke brain. Not till my head works better.*

My gaze remains fixed on our red squared carpet floor. "Yes, Sir."

Doc's arm stretches right, over his desk, inches from his deep maroon wall. "Think back to when we began our work. Do you remember our broken leg analogy? Let us say before your bone heals you get on a bull at a rodeo. Stress of such an activity would shift bone on bone. Such shifts would negate one's healing prior to mounting the bull. Furthermore, should you be thrown off and re-break the same bone, you see the point."

My head leans right. "Have I made progress? Images, flashbacks, are still there." My shoulders shrug and head turns to Doc. "I still don't sleep. Yell, or kick when I do sleep, and wake up in puddles of sweat."

My head flows to my right again. I gaze beyond the rose.

*Flashbacks at home, mortar strikes in church, an ambush in route to pick up my daughter, a dead Hadji by the gas station on my way to town. I still see sh' every day.*

My gaze locks on that Hadji who lost both legs. I say, "Have I made progress or have I just gotten skills to cope? It seems the same to me as it was. When I limit time with people, don't watch violent movies, look at pictures from the Stan, or talk to people I was over with, I can stay calm longer. But drivin' at night, or on unfamiliar roads, and ah hell here we go again."

*Bandages on his stumps are a deep maroon brown. Stumps.*

Doc says, "Your sub-conscious still tries to protect you from eventualities you saw or experienced. You have memories of horrible events in your mind. Your subconscious does not want these to surprise you again, or hurt you. Your subconscious wants to survive. Though vital to your survival there, here it distracts, upsets, and frustrates. As one works with someone in your situation, we strive to ensure you and your subconscious know you are safe. This is to prevent your minds creation of relationships between here and events over there. This takes much more time than it took you to develop this subconscious skill, which served you and your men so well in combat.

*Hadji's eyes, he stares in mine. Did he lose his legs because I failed to find a bomb? Is it my fault? Fu' it. Damn, Doc, you're gonna use up your comfort voice, ain't you?*

My eyes return to Doc's.

"Please keep in mind, Dale; it is not weakness on your part. It is a process learned in combat, which brought you home. Methods to turn it off, or control it, are as varied as soldiers experiences in combat, as complex and diverse as the soldiers themselves."

"Yes, Sir. We talked about that. I am, at times, able to understand what brought up a memory, not at first but soon after I have one. It just sucks you know. I do all this therapy in here with you, three times a week, for eight weeks now. And another once or twice a week with my Christian counselor, and every month or so at the VA clinic. And I still ain't done enough to be ready for work."

Doc leans forward, reaches out, palm down.

*You gonna touch my leg?*

He says, "Dale you have done an immense amount of work in here, and on your own. Your journaling, Scripture study, meditation, and contemplation amaze me. Your dedication to this process is exemplary. Nevertheless, effort, devotion, and work do not always determine progress. There remain things we do not know of the subconscious mind. Studies continue on post-traumatic stress' both cause and effect. Why one person is injured and another, in the same situation, is not. Why one heals with one method, and to another that same modality is useless. You have done all you could have done. We have done all we could do. You have made progress in both coping and healing. We must realize and appreciate your progress but not strive for unrealistic measures. When will you be 'normal' as you say? Most likely, you will never be the old normal. Together we must find your new normal, a new way to live your life."

"Yes, Sir. I see that. I can't go back to before. Scars remain. Even my pain is still here. I'm just disappointed. All this effort, all these journals, sessions, time, to still not be able to work."

"I understand. There is little way for you to escape frustration. Remember though, our measure is not what you were, but what you can become. Not who you were before this third deployment, but who you can become after it. As you embrace post-traumatic stress, your experiences and develop new perspectives on both, along with skills to cope, you can have a productive life. Again, no one can give a time, date, or even a full measure of completion. We must continue until we see you are stable and consistent for an extended period. Let us not give up yet. We should say not now, but it is not time to say not ever. Agreed?"

"Agreed, I guess I need a letter for my boss."

"We need at minimum four additional weeks. How are your medications?"

"I get 'em from the VA clinic now. They help, except when I forget to take 'em."

"Is forgetting them a problem? Does your wife help you remember?"

"She loads a weeklong pill keeper for me. I have it on my phone to remind me in the morning. Nighttime stuff I remember when I can't sleep."

"Good, good. You are developing methods to help you live your new life, whatever you find or decide your new existence to be."

"I guess."

"I'll draft a letter and have it ready for you this afternoon. Do you think that will suffice?"

"Roger, Sir. time to go."

"Ok, Dale. I'll ask our people to call when your letter is ready."

I pack my journal in my bag and shoulder it as I stand.

"Thank you, Sir."

Doc stands, plops his notebook and pen on the footstool. "Remember Dale do not think of these eight weeks as a failure. You are not ready for work, but you are not where you were. Agreed?"

Two steps to my exit, I pause and turn toward him. "Roger, I won't. I have learned, grown, adjusted. We just ain't done."

"Perfect. Have a good day, Dale."

"You too, Sir."

I turn, exit his office, proceed to check doors, halls, rooms, porch and parking lot. Bag drops on my car hood and I step under my tree to smoke before I have to drive.

*Karen's Journal June 2012*

Life is different and I mean really different. But yet life is good. I keep my focus most of the time on the positive—the blessings. I see soldiers coming home without arms, legs, etc. I see soldiers fighting physical battles and mental ones and I pray. My husband wages his battle in his mind. But God is there and ultimately he fights our battles for us; so I continually give my husband to God over and over.

I give Him my disappointments also. My dreams of still having a great life, of continued and complete healing of Dale in His will. Always praying for His will not mine since we are on the path for God's way to be done in our lives.

I know our weaknesses are perfected in His strength so I pray healing for Dale in accordance with His will.

Does that sound harsh? Perhaps it is. But we serve a loving, just and wise God who has plans for our lives—and ultimately that is what life should be about—serving God and fulfilling His plan for our lives. That is why we are here. Not for the cushy blessed life where we compete and compare ourselves to others, but to love and serve others. To let our lives speak volumes of who God is and His love for people. I am attending a class on coping skills for caregivers soon. I still look for ways to improve Josh's condition.

I nag dale then wish I didn't. His long trips to the bathroom have become the norm. At first, I was impatient and thought he was in there avoiding me. How selfish we are as people—always taking someone's actions and turning them toward ourselves. He has IBS.

Our days have changed—sleep patterns, daily medications, the way we disagree and how we discuss it, attending social functions, making phone calls, a slower pace of life.

Yet again, I can see the blessing in these changes. I know I keep going to the upside of these issues, but I see how God has been there and changed my view of things. How incredibly blessed we are to be together, just to live each day; it really is a gift.

*Dale's Text To Doc*

181010Sep11     At Church

I left Sunday school early for break. Don't wanna be around people. Prayer requests like spider bites. Give me a freaking break!

Felt surreal in class. Mind jumps from Iraq, to Afghanistan, to meetings with medical, to troops thinking of suicide. Won't focus.

Having smoke and chilling at BBQ pit now. At a loss as to the point of it all. Why chit chat, why try, what is the damn purpose? Often think "just enjoy where I am." But I don't like where I am. Does it matter my brain functions below average?

Who cares if I serve no purpose? Is there a purpose? What is the point with no mission, no risk to take, no one to sacrifice for?

Woke wife up last night. Another bad dream. Don't remember what it was. Who is running my thoughts now? Screw it. I'll do what I feel like and try to find enjoyment. Birds sound pretty. Squirrels are fun to watch.

Meaning in life is a farce. Beyond living in God's presence, there is nothing. I sound like Old Testament rambling. Guess I just needed to ramble, get crap out of my head. Have a good day. See you Wednesday.

I look at my arms, my hands. Places they've been. What they've done. What else will they do? Scars are real. Clean and healed now but dirty and hurt before.

I'm the same. Been lonely, hurt, tired and done things I shouldn't have or wish I hadn't had to. Where does this body go from here? Used up by the Army. Cast to the side by civilians. Fat, lazy, tired, and can't do what it used to. Where is the motivation when there is no "what must be done for our fellow man?" Boredom, complacency, monotony. It sucks is all I have to say.

*Josh's Journal*
17JUL2011 Home
Wow. Time flies. I'm home now. I guess that's obvious. Sitting in my room searching for hobbies I can find and do at home.

Life's interesting. I don't do much of anything these days. I sit at home, drink, smoke cigarettes and watch television mostly. So life hasn't really taken me where I've expected to go.

But I guess while I've dedicated some time to document the downward spiral that is my life. I should go ahead and recall all that I can.


19 October 2010.
That's an interesting date to leave off on. That's the date that started it all. Well, at least the October 19 part. It's the day I started basic training. The day I became a "sh' bag, guy, low speed slug" etc...

But this was a different October 19—very much so. I was still in ACU's and combat boots. I was still a Private in the US Army. I just had the opportunity to be in Afghanistan. A Private in an RCP is the most expendable person in that f'in country.

That's true. But as you can see, I made it out. So anyway, back to the war. Time sped up for us. All the talk about the summer being the hottest months as far as action may be true in most cases. Unfortunately for us, it was not.


December 2010
When I left off I was just a few weeks from going home for my leave. I can't remember ever being so happy in my life. I just knew I had to make it to that date. I spent most of the days off mission then diving back into my plywood box when we got "home" to see what people back home were doing.

I still stalked my ex. As stupid as that was, she dumped me while I was in f'in basic.

All I cared about was being able to get home and relax for a few weeks. But of course, the pace picked up. Not sh' was really going on honestly. Penguin stayed pretty clean for the most part around this time thanks to Dad and 154 running it like every other day.

So we were put on for a weeklong trip down to Sharana. Perfect. I remember being so pissed off that I couldn't stand it. The mission was to escort an entire division of ANA from FOB Bravo to some place around Sharana. Wherever the hell those fu'ers went to I don't care.

The mission was going pretty well as I recall. We made it to the sandpit as we called it. The place where I remember telling Lt. would be a great place to bury the IED's before it actually became a great place for them to bury IED's.

I was gunning the truck for Lt. Everything seemed to be going good. I remember for some reason we were behind this Hadji in his jingle truck for this part of the trip.

Then a blast.

"Mother f'errrrrrrrrrrrrrrrr." I hated blasts when I was gunning because I always thought it was me. About 200 meters ahead of us a husky had been hit.

I began scanning and checking my sector's hard.

But as usual, no contact here. Just an IED. Cowards.

"Hell, Byson Two Seven this is Husky two uhhh, I think I found one".

"Roger that, reaper this is Byson two seven."

Time for cleanup. This was going to be a long day. We Charlie Miked. The blast didn't really do too much damage to the husky. But I don't remember how the recovery actually happened. I do remember sitting and waiting for a long-assed time.

The Hadji in front of us took a seat on his jingle truck and began making chai. He shared with the ANA, who were now dismounted on foot patrol. About ten minutes later, they came and told us they found a mine on the side of the road.

A mine? F'in really ANA you think you found a mine? It turned out to be another waste of time as it was just some kind of debris. We made it through the rest of Penguin without incident. Then on the outskirts of the NAI a blast occurred 150 meters behind us. This one sounded big.

I looked through my NVG's but all I saw was smoke. This mission had us in the lead, the ANA division, then 128 in the rear. I knew this blast was too close to be 128 so it must have been ANA. I heard yelling and screaming from the area which was struck. But still saw nothing but smoke.

Everyone turned their lights out. Then when the smoke settled I saw it. It was an ANA truck that was hit, but not much damage was done.

I just remember thinking, "stupid fu's." Apparently, it's ANA TTP to jump out of the truck into the prone position when there is a blast. Wow. Another reason they suck. Who's to say they wouldn't counter that with secondary command wire on the side of the road for that sh'? I know *I* would.

They were alright and probably smoked some hashish to calm their nerves. The rest of the trip took what seemed like forever, but we finally made it.

# 18

Doc Taylor steps into the hall, holds his door open, and shuffles to my right. "Can I get you a water or coffee? You need a drink before we begin?"

I pass him on a b-line to my corner couch refuge. "No, Sir. I'm good."

*Déjà vu, he's about to say, "How are you today?", or "What's on your mind Dale?"*

Doc sits and sips his water. "Are you still considering sharing your journey?"

*Like anyone gives a sh' what I think. He did shake up our monotonous duplication though.*

"Yes, Sir. I typed a bunch of it, been a good review. But all the spiritual sh' will have to come out of it."

Doc looks at me, left hand on his beard, and says, "Isn't your spiritual journey a large part of your development."

"Yes, Sir, but there is too much of it."

"I understand. Do you have a particular topic you would like to discuss today, Dale?"

"Not really. Still don't sleep well, see stuff, think too much, same ole sh'."

"I would like to follow up on our last session if we could. If memory serves, Josh was in an ambush; you and your men were not far away. Can we pick up there today?"

"Yes, Sir. We didn't finish it did we?"

"I think there is more there worthy of our attention."

"Yes, Sir. My choice to let Josh die rather than increase risk for my men."

"Let's pick up right there."

"Yes, Sir…"

\*\*\*

To know Josh's vehicle is broke down, in a kill sack, taking small arms, mortar and RPG fire, rattles me. Haste in his direction could get my men hit by an IED.

*Dudes from Sharana had a 300-pound IED flip one of their VICs near here. Our mission is to clear for our brothers. No one else will insure we, or Josh's platoon, don't get blown up—that's our job. Find bombs, or make 'em blow up on us. Hell, we are s'pose to be blown up.*

I broadcast, "Husky Two get us up there, clear as you go, don't get us blown the hell up, over."

One after another, in order, my men's impatient voices confirm my order. Like a family who learn their youngest brother is hurt at school, everyone wants to get there, to help, to make him feel and be safe, and insure little brother is not hurt again.

*Locals ambush us to push us into IEDs. Can't risk my platoon to save Josh. Our NCO creed says, "I will not use my grade or position to attain pleasure, profit, or personal safety." I cannot risk my men, for my son's safety.*

Massive tires of our trucks pound gray powder of another dirt road, bellowing clouds of dust in an evening sun. Josh and our brothers receive and return fire, our IED search north drags on.

*Could take just my VIC and rush to their aid, to his aid. Not good, Sarge. You get blown to pieces and your troops will have to pick up another Plat Daddy. You know better, Sarge. We ain't no help if we're blown up.*

Out Miller's window, I see a familiar abandon qal'at.

*Ain't that?*

*Yup, we found a pipe bomb with shards of glass and metal, right there, in front of that run down qal'at.*

Seconds are minutes, minutes—hours. We want to engage, but are not. Want to get there, but cannot.

Lutz's vehicle clears through our next choke point. Josh's platoon frequency is on our second radio. Screams over the radio impale my ears, and slaughter-crushing silence in our truck. Our desperate hunger for information chokes on screams of enemy positions, weapons fire identification, and targets engaged. These blasts I hear, smoke I see, and details in my ears all describe what I've done to my son.

Smith broadcasts, "Wrench, go drag Nine out. Break. Anyone got a target, anyone takin' fire?" To confirm today's enemy are "suppressed." If so, he can prepare for and continue their mission. Several VICs report "all clear."

Smith's radio traffic slows. I key up on Smith's frequency. "Two Nine, this is One Nine, over"

"Go for Two Nine"

"Two Nine, we'll be at your location five to ten mikes."

"Roger One Nine, I think we're good."

"Roger Two Nine, let me know what you need us to do."

"Wrench, this is Two Nine. Need any help?"

"Two Nine, this is Wrench. 'At's a negative, 'bout got her did. Over."

Sergeant First Class Smith communicates with his team and squad leaders as recovery continues. He checks for vehicle for damage, injuries, and ammunition status.

Miller eases Lu Lu through another huge blast hole. Our gunner and my head slam side to side; Lu Lu creaks and cries as she has for months. One more choke point, ditch perpendicular to our path on both sides, after this one to get to Smith, our men, and Josh.

*This choke point is where Ramirez' soccer ball was blown out of French's truck, didn't even go flat. That was funny. Here we go, first VIC…Second…Third…probably no IED here today.*

Wrench broadcasts on Smith's frequency, "Wrench's ready to Charlie Mike."

Smith responds, "Husky let's Charlie Mike."

I key my headset. "Two Nine, this is One Nine, over."

"Go for, Two Nine."

"Two Nine, you need me to cross load ammo, water or anything?"

"One Nine, my rear two VICs could use some 50-Cal. if you can spare it."

"Two Nine, take a Papa Bravo when you're even with my VIC and we'll get it done."

"Appreciate it, One Nine."

"Roger, One Nine out."

"Two Nine out, break. Husky you copy? Halt a little past their last truck."

"Husky One, roger"

I halt my platoon. Smith does so next to us. I see my son, here, in combat, AK bullet scars, and rocket propelled grenade blast marks decorate his truck in tow. I wave, Josh smiles and waves back, as if we pass on a safe road back home.

*I am not telling Karen this one. She'd freak out. Josh looks good.*

*Why did I drag him here?*

*How could I leave him to die?*

*Shut up, Sarge, get Smith his Ammo, and get back to work. Drop the emotional BS.*

*Back to work, Sarge.*

\*\*\*

Doc says, "How do you view your choice today?"

"Lotta people would John Wayne it. Floor it and get up there. People been blown up doin' that. I brought my men home. Josh came home. Taliban had to stack rocks after playtime, more than once. That's all anyone can do, do the job"

Doc's brow curls and eyes squint. "Stack rocks?"

"Some who shot at us won't be shootin' again."

"I see. You said at our last session this began a new perspective for you."

"I found myself in freedom from defining myself."

Doc resituates in his chair, swaps to right over left crossed legs, and back to left over right. "Yes, yes. I love that statement, please elaborate."

*Need to pee, Doc?*

With palms facing skyward over my lap, I say. "Like that ambush, I don't matter. My son don't matter." Right hand elevates to my right front, my left plops on the armrest. "All my definitions of myself are gone." I point right. "I can't do what I've done." Both hands pat my chest. "I'm not who I was. I'll never be any of that sh' again. None of it matters. None of it defines me.

Hands fall to my lap, shoulders shrug, and my eyebrows raise. "We have to find new ways to live, now, after. My wife, daughter, son, and me, we all do. I had to start with 'who am I?'"

His left index finger on his lips, Doc nods, closes his eyes, and nods again. "How a man perceives himself has an enormous impact on him and everyone around him. What defines you now?"

*There's my rose. Right where it is every time I come here.*

I stare at my rose and wave a hand toward Doc. "When we started this I defined myself as a broke down useless soldier. One more name on a sick, lame, and lazy list. Can't go to war. Can't live here after it. Can't, Can't, Can't. I decided that's the same as what I did before."

I look to Doc's open eyes. He asks, "Same as before. How?"

I refocus on my rose. "I once defined myself by what I could do, what I had done, and what people expect me to do. Then, like a pendulum, I swung to what I can't do, what I fail to do, how I disappoint everyone."

"I see. First you chose to define Dale by his actions, and then by his inability to act."

I look back to Doc. "Yes, Sir. In Scripture I found a third option."

Doc looks up from his notebook. "And that is?"

"The Bible tells us God created us in His image, right?" My left arm, on the armrest, turns palm up and waits for a response.

"That has long been a basic belief of Judeo-Christian theology."

*I never get a yes or no from this guy.*

I give him a nod. "If our being created in His image is true, we need to know who He is to know who we are."

"That stands to reason. There are many definitions of God, from as many religions. Of course, you subscribe to Judeo-Christian beliefs. How do you now define God?"

"I tried to find Scripture where God defines himself. Opinions of preachers, professors, and our own may be well thought out. But who does God says he is."

Both corners of Doc's lips drop. "Go on."

My hands raise and make quotation marks. I say, "'I am, '" and drop my hands. "Again and again when God defines Himself, He begins with or simply says, 'I am.' Well I am created in His image. I am to strive to be like Jesus, who is God in flesh. Then perhaps I should define myself as He does."

"You exist, why strive for finite definitions?"

"A definition of self as" Again I motion quotation marks. "'I am' sets me free to-not-be the old Dale. To leave details of who I am, or will be, undefined. 'I am' brings freedom to enjoy, as best I can, who 'I am' now. Coping skills help with my P-tids. Am I P-tids? Or do I have P-tids? Who cares? A specific definition of who I am no longer matters, just don't matter."

"I see freedom for you in this."

"Yes, Sir. Don't stop flashbacks, dreams, or fix my bad back, migraines, or any of that sh'. If 'I am' now, then I can live now. I can enjoy something. I can offer something. I may never work full time again, who knows. God will provide for my family and me. I just do what he asks. Meanwhile, I am who I am, and that's all that I am."

Doc laughs, puts his pen down, and looks at me. "Popeye had no idea what a great philosophy he had did he?"

"No, Sir. I'm gonna go. Gonna catch the chiropractor before he closes at eighteen-hundred."

"Ok, Dale. Great talk today. I hope you catch the chiropractor. The ladies out front are gone I think. Can you call back tomorrow to schedule another visit?"

"Roger. Well, Karen probly will."

# EPILOGUE JOURNAL ENTRIES

*Karen's Journal July 2012*

Looking back, I see the good from a third deployment but while you are going through it's a different story entirely. One good thing—I have so much more patience now—which I use currently just about each day. Our lives are different now. The last deployment took more than we realized as Dale deals daily with PTSD, anxiety and depression. It's been a year since they returned at this writing, and I am still so amazingly grateful to God that they are home. I think I told Dale that every day for a month or two then weekly after that and still tell him now the same about four times a month.

Our situation reminds me often that we have so much to thank God for. That we are here together as a family means so much. Our family is precious. My hopes for us were not fulfilled before the last trip, and I was disappointed, but now I am so glad that we are the family we are. I give my expectations for us to God and He blesses me in so many ways I was not willing to see before. We are the family God created us to be just as we are. I don't wish we were different now. God is using our family for His glory and that is more than enough for me.

I remember praying, praying, and searching God's face on Dale's decision to go this last time. I had nothing left in me to pray. I had reached the end and knew it was done. He was going. I remember the night like yesterday when he was on the couch and I asked him if he was prepared to pay a price for going. Like permanent disability, death, etc. He looked at me and nodded his head. He was going. Little did we know that evening how much it would cost us. I remember asking almost as if God were asking through me. It was that calm—that serene. A knowing of sorts I think was set that day—of what was to come. A forecast. A look into our future.

My feelings for Dale ranged from anger to resentment to pride and back over and over, again and again. Every emotion is present in deployments. Each one is valid. They serve for love of country. You serve for love of them. Loving a person is costly—they hurt you with their choices, intentionally sometimes and sometimes not. Either way, loving another person is tough. Loving God though is something greater and far more fulfilling. It is our purpose for being here. There were times I stayed with Dale out of love for God. I am sure he could say the same for me. That is what marriage at its best is. Staying together when it's tough because God ordains it. Because it is best for man and wife.

## Helpful Websites

www.caregiver.com
www.VFW.org
www.legion.org
www.va.gov
www.woundedwarriorproject.org
www.nacvso.org
www.chog.org
www.veteranscrisisline.net
  1-800-273-8255
www.military.com

*Dale's Journal*
   061042JUN2012     At home

They tell me I have Post Traumatic Stress. What is it? What do I do about it? Wikipedia, Jun 6 2012 defines PTSD this way:

(PTSD) "is classified as an anxiety disorder in the DSM IV; the characteristic symptoms are not present before exposure to the violently traumatic event. In the typical case, the individual with PTSD persistently avoids all thoughts and emotions, and discussion of the stressor event and may experience amnesia for it. However, the event is commonly relived by the individual through intrusive, recurrent recollections, flashbacks, and nightmares. The characteristic symptoms are considered acute if lasting less than three months, and chronic if persisting three months or more, and with delayed onset if the symptoms first occur after six months or some years later."
   http://en.wikipedia.org/wiki/PTSD

Wikipedia is open for changes by nearly anyone. The FREE Dictionary by Farlex web site says:

"Posttraumatic stress disorder (PTSD); an anxiety disorder caused by exposure to an intensely traumatic event,…Characteristics include re-experiencing the traumatic event in recurrent intrusive recollections, nightmares, or flashbacks; avoidance of trauma-associated stimuli and a generalized numbing of emotional responsiveness; and hyper-alertness with difficulty in sleeping, remembering, or concentrating. The onset of symptoms may be delayed for months to years after the event"
© 2003 by Saunders, an imprint of Elsevier, Inc. All rights reserved
http://medical-dictionary.thefreedictionary.com/PTSD

Who would know more about it than the VA. They get all of us. The VA mental health website says:

"… (PTSD) is an anxiety disorder that can occur after you have experienced a traumatic event. PTSD symptoms usually start soon after the traumatic event, but they may not happen until months or years later. They also may come and go over many years. If the symptoms last longer than 4 weeks, cause you great distress, or interfere with your work/home life, you probably have PTSD. Symptoms of PTSD include reliving the event, avoiding places or things that remind you of the event, feeling numb, and feeling keyed up (also called hyperarousal)."
   http://www.mentalhealth.va.gov/PTSD.asp

The American Psychological Association On page 17 of The Psychological Needs of U.S. Military Service Members and Their Families states:

A Preliminary Report

American Psychological Association Presidential Task Force on Military

Deployment Services for Youth, Families and Service Members
February 2007
"Given the risks associated with the stress of deployment and exposure to combat, it is not surprising that military service members and their families may be suffering significant mental health problems in the wake of current military operations."
http://www.ptsd.ne.gov/publications/military-deployment-task-force-report.pdf

Everyone and their cousin wants to talk about PTSD. Go here, go there, do this, do that, take this, drink that, get a hobby, get a dog. Everybody has advice. I gotta start with what is it?

My shrink tells me my subconscious mind brings back memories and images in an effort to protect me. Just like when we were entering an area we knew we would have issues overseas. We would remember all the issues we had there before. That makes sense. My subconscious doesn't know I am "safe" at home. So when I get stressed or anxious, which happens a lot, my subconscious wants brings to mind experiences which may apply. It prepares me for painful possibilities.

As to nightmares, counselors tell me my mind is bringing back things I have yet to deal with. Events or memories I have not come to terms with, are incomplete, or significant. Recalling significant emotional events, I am able to relive them until I come to terms with what they were. Better yet, to redefine my perceptions so the memory or event does not bother me as much.

Then there are my leadership regrets and issues. Thousands of *what if*'s swirl through my head in the middle of the night. I should have done better. What I should have taught my men. Now that I am no longer with them, how much I let them down. Doc says these are part of my own perceptions of my past. My over judgmental attitude toward what a poor job I did with my men, not part of the PTSD.

Seeing stuff when I drive is my subconscious bringing crap up again, Doc says. Memories I should consider to keep my physical body safe. Don't forget this or that because bad guys might do it again. Really? In church, my subconscious wants to remind me of possible danger. Yeah, mortar rounds five pews in front of me, real possibility. I know the preacher yells sometimes, but he won't mortar me to get my attention.

Neuroplasticity of the brain allows the brain to change its make up, the connections between data so new memories, perceptions and emotions attached to those memories are possible. They say an understanding of the brains neuroplasticity can be helpful during our recovery process. The same way connections were made in combat between things and significant memories are burned into our memory, we gotta work for years to change those connections.

Okay so neuroplasticity, man that is a big word. What the heck is "nerdo"-plasticity? I dumb it down to the ability of the brain to attain new reflex responses. Just like when we practice reflexive fire drills over and over again. The more we do it, the quicker and more accurate our response, ability and skill. People call it muscle memory but the brain is still involved. The muscles have no memory. It is a learned response to a threat. The brain memorizes the movement and eventually it becomes nearly as natural as breathing or our own heartbeat. Once this happens, the thought process behind what to do is unconscious to us. We hear a sound, see a bad guy, receive fire or whatever and our mechanical response is so programmed it happens without our giving conscious thought to it. Expand that to thought processes, recovery of applicable memories and such. Our subconscious brings us information to consider in case it is applicable today.

My increase in anxiety around a crowd is enough to trigger it. Trying to meet others' expectations of me or perform tasks I get confused about, like counting change, has triggered it as well.

My definition:
PTSD is trained into our head with this "nerdo"-plasticity. The nervous responses, over vigilance, constant alertness, inability to feel safe and secure, etc. kept us alive. Why would our brain leave those things behind just because we got on a plane and came home? We are survivors. Our mind and body wants to survive and propagate the species. (Soldiers terms, live and have sex.) Our mind remains vigilant, to remind us what we did, or happened to us.

Add the emotional strain the military never trains us to handle, and we end up confused, alienated, and depressed. We all think, "no one else feels this way." I need to just "suck it up and drive on," or "get the sand out." Deal with my issues on my own time and Charlie Mike. Thinking nobody else has any negative emotions about what we did or went through. I am the only one. Everybody else is fine.

Other troops continue what they need to do, so I must be a wimp or something. Soldiers are not supposed to have emotions. Doc says we do have emotions. We just turned them off for a while to do what we had to. Now we have piles of memories, emotions, regrets, and guilt in our head we haven't dealt with. Our brain is like *WTF?*

We get mad because there is so much going on in our head, we can't handle one more thing—even a little thing. We have to take the time to deal with our memories, learned responses, and grief before we can hope to move forward. Just like clearing for bombs. No one did it for my platoon. For us and others to survive we had to clear the way.

Drugs are another issue, legal and illegal. Some places they give us enough drugs to make us zombies, who cannot feel none of our old or new emotions. We feel better, we behave better because we don't yell and shout as much. However, we don't deal with the septic tank of our mind, so we don't get better. Our mind does not come home. We just survive, day to day rather than thrive. I'm on anxiety and depression medicine as I write.

My wife worked with Doc to keep my dosage low enough I still have problems, so I can learn to deal with them. I just take a large enough dose to appease the problems so my mind will be calm enough to start dealing, processing and working through all this in prayer, counseling, reading, journaling and talking to my wife and son.

We return home with all these memories, and other emotions arise which compound our confusion. Why am I still here? Why did he have to die in my place? Why did we have to kill those people? Why did I do this or that? I am not a cruel person. What do I do with it all? A common result is to delve further into confusion and depression.

We soldiers ignore our emotions—especially fear—and Charlie Mike. Ever forward, never look back, prepare for the next mission, no time for emotions in our business. Doc says all humans have emotions. Even if we will not admit, or recognize them, we do have them. The more we deny self, or parts of self, the larger our pile of garbage grows. Until its weight breaks us down. We become dysfunctional, or out of control and must face our past.

That is why some of my troops have had their PTSD kick in months after our return. They get a divorce, a family member or brother in arms dies, or they lose a job. Suddenly emotions are no longer ignorable. The straw that broke the camel's back, if you will. We push things down, hold them in until the pile is so big the dam breaks and we're completely broken.

My dam broke while trying to work back here as a civilian. My mind does not perform the way it used to. I have trouble learning new things and remembering old ones. My drop in job performance brings more stress. I've become unable to perform the simplest of tasks. I've thrown up more than once on my way to work. Simple decisions are impossible for me. Much of this remains now, after I left my job to start this "recovery" journey.

With reduced stress of not working and medications, I am able to spend time daily working through my issues. Doc says if I'm healed in ten years, he would be surprised. That it would be a miracle. However, I will be able to live, and relearn how to enjoy life. Suicidal thoughts are not as much of an issue for me now. A visit to my old civilian job two weeks ago proved I am still not ready for the stress of work. I can't be around people, even my eleven-year-old daughter, for more than a couple hours a day. I have to have "me" time to function at all.

So how do we move forward? I told one of my troops we must learn a new way to live. We are not who we were. We may never be again. However, we can learn coping skills, process our memories and learn to enjoy the life we worked so hard to protect.

We, more than any American, deserve to enjoy our freedom. We, as God's creation, deserve to sleep at night. We can get to a point we can enjoy parts of life again. Will our flashbacks, memories, and anxiety ever go away completely? I don't know. I have found by taking my dog with me wherever I go, spending the time I need alone, getting back into my art, has helped me spend time with people without freaking out.

I haven't wanted to raise my M4 in church in over two months. I often have to leave because I see stuff and get too fidgety. My wife asks me to leave when my leg tapping distracts people. I do what I can, and it's ok if I have to get away from everyone on Thanksgiving. It's fine if the crowd at Christmas is getting to me and I take a half hour to myself outside or watching TV alone in the other room.

What are the steps to recovery? You see so many "treatments" out there for PTSD. Force yourself to discuss the deployment. Wait for the memories to come to you then discuss them. Spend time in PTSD groups, in-patient treatment, outpatient treatment. So how do I move forward? How is my wife supposed to help me? The process isn't a defined step 1, then 2, then 3.

God created each of us differently. I am nothing like you. My wife is nothing like me. My son has had completely different experiences in both civilian and military life than I have. We are born different, raised different, conduct different missions, deal with different emotions and experiences. So how in the hell could the recovery process be a generic or uniform process?

Every mission we did in Afghanistan was different. We left at different times. The threat was higher or lower. The road changed. The weather was different. The insurgents tried different things. We changed how we did things to minimize patterns in our behavior. Considering this along with the fact each soldier or marine is as different as the missions are, we must customize our recovery process. For anyone to say you must do x, y and z is as ignorant as saying we are back on the same route so let's do everything the exact same way as last time. It's a new day with new people and situations to deal with.

My recovery process includes counseling Christian and secular, Bible study and prayer. Lie still and ask God to heal me and bring to mind what to deal with, journal or discuss in counseling next.

My coping skills center on avoiding "triggers" for my flashbacks such as crowds, driving, stress and being in uniform. Taking my dog with me nearly everywhere I go. Exercise helps but my doc will not allow me to run, bike or even do pushups and sit-ups.

Family support begins with my wife. She issues my medications and is understanding to my need for reduced stress, to talk out memories with my son and other soldiers, getting into my art, and writing.

I spend time with small groups of people in prayer for others and myself. Study what God says about who He is and who I am. Try to observe my flashbacks rather than experience them. Praying through and discussing my regrets and the "why am I here and they aren't" sh'.

To focus too long on all this crap is not good for me. I enforce limits on time in this text to prevent "increased anxiety." I continue to check psychological concepts against God's word. I'm surprised how many authors repackage Jesus' teaching as new age thought and leave Him out to sell books and look smart.

I am not "healed." Just yesterday, I had to get away from all my family members because I had been around people too long. I continue to learn coping skills which enable me to live my life in spite of my issues rather than depressed about not being over or past them.

I began my journey desperate to find a rock solid truth on which I could rebuild my old life. I have found some truth. However, I embrace that search as my new life.

The End

# APPENDIX I MILITARY INFORMATION

## Soldier's Creed

I am an American Soldier.

I am a warrior and a member of a team.

I serve the people of the United States, and live the Army Values.

I will always place the mission first.

I will never accept defeat.

I will never quit.

I will never leave a fallen comrade.

I am disciplined, physically and mentally tough, trained, and proficient in my warrior tasks and drills.

I always maintain my arms, my equipment, and myself.

I am an expert and I am a professional.

I stand ready to deploy, engage, and destroy, the enemies of the United States of America in close combat.

I am a guardian of freedom and the American way of life.

I am an American Soldier.

http://www.army.mil/values/soldiers.html

# NCO Creed

No one is more professional than I. I am a noncommissioned officer, a leader of Soldiers. As a noncommissioned officer, I realize that I am a member of a time honored corps, which is known as "The Backbone of the Army." I am proud of the Corps of noncommissioned officers and will at all times conduct myself so as to bring credit upon the Corps, the military service and my country regardless of the situation in which I find myself. I will not use my grade or position to attain pleasure, profit, or personal safety.

Competence is my watchword. My two basic responsibilities will always be uppermost in my mind—accomplishment of my mission and the welfare of my Soldiers. I will strive to remain technically and tactically proficient. I am aware of my role as a noncommissioned officer. I will fulfill my responsibilities inherent in that role. All Soldiers are entitled to outstanding leadership; I will provide that leadership. I know my Soldiers and I will always place their needs above my own. I will communicate consistently with my Soldiers and never leave them uninformed. I will be fair and impartial when recommending both rewards and punishment.

Officers of my unit will have maximum time to accomplish their duties; they will not have to accomplish mine. I will earn their respect and confidence as well as that of my Soldiers. I will be loyal to those with whom I serve; seniors, peers, and subordinates alike. I will exercise initiative by taking appropriate action in the absence of orders. I will not compromise my integrity, nor my moral courage. I will not forget, nor will I allow my comrades to forget that we are professionals, noncommissioned officers, leaders!

http://www.army.mil/values/nco.html

# REFERENCES

1. http://en.wikipedia.org/wiki/24-hour_clock#Military_time

2. http://www.merriam-webster.com/inter?dest=/dictionary

3. http://www.army.mil/values/nco.html

4. http://www.army.mil/values/warrior.html

5. http://www.armystudyguide.com/content/army_board_study_guide_topics/communications/phonetic-alphabet-military.shtml

6. http://www.armystudyguide.com/content/army_board_study_guide_topics/communications/phonetic-numerals-military.shtml

7. http://en.wikipedia.org/wiki/PTSD

8. © 2003 by Saunders, an imprint of Elsevier, Inc. All rights reserved http://medical-dictionary.thefreedictionary.com/PTSD

9. http://www.mentalhealth.va.gov/PTSD.asp

10. American Psychiatric Association (1994). Diagnostic and statistical manual of mental disorders: DSM-IV. Washington, DC: American Psychiatric Association. ISBN 0-89042-061-0.[page needed]; on-line.

11. http://www.ptsd.ne.gov/publications/military-deployment-task-force-report.pdf

12. Rothschild, Babette (2000). The Body Remembers: The Psychophysiology of Trauma and Trauma Treatment. New York: W.W. Norton & Company. ISBN 0-393-70327-4.[page needed]

13. Kaplan, H. I.; Sadock, B. J. (1994). Grebb, J. A., ed. Kaplan and Sadock's synopsis of psychiatry: Behavioral sciences, clinical psychiatry (7th ed.). Baltimore: Williams & Williams. pp. 606–609.[page needed]

14. Satcher D (1999). "Chapter 4". Mental Health: A Report of the Surgeon General. Surgeon General of the United States.

15. Robinson, Maisah (May 27, 2006). "Review of Francisco Goya's Disasters of War". Associated Press.

16. "Post-Traumatic Stress Disorder (PTSD)". U.S. Department of Health and Human Services. National Institute of Mental Health (NIMH). Retrieved 2011-12-16.

17. Mayo Clinic staff. "Post-traumatic stress disorder (PTSD)". Mayo Foundation for Medical Education and Research. Retrieved 2011-12-16.

18. Fullerton CS, Ursano RJ, Wang L (2004). "Acute Stress Disorder, Posttraumatic Stress Disorder, and Depression in Disaster or Rescue Workers". Am J Psychiatry 161 (8): 1370–1376. doi:10.1176/appi.ajp.161.8.1370. PMID 15285961.

# THE STAN
## Father and Son Find Bombs

"The Stan" shares private thoughts, therapy sessions, journal entries, and memories of our family of four as father and son deploy to combat. A rare opportunity to experience deployment as we say goodbye, sacrifice for others, struggle inwardly, attempt to heal, and move on with life from differing, even opposing, perspectives. Observe unspoken emotions, hopes, and dreams common to military families.

# ABOUT THE
AUTHOR

Dan Talley is a veteran of a twenty-six year marriage, twenty-eight year military career and three wars. His varied occupations include years of leadership in military, educational, industrial, religious, and civic organizations. God, through this experiential education, amassed within this storyteller numerous tales to be told. Dan is winner of both visual art and literary contests. His experience, quest for understanding, creativity, and artistry enable story-telling which guides others to comprehend truths from ordinary and extraordinary situations. Serving in combat with his son in 2010 brought new perspectives on Jesus' sacrifice and God's love. Subsequent depression, suicidal thoughts, and PTSD, contrast with a mission trip in India to grow greater compassion for others and a desire to assist in their personal growth.

Made in the USA
Charleston, SC
04 October 2016